Odense University Literary and Cultural Studies vol. 8

Folkways and Law Ways:
Law in American Studies

Folkways and Law Ways: Law in American Studies

Edited by
Helle Porsdam

Odense University Press 2001

Published with support from the Danish Research Council
for the Humanities

© The Contributors and Odense University Press 2001
Set by DTP-Funktionen, University of Southern Denmark
Cover Design by UniSats
Printed by Narayana Press, Gylling, Denmark
87-7838-583-0

Odense University Press
Campusvej 55
DK-5230 Odense M

Phone: +45 66 15 79 99
Fax: +45 66 15 81 26
E-mail: press@forlag.sdu.dk
www.oup.dk

Customers in the United States and Canada please contact:

International Specialized Book Services
5804 NE Hassalo Street
Portland, OR 97213
USA

Phone + 1-800-944-6190
E-Mail: info@isbs.com

Contents

Helle Porsdam Introduction 9
1. *Irmina Wawrzyczek* Plantation Economy and
   Legal Safeguards of Sexual Discipline in
   Early Tobacco Colonies 33
2. *Saul Cornell* The Irony of Progressive Historiography:
   A Critical Comment on the Revival of Anti-Federalism
   in Contemporary Constitutional Thought 53
3. *Niels Bjerne-Poulsen* "Hunting in the Pond Where the
   Ducks Are": Conservative Opposition to Civil Rights
   Legislation in the 1964 Election and Beyond 73
4. *Mark Gibney* Protection under United States Law?:
   It Depends on Who You Are, Where You Are,
   What Aspect of Your Job You Are Talking About, and
   Who Is Trying to Hurt You 89
5. *Bosse Ekelund* Recognizing the Law:
   Value and Identities in William Gaddis's
   A Frolic of His Own 113
6. *Peter Schneck* Dissenting Opinions:
   William Gaddis and Alan Dershowitz on the
   Spectacles of Justice 139
7. *Marcus Bruce* "The Promise of American Life":
   Derrick Bell, Critical Race Theory, and the
   American Jeremiad 165
8. *Christophe Den Tandt* Hollywood Courtroom Dramas:
   The Politics of Judicial Realism 183
9. *Eric Guthey* A Brief Cultural History of Corporate Legal
   Theory and Why American Studies Should Care
   About It 209

10. *Michael Böss* American Links to Legal Reform in
 Ireland, 1937-1997: A Study in the International
 Impact of American Constitutional Law 229
11. About the Authors 254

Preface

From different perspectives, the essays in this volume highlight the importance of the law for the study of the culture of the United States. Thoroughly interdisciplinary and wide-ranging in their scope, they embody all that is best about American studies. The contributors represent five different European countries as well as the United States, and many of them first met to discuss their work at the 1998 European Association of American Studies conference in Lisbon, Portugal.

The idea to put together this volume grew out of a wish to draw the attention of fellow Americanists on both sides of the Atlantic to the emerging field of law and culture. After such recent events as the impeachment proceedings of President Bill Clinton and the 2000 presidential election, the way in which every major political discussion inevitably turns into a legal one in the United States should be obvious. Most often, however, American studies scholars seem to think that the law has nothing to do with us in American studies Ð that we ought to leave it to our colleagues in the fields of law and political science. That is a shame; all we have to do is to look at the cultural life of the nation. It is hardly possible these days to see an American movie or television series without law and lawyers. The interest of the American people in matters relating to law and lawyers, reflected in these cultural texts, ought to alert us to the fact that law is an important cultural factor.

In editing this volume, I owe a debt of gratitude to editor Ann Gross of the *William and Mary Quarterly*. Spending a year in Odense together with her husband, Robert Gross who held the 1998-99 Fulbright Chair in American studies at the University of Southern Denmark-Odense University, Ann helped me create out of articles written by scholars from six different countries a coherent volume of essays.

Odense, April 2001
Helle Porsdam

Introduction

Helle Porsdam

Rumor has it that the character of Professor Nicki Morris in *One L,* Scott Turow's memoir of his first year at the Harvard Law School, is based on Professor Duncan Kennedy. If true, Kennedy has every reason to be pleased: Nicki Morris is one of young Turow's legal heroes. Unlike certain other Harvard law professors, Morris sees the law's search as profound and wide-ranging. In his class, Turow feels the gap between legal ideas and those he has encountered in other fields of study close down. Things make sense to an extent that they never do in other classes. In the end, it is Morris who puts into words Turow's feelings and thoughts about the law.

> The law, Nicki said, ... is a humanistic discipline. It is so broad a reflection of the society, the culture, that it is ripe for the questions posed by any field of inquiry: linguistics, philosophy, history, literary studies, sociology, economics, mathematics.[1]

The themes and arguments of Kennedy's two latest books, *Sexy Dressing Etc.* (1993) and *A Critique of Adjudication (Fin de siècle*) (1997), indicate that the rumors have a factual basis.² The four essays that make up *Sexy Dressing* concern "the power and politics of cultural identity." The subtitle is well-chosen. *Sexy Dressing* covers a lot of ground. So does *A Critique of Adjudication,* which addresses in particular "the role of political ideology, in the simple sense of, say, 'liberalism' or 'conservatism,' or 'states' rights' and 'abolitionism,' in the part of judicial activity that is best described as law making."³ But in discussing the grand questions concerning the meaning and effects of adjudication in society, Kennedy touches on every major issue currently the subject of intellectual and cultural debate.

That Kennedy, a co-founder of Critical Legal Studies (CLS), sees the law as a broad reflection of American society and culture should come as no surprise. Since its tentative beginnings in the late 1970s, CLS has been an interdisciplinary endeavor. As Kennedy and other "Crits" see it, questions concerning cultural identity, power, and law in today's multicultural America can only be successfully dealt with if legal scholars draw inspiration from both the humanities and the social sciences. What is perhaps more surprising is that legal scholars of a more traditional "observation," for whom the postmodernist turn of CLS and its offspring such as Critical Race Theory (CRT) is dangerous and reprehensible, have also come increasingly to acknowledge a broadening of interests within contemporary American law. Richard A. Posner, one of the founders of the Law and Economics movement, is a case in point. Posner has mostly found the tools and methodology of economics useful in his analysis of American law. Yet, in his preface to *Overcoming Law* (1995), he tells his reader to prepare herself for an approach that is far from being exclusively economic.

> We live at a time when economists, like Ronald Coase and Gary Becker, philosophers, like John Rawls and Richard Rorty, and literary critics, like Stanley Fish, are real presences in legal scholarship. So the reader of this book will find, along with chapters on judges, the legal profession, legal scholarship, the Constitution, and the regulation of employment contracts, chapters that deal with sex-

uality, social constructionism, feminism, rhetoric, institutional economics, political theory, and the depiction of law in literature. Even my forays into topics as remote from the conventional domain of legal theory as the ancestry of Beethoven, feuds in medieval Iceland, child care in ancient Greece, and the education of deaf children have grown out of my professional interests as a judge and legal scholar.[4]

What Posner has come to realize – and what legal scholars such as Kennedy have been aware of for quite some time – is that American law has everything to do with American identity, American culture. Foreign observers of America have always been puzzled by the invocation in all kinds of unlikely contexts of judicial authority, by the constant reference to personal rights and freedoms, and by the way in which any topic – be it political, moral, social or cultural – invariably turns into a legal one. Permeating, as it does, all levels of American society and penetrating all corners of American culture, the law therefore makes an obvious area of study for anyone interested in American Studies.[5] Where legal scholars have long focused on the role of law in the shaping of American identity, it is only within the past ten to fifteen years that American Studies scholars have shown a serious interest in law. This is somewhat puzzling – especially because American Studies prides itself on being a thoroughly interdisciplinary field whose areas of interest are the totality of American culture and the formation of American identity.

Books such as Jerold S. Auerbach's *Justice without Law?* Richard H. Weisberg's *The Failure of the Word,* Robert A. Ferguson's *Law and Letters in American Culture,* and Carl S. Smith, John P. McWilliams, Jr., and Maxwell Bloomfield's *Law and American Literature* from the mid-1980s really drew the attention of American Studies scholars to the law as an important cultural factor.[6] Historians and literary scholars have always written on various aspects of American law, but only rarely have they attempted to relate these aspects to more general American Studies discussions concerning American ways of thinking about and formulating social, political, moral, and cultural issues. Auerbach set the scene for such discussions when he noted that,

> by now the predominance of law as a cultural force is beyond dispute. It might be measured by the assertive role of the Supreme Court (whether heroic or villainous is beyond the point); by the hypnotic allure of the courtroom trial as a staple of national melodrama; by the astonishing attractiveness of the legal profession as a career choice. No longer is it possible to reflect seriously about American culture without accounting for the centrality of law in American history and society, and in the mythology of American uniqueness and grandeur.[7]

The years since *Justice without Law?* have seen many important works on the role of law in American culture. They may roughly – and at the risk of grossly generalizing – be divided into three categories: law and history, law and literature, and law and popular culture. In the following, I take a look at each of these categories. Law and literature is the best established of the three, and many of the discussions going on in law and history and law and popular culture have their origin in debates taking place within law and literature. In practice, these issues and debates overlap, so that it is not always possible – or indeed desirable – to say of a particular issue whether it "belongs" to one category or another.

With the possible exception of the final essay, which forms a category in and of itself, the ten essays in this volume may all be said to fall into one of the three categories. The thematic approaches of the ten essays are very different and wide-ranging. What the authors of the essays all have in common is a concern for American law and legal discourse as these relate to American culture. Incorporating into the field of American Studies legal concerns and legal issues presents both methodological and ideological problems. Several of these are intrinsic to the very attempt of doing interdisciplinary work and consequently concern the nature of American Studies itself. Addressing these problems as they crop up in relation to the works discussed, the contributing authors show that, just as it is in the field of law that some of the most interesting cultural and political discussions are taking place these days, so it is in law and American Studies that some of the most fertile debates of our discipline may be found.

Law and history is not a movement or even a field in the same way that law and literature is, although historians have always been aware of the importance of law for American history. In the preface to his famous book on Blackstone's *Commentaries, The Mysterious Science of the Law* (1941), Daniel J. Boorstin writes, for example, that the book "is designed to suggest how [the lawyer], in common with the rest of the community, employs the ideas and assumptions of his day about the whole of human experience" and to give evidence that "the lawyer's work, whether or not the lawyer is aware of it, is in the main stream of the history of thought."[8] Likewise, in his seminal *The Life of the Mind in America* (1965), Perry Miller writes about the rise of a legal mentality among Americans.[9] As a field in and of its own right, however, legal history is not that old. Many courses were offered in American constitutional history during the first half of this century, but "even as late as the 1950s, historians of the United States did not think of legal history as a field at all."[10] When historians finally did discover legal history, they occupied themselves with statutes and doctrines, appellate judicial opinions, and other material internal to the legal system. To some, it was the whole institutional process concerning the passage of laws and statutes that merited their attention.[11] Others found the legal profession itself and its role in American society interesting[12] and concentrated their efforts on describing the origins and the status of lawyers and writing biographies of great American jurists.[13] A third group of legal historians investigated issues relating to the police and the enforcement of laws,[14] issues that led in turn to an interest in crime levels and social deviance.[15]

"Whatever its pretense to autonomy," argues Anthony Chase, "law cannot be adequately understood when separated from historical context."[16] Ever since Lawrence M. Friedman introduced and popularized the concept of an American "legal culture" in the 1960s and 1970s, members of the legal academy and others interested in American law have engaged in lengthy debates as to whether or not it is necessary to look beyond legal scholarship itself to understand the place of law in American culture and society. As Friedman saw it, a legal system consists of three components: institutions and their processes, rules, and a legal culture. The two former components make up the internal workings of the legal system, whereas the latter is directed toward the external aspects of law, "the ideas, attitudes, values, and beliefs that people hold about the legal system."[17] Though some legal scholars would still want to keep the law "pure," as it were, the sizable number of articles in the country's best law journals devoted to issues that link law and its practitioners to American society and culture in general testifies that Friedman's concept of legal culture has by now become a mainstay in legal history scholarship.

In the 1970s and 1980s, inspired by scholars such as J. Willard Hurst and, as we just saw, Friedman, social historians began looking beyond legal statutes and doctrine toward legal records of all kinds.[18] Court cases and legal codes were now of interest, less for what they might reveal about the workings of the judicial system itself, than for what they might tell us about the general history and development of the United States. Whether the specific area of interest was the origins of slavery and segregation,[19] bastardy and bridal pregnancy,[20] privacy,[21] family and gender relations,[22] or legal reform movements, law codes and court cases were perceived as sources for social history.[23] The preoccupation of the older generation of legal historians with the highest level of the American judicial system, notably the Supreme Court and its decisions, moreover, was viewed as too narrow. From now on, every level of the judicial system, from the Supreme Court to local common councils, was seen as worthy of investigation.

From the insistence of the new social history on recovering legal records of all kinds and from all levels of society, it is but a short jump to the interdisciplinary orientation of recent legal historiography. The blurring of boundaries between established fields of study such as history and law, which is implicit in the assertion made by Friedman, Hurst, and others that a true understanding of how law operates in society may only be gained if we stop looking at legal history as a specialized, narrow inquiry, does present problems. Most important, there is the question of methodology (and ideology) – whose methodology (and ideology) prevails, that of history or that of law? The claim that law can play an important role in highlighting and making intelligible the past is pretty much accepted by both legal theorists and historians. "Like the discipline of history, the law remains anchored to a factual record that must be investigated and probed with an eye toward organizing events and actions into a coherent narrative embedded within a narrative framework."[24] But when legal historians start to experiment with what does and does not constitute a "proper" historical source by including in their research the materials of popular culture, oral history, local archival work, and participant observation, for example, there is a danger that they end up using legal culture as "a catchall" that can include "what we want grouped together and exclude what we want left out."[25] While legal culture "remains murky in theory and elusive in practice," as Richard J. Ross puts it, the concept invites historians to broaden the context of what they intuitively consider relevant.

> Yet despite its murkiness – or, to some extent, because of it – the concept [of legal culture] has invigorated recent historiography. Its lack of clarity and rigor makes it a useful heuristic and scholarly catalyst. The alluring ambiguity of legal culture offers a standing invitation to arrange seemingly unconnected bits of the past in new and revealing patterns without dampening enthusiasm or imagination by suggesting in advance what should or should not matter or by prejudging how the elements might be arranged.[26]

According to Ross, that is, it is primarily the interdisciplinary quality of the notion of legal culture that makes it useful to historians. As is the case with American Studies, of which it forms an important part, nothing – no concern, topic, or element, however trivial – is off-limits to the legal historiographer. Inclusiveness, intellectual diversity, and flexibility are the keywords here; in the opinion of young legal historians such as Ross, they are what make for good, innovative legal historiography.

"Much of contemporary legal scholarship," writes R. Richard Banks, "expresses a narrative impulse. Eschewing the traditional norms and forms of legal scholarship, many professors have turned to storytelling to capture issues not easily elucidated through more conventional approaches."[27] The narrative approach has been gaining prominence through the writings of Critical Legal Feminist and CRT scholars.[28] Within the past ten years, intellectuals and writers have produced a significant amount of "different," nontraditional – often very personal – writing about gender, race, and law. This writing, which includes personal essays, memoirs, and full autobiographies, is often written for a broader audience than that of traditional legal scholarship.[29]

In using storytelling as a way of alerting lawyers and non-lawyers alike that, as Robin Williams puts it, "laws have a profound impact upon the subjectivity of people, children, slaves, women, and other living things who either might or might not participate in their textual production, interpretation, or critique," CRT scholars build on and further develop concerns that have been present in the law and literature movement since its tentative beginnings in the 1970s.[30] Law and literature is "a project that is most easily defined as a process of reading and comparing literary and legal texts for the insight each provides into the other, and whose combined force illuminates our understanding of ourselves and our society."[31] The project or movement consists of two somewhat different enterprises or concerns. Roughly speaking, there is "law-in-literature" and there is "law-as-literature." The distinction is Robert Weisberg's and was introduced in his influential and much-quoted 1988 article, "The Law-Literature Enterprise."[32] The distinction, as Weisberg himself points out, is most useful in terms of sorting out existing scholarship in the field. In practice, "the best works on the two sides of the line tend to converge, because they constitute the work that captures the best insights about the relationship between the aesthetic and the political-ethical visions and forces in society."[33]

Law-in-literature scholars pursue the detailed study of specific authors and texts for the light they shed on legal issues and their impact on our lives. The area is not new. In the nineteenth century, English lawyers were interested in the ways in which Shakespeare, Dickens, and others dealt with the legal system. In an American context, it is somewhat more recent that critics have realized the extent to which law plays a prominent part in American letters.[34]

Underlying – and partly shaping – the discourse of law-in-literature are two basic assumptions: first, law and legal thinking have always been or are increasingly becoming too rigid, technical, and abstract, and, second, precisely because the law is a generalizing and abstracting mechanism, it may at times be necessary to supplement its professionally detached and rational voice with a more human and passionate one. This is where literature comes in. Posner, a key player in the law-in-literature debate, cites a number of important connections between law and literature: the issue of interpretation is central to both; legal texts resemble literary texts in being highly rhetorical; literature is subject to legal regulation under such rubrics as defamation, obscenity, and copyright; and judicial opinions often employ literary devices. Finally, the legal process has a significant theatrical dimension to it, which is attractive to writers of literature.[35]

What chiefly interests Posner, a one-time law professor turned judge, is what lawyers can learn from literature and literary theory. Expressing "a warm though qualified enthusiasm for the field of law and literature," he points to the way in which literary works can teach lawyers empathy and give them insights into the concerns and problems of other people.[36] When it comes to some of the larger and more ambitious claims made on behalf of law and literature by post-structuralist critics, however, Posner's attitude is less positive.[37] Other participants in the law-in-literature enterprise see greater potential in the new, interdisciplinary field. James Boyd White, Richard Weisberg, and Robert Weisberg, for example, do not limit their interest to literary texts and literary theory that may clarify the place of law in society.[38] They are willing to confront some of the more politically controversial consequences of bringing together two different fields of inquiry.[39] These consequences – and the willingness to confront them – take us to the law-as-literature part of the law-literature enterprise.[40] This is the more elusive and hard-to-define part. Whichever way one looks at it, however, the essence of law-as-literature is "the suggestion that the techniques and methods of literary theory and analysis are appropriate to legal scholarship."[41] The belief in the usefulness of literary scholarship to legal scholarship has led law-as-literature scholars to pursue two different areas of inquiry: hermeneutics and rhetoric. As some scholars see it, questions relating to the interpretation of legal texts are the most pressing; for others, a focus on how legal arguments attempt to persuade is more relevant.

Inspired by post-structuralist and deconstructionist thinking, scholars such as Stanley Fish, Ronald Dworkin, and Owen M. Fiss stress that legal practice is legal interpretation and that legal scholars may learn a thing or two from their colleagues in the humanities who are engaged in literary analysis and interpretation.[42] What occupies all three is that, with the recognition that any critical approach is at root textual and that the literature of law is inevitable, the possibility that texts are radically indeterminate becomes an ever-present reality. Fish is somewhat more at ease than are Fiss and Dworkin with the dangers of excessive interpretive freedom. For the latter, the specter of the unconstrained judge who can interpret and apply the law according to her own subjective whims looms large and suggests a dangerous slide toward nihilism.

If Fish and Company wish to make us conscious that the law is what we make of it and that this state of affairs presents problems in relation to the interpretation of legal texts, other critics wish to draw our attention to the ways in which the law manages to cover up how it works and manipulates. Gerald Frug suggests, for example, that "we look at legal argument as an example of rhetoric," just as James Boyd White wishes to replace the focus on the problem of indeterminacy with a focus on how legal writers read and write texts.[43] A thematic or a textual approach, or both, to law may distract us from the politics of law, these writers feel. Neither approach quite catches the way in which a text "assumes an equality of voices" and thereby "obscures – precisely by equating – speakers of different genders or races or classes."[44] Legal writing is as open to the uses and misuses of power as any kind of writing, and it is only by emphasizing the dimension of figurative description or style that we may successfully expose legal writing as a vehicle for the distribution and use of power. Indeed, for Robin West, law is politics and power relations, not textual interpretation. The analogy between law and literature, she suggests, should not be carried too far. Adjudication may be interpretive in form, but in substance it is an exercise of power in a way that literary interpretation is not.[45] For the past decade or so, West has used the forum of law and literature to champion the needs of "the textually excluded – those robbed of subjectivity and speech."[46] The true promise of law and literature, as she sees it, lies in its ability to educate about the *politics* of law. Though at odds with colleagues who see the study of literature as an exercise in liberal education, West thus ultimately has as much of an educational ambition for law and literature as they do.

When we get to the emerging field of law and popular culture – or, as some scholars call it, popular legal culture – it no longer makes sense to employ categories such as literature and history.[47] Law and popular culture is an interdisciplinary field; its practitioners consciously seek to blur the boundaries between older, more traditional fields of study. Yet the interest in the ways in which the realities of law and justice are changed, not merely because of legal scholarship, but also because consumers take the attitudes and ideas of the legal stories to which they have been exposed with them into places of power where they take root, recalls debates going on within the field of law and history. Likewise, the interest among these practitioners in legal storytelling, in what kinds of legal stories are told and how they are being constructed, and in what ways the people who consume these legal stories are affected by them, is immediately familiar to us from the law and literature debate.

What gave rise to the field of law and popular culture was the realization that there is a complex relationship among popular culture, the day-to-day operation of the legal system, and the ideas that books, films, and television shows attempt to convey. Most Americans learn about their legal system indirectly, from novels, newspapers and magazines, and perhaps most of all from films and television. These are the media that tell those legal stories that "bring us into contact with a cultural repository of common knowledge and popular belief concerning law, truth, and social justice in our time."[48]

Legal storytelling merits our attention for several reasons. First of all, what people consider necessary, acceptable, or just may form the basis for their support of the legal system. If we concentrate our efforts at understanding the place of law in society around the reading of specific legal rules and the operation of the legal system, we miss out on one very important source of law: the popular imagination. Second, the popular myths, images, and storytelling conventions that help shape the popular imagination remind us that we are surrounded by a plurality of legal meanings. For legal officials and law professors, whose working lives are intimately related to law, legal ideas and symbols are bound to have a different meaning from the one they hold for lay persons. Similarly, various groups in a nation or culture may experience and therefore think very differently about the law and its practitioners.

Beyond teaching practical lessons about the variety of legal sources and legal meanings, the pursuit of legal storytelling may be beneficial in a more theoretical way, participants in the law and popular culture debates claim. Legal storytelling may expand not only the traditional range of legal studies, but also the traditional range of American Studies. Here is Richard Sherwin on the attempt to transform traditional legal studies:

> [The study of law and popular culture] seeks to include what has often been omitted, such as the feelings, desires, conflicting impulses and wishes that circulate within the law, from its narrative construction to its (at times violent) social effects. To recognize this part of legal reality is to recognize as well the evisceration of the legal fictions that in the past succeeded in keeping this domain in the shadows. This includes the fiction that law derives from dispassionate reason, that it is the product of objective analysis disengaged from feeling or desire, and the fiction that legitimate legal decision making cannot occur in the absence of deductive or inductive logic, strict causal analysis, and well-reasoned explanation.[49]

The echoes of a CLS-inspired attack on law's rationality and neutrality as well as a Robin West-inspired call for the inclusion of "other voices" are unmistakable.

Scholars believe that important and innovative interdisciplinary work may result when they venture into this sphere. The parameters are not yet fixed; opinions as to how the domain is constructed, what and who it includes and excludes, and how it should be approached and analyzed vary. As Steve Redhead sees it, for example, the disciplinary terrain of "popular cultural studies" arises "where 'law' and 'popular culture' meet; where the battle over terms such as 'unpopular' and 'popular,' 'legal' and 'illegal,' 'normal' and 'pathological,' 'straight' and 'deviant' are fought out."[50] Redhead wants to explore "the diverse languages of law (of law as made up of a body of texts and institutions and personnel) within a narrative and historical setting," and he proposes three areas of study as particularly relevant for the field of law and popular culture: the role of law in licensing popular entertainment and regulating public spaces, the role of legal institutions in the changing forms of ownership and control of cultural goods and services, and the involvement of law in moral censure, particularly in the domains of domesticity and sexuality.[51]

For Sherwin and for Stewart Macauley, the worlds of law, film, and television increasingly overlap, and this calls for a careful examination of the images and stories furnished by popular culture.[52] David Ray Papke's research reflects a "concern with the dominant American culture's most basic law-related faith, institutions, motifs and disbelievers."[53] It is, he argues, in attention to cultural configurations and conventions such as courtroom trials, lawyer novels, and films that the analysis of law and popular culture must begin.[54] John Denvir concentrates his scholarly efforts on Hollywood films. Unabashed products of "mass" culture, Hollywood films turn out to provide a comparative advantage over "serious" narrative texts, he argues, in that they "draw upon a broader variety of communicative tools than novels in their attempt to engage our emotional response."[55]

Finally, many researchers are looking into how the law and lawyers are presented to the public. Are lawyers heroes or villains? Is the legal system portrayed as a well-functioning part of the American democracy or as a part that can no longer be trusted to work fairly and impartially? What role do gender, race, and class play in the day-to-day operation of the American justice system, and how are these reflected in the media? These are but some of the questions raised by law and popular culture scholars.[56] As these scholars see it, representations in popular culture of law and lawyers are a cultural barometer that can provide useful information about current norms and values as well as about alternative normative possibilities and ways of thinking. And precisely because the law is such an important cultural factor in American history and society, law and popular culture scholars feel a need to intrude on the kind of scholarship traditionally undertaken by legal scholars.

Irmina Wawrzyczek, Saul Cornell, Niels Bjerre-Poulsen, and Mark Gibney all consider issues relating to debates carried on among law and history scholars. Wawrzyczek's contribution, "Plantation Economy and Legal Safeguards of Sexual Discipline in Early Tobacco Colonies," is a study of the legal behavior of the settlers in Virginia and Maryland in the seventeenth century. She argues that the white male planter-lawmakers and law officers used the legal apparatus and legal discourse in their efforts to control the sexual activities of their indentured servants and African slaves. In "The Irony of Progressive Historiography: A Critical Comment on the Revival of Anti-Federalism in Contemporary Constitutional Thought," Cornell offers a critique of the constitutional canon. Unlike many other fields within the humanities and the social sciences, American constitutional history has never really been deconstructed so as to include alternative voices and sources. Only when the canon of constitutional history is deconstructed, Cornell argues, may the field be re-conceptualized.

Since its emergence in the late 1940s, and especially since the Supreme Court's famous decision in *Brown* v. *Board of Education of Topeka* in 1954, the American conservative movement has been heavily opposed to judicial activism. With the appointment by Ronald Reagan in the late 1980s of conservative Supreme Court judges, however, this attitude has changed. In "'Hunting in the Pond Where the Ducks Are': Conservative Opposition to Civil Rights Legislation in the 1964 Election and Beyond," Bjerre-Poulsen shows how conservative attitudes toward constitutional interpretation in the area of civil rights have changed since the 1960s and how many conservatives have come to see the court as a possible engine for their own cultural counterrevolution. Gibney explores the intersection of citizenship and nationality. His essay examines under what circumstances that firm American belief in living under the rule of law is (still) justified. As implied by his provocative title, "Protection under United States Law?: It Depends on Who You Are, Where You Are, What Aspect of Your Job You Are Talking About, and Who Is Trying to Hurt You," he believes that the protection of American law is mainly reserved for American citizens. Whether they are the targets of American criminal investigations or merely innocent bystanders caught up in American law enforcement activities, foreigners receive little protection.

Bosse Ekelund, Peter Schneck, and Marcus Bruce take us into law and literature. According to Ekelund, William Gaddis's novel *A Frolic of His Own* constitutes an astute analysis of a contemporary America in which law, art, and politics are all affected by the forces of spectacle. Ekelund's argument, in "Recognizing the Law: Value and Identities in William Gaddis's *A Frolic of His Own*," is that Gaddis attempts in his last novel to mount a defense of the values of art and law from the forces of spectacle, that is, the combined power of the press, Hollywood, and populist politicians. Schneck is also interested in Gaddis and his concern that the legal process in the United States threatens to turn into a mindless spectacle, staged exclusively for the media and directed by the petty personal interests of the lawyers, judges, and journalists involved. By comparing, in "Dissenting Opinions: William Gaddis and Alan Dershowitz on the Spectacle of Justice," Gaddis's *A Frolic of His Own* to Dershowitz's *The Advocate's Devil* (both from 1994), Schneck shows how, for all their obvious differences of opinion about American law and culture, both writers share a concern for what they see as a distortion of public and private notions of justice and truth by the dominant media. In "'The Promise of American Life': Derrick Bell, Critical Race Theory, and the American Jeremiad," Bruce discusses one of the most promising new fields in law and literature, Critical Race Theory. He relates Bell's attempt to renew the genre of legal writing in such novels as *And We Are Not Saved* (1987), *Faces at the Bottom of the Well* (1992), and especially *Gospel Choirs* (1996) to the tradition of the American Jeremiad described by Sacvan Bercovitch and shows how Bell points toward the theme of Christian love in his latest novel to ameliorate messages of bitterness and defeat in matters relating to race relations in the United States.

Christophe Den Tandt's essay on "Hollywood Courtroom Dramas: The Politics of Judicial Realism" and Eric Guthey's essay on "A Brief Cultural History of Corporate Legal Theory and Why American Studies Should Care about It" belong to the category of law and popular culture. Den Tandt focuses on courtroom dramas both in Hollywood films and on television from the 1930s to the present. He contends that these dramas have largely been vehicles for liberal politics by fostering trust in the federal judicial system whenever race and other discrimination have been excused in the name of states rights. Growing skepticism about the liberal foundation of American democracy notwithstanding, recent film and television productions have not fundamentally challenged the belief in law's promise, but have instead insisted on pursuing – and (re)constructing – the liberal American self. Guthey's focus is corporate legal theory and its influence on individual and collective conceptions of American identity. He surveys the cultural work performed by the real entity theory of the corporation, from its prehistory in the *Dartmouth College* v. *Woodward* decision (1819), through its more complete articulation in turn-of-the-century jurisprudence, to its replacement by the nexus-of-contracts theories currently in vogue. By relating this cultural work to media legends such as Ted Turner, he shows how the various transformations in corporate jurisprudence have contributed to considerable confusion about the distinctions between the public and the private spheres in American social life.

In "American Links to Legal Reform in Ireland, 1937-1997: A Study in the International Impact of American Constitutional Law," Michael Böss discusses the way American constitutional law has inspired Irish lawyers and politicians, notably Mary Robinson, in their attempts to create political and legal reform in the Republic of Ireland from the 1960s to the present day. His is a new and interesting approach to the international theme, an approach that links law to American culture but does not directly fall into law and history, law and literature, or law and popular culture. In identifying what the Irish find so attractive about American law that they wish to import it into their own system, Böss's essay nicely sums up ideas about American law and culture, thereby providing a fitting conclusion to this volume.

Notes

1. Scott Turow, *One L* (New York, 1977), 200.
2. Duncan Kennedy, *Sexy Dressing Etc. Essays on the Power and Politics of Cultural Identity* (Cambridge, Mass., 1993), and *A Critique of Adjudication (Fin de siècle)* (Cambridge, Mass., 1997).
3. Kennedy, *A Critique of Adjudication,* 1.
4. Richard A. Posner, *Overcoming Law* (Cambridge, Mass., 1995), vii.
5. For a brief overview of some of the ways in which Americans find and construct meaning with reference to law, see David Ray Papke, "Law in American Culture: An Overview," 15 *Journal of American Culture,* 3 (1992). See also Helle Porsdam, *Legally Speaking: Contemporary American Culture and the Law* (Amherst, Mass., 1999).
6. Jerold S. Auerbach, *Justice without Law? Resolving Disputes without Lawyers* (New York, 1983); Richard H. Weisberg, *The Failure of the Word: The Protagonist as Lawyer in Modern Fiction* (New Haven, 1984); Robert A. Ferguson, *Law and Letters in American Culture* (Cambridge, Mass., 1984); Carl S. Smith, John P. McWilliams Jr., and Maxwell Bloomfield, *Law and American Literature: A Collection of Essays* (New York, 1983).
7. Auerbach, *Justice without Law?* 115.
8. Daniel J. Boorstin, *The Mysterious Science of the Law: An Essay on Blackstone's Commentaries* (Chicago, 1996; orig. pub. 1941), xvii.
9. Perry Miller, *The Life of the Mind in America: From the Revolution to the Civil War* (New York, 1965). Book two is called "The Rise of the Legal Mentality."
10. Stanley N. Katz, "Explaining the Law in Early American History," *William and Mary Quarterly,* 3d Ser., 50 (1993), 4. See also Katz, "The Problem of a Colonial Legal History," in Jack P. Greene and J. R. Pole, eds., *Colonial British America: Essays in the New History of the Early Modern Era* (Baltimore, 1984), 457-89.
11. The following notes are merely meant to suggest what has been written in these areas of interest to legal historians; they are by no means exhaustive. See, e.g., Irving Brant, *The Bill of Rights: Its Origin and Meaning* (New York, 1967); Edward P. Hutchinson, *Legislative History of American Immigration Policy, 1798-1965* (Philadelphia, 1981); John V. Orth, *The Judicial Power of the United States: The Eleventh Amendment in American History* (New York, 1987); and Alfred H. Kelly, Wilfred A. Harbison, and Herman Belz, *The American Constitution: Its Origins and Developments* (New York, 1991).
12. See, e.g., Auerbach, *Unequal Justice: Lawyers and Social Change in Modern America* (New York, 1976); Morton J. Horwitz, *The Transformation of American Law, 1780-1860* (Cambridge, Mass., 1977), and *The Transformation of American Law, 1870-1960* (Cambridge, Mass., 1991); Michael G. Kammen, *A Machine That Would Go of Itself: The Constitution in American Culture* (New York, 1986); Henry J. Abraham, *Freedom and the Court: Civil Rights and Liberties in the United States* (New

York, 1988), and *Justices and Presidents: A Political History of Appointments to the Supreme Court* (New York, 1992); William M. Wiecek, *Liberty under Law: The Supreme Court in American Life* (Baltimore, 1988); Richard L. Abel, *American Lawyers* (New York, 1989); Kermit L. Hall, *The Magic Mirror: Law in American History* (New York, 1989); and Peter Charles Hoffer, *The Law's Conscience: Equitable Constitutionalism in America* (Chapel Hill, N. C., 1990).
13. See, e.g., G. Edward White, *The American Judicial Tradition: Profiles of Leading American Judges* (New York, 1976), *Earl Warren* (New York, 1982), and *Justice Oliver Wendell Holmes: Law and the Inner Self* (New York, 1993); Sheldon Novick, *Honorable Justice* (Boston, 1989); Charles F. Hobson, *The Great Chief Justice: John Marshall and the Rule of Law* (Lawrence, Kan., 1996); and Jean Edward Smith, *John Marshall: Definer of a Nation* (New York, 1996).
14. Robert M. Fogelson, *Big-City Police* (Cambridge, Mass., 1977); Francis A. Allen, *The Decline of the Rehabilitative Ideal: Penal Policy and Social Purpose* (New Haven, 1981); Norval Morris and Michael Tonry, *Between Prison and Probation: Intermediate Punishment in a Rational Sentencing System* (New York, 1990); Gary Kleck, *Point Blank: Guns and Violence in America* (New York, 1991); Marvin E. Frankel, *Criminal Sentences: Law without Order* (New York, 1993).
15. Anthony M. Platt, *The Child Saver: The Invention of Delinquency* (Chicago, 1969); S. Brown, *Objectivity and Cultural Divergence* (New York, 1984); James B. Gilbert, *A Cycle of Outrage: America's Reaction to the Juvenile Delinquent in the 1950s* (New York, 1986); Victoria E. Bynum, *Unruly Women: The Politics of Social and Sexual Control in the Old South* (Chapel Hill, N. C., 1992); Marie-Christine Leps, *Apprehending the Criminal: The Production of Deviance in Nineteenth Century Discourse* (Durham, N. C., 1992); Michael Cruit and Pat Lauderdale, *The Struggle for Control: A Study of Law, Disputes and Deviance* (New York, 1993); L. Calhoun, "Institutions and Deviance – Art and Psychiatry," *Critical Review,* 8 (1994), 393; J. M. Lehman, "Durkheim Theories of Deviance and Suicide: A Feminist Reconsideration," *American Journal of Sociology,* 100 (1995), 904; C. Stanley, "Teenage Kicks: Urban Narratives of Dissent Not Deviance," *Crime Law and Social Change,* 23 (1995), 91.
16. Anthony Chase, "Historical Reconstruction in Popular Legal and Political Culture," *Seton Hall Law Review,* 42 (1994), 1992.
17. Lawrence M. Friedman, "Legal Culture and the Welfare State," in Guenther Teubner, *Dilemmas of Law in the Welfare State* (1985), reprinted in *Law and Society: Readings on the Social Study of Law,* ed. Stewart Macauley, Friedman, and John Stookey (New York, 1995), 269.
18. See, e.g., J. Willard Hurst, *The Growth of American Law: The Law Makers* (Boston, 1950); *The Legitimacy of the Business Corporation in the Law of the United States, 1780-1970* (Charlottesville, Va., 1970); *Law and the Conditions of Freedom in the Nineteenth Century United States* (Madison, Wis., 1964); and *Law and Economic Growth: The Legal History of the Lumber Industry in Wisconsin* (Madison, Wis., 1984).

19. See, e.g., Richard Kluger, *Simple Justice: The History of Brown v. The Board of Education and Black America's Struggle for Equality* (New York, 1975); John W. Blassingame, *The Slave Community: Plantation Life in the Ante-Bellum South* (New York, 1979); J. Harvey Wilkinson III, *From Brown to Bakke: The Supreme Court and School Integration, 1954-78* (New York, 1979); Elizabeth Fox-Genovese and Eugene D. Genovese, *Fruits of Merchant Capital: Slavery and Bourgeois Property in the Rise and Expansion of Capitalism* (New York, 1983); Donald G. Nieman, *Promises to Keep: African-Americans and the Constitutional Order, 1776 to the Present* (New York, 1991); and Eugene D. Genovese, *The Southern Front: History and Politics in the Cultural War* (Columbia, Mo., 1995).
20. See, e.g., Peter Laslett et al., eds., *Bastardy and Its Comparative History: Studies in the History of Illegitimacy and Marital Nonconformism* (Cambridge, Mass., 1980); Rickie Solinger, *Wake Up Little Susie: Single Pregnancy and Race Before Roe v. Wade* (New York, 1992); Marie Mac Lean, *The Name of the Mother: Writing Illegitimacy* (New York, 1994); and Llewyllyn Hendrix, *Illegitimacy and Social Structures: Cross-Cultural Perspectives on Nonmarital Birth* (Westport, Conn., 1996).
21. See, e.g,. Richard F. Hixson, *Privacy in a Public Society: Human Rights in Conflict* (New York, 1987); Julie Innes, *Privacy, Intimacy, and Isolation* (New York, 1992); Vincent J. Samar, *The Right to Privacy: Gays, Lesbians, and the Constitution* (Philadelphia, 1992); David J. Garrow, *Liberty and Sexuality: The Right to Privacy and the Making of Roe v. Wade* (New York, 1994); Michelle Perrot, *A History of Private Life* (Cambridge, Mass., 1994); Deckle McLean, *Privacy and Its Invasion* (Westport, Conn., 1995); and Patricia Boling, *Privacy and the Politics of Intimate Life* (Ithaca, N. Y., 1996).
22. See, e.g., William H. Chafe, *Women and Equality: Changing Patterns in American Culture* (New York, 1977); Rudy Ray Seward, *The American Family: A Demographic History* (Beverly Hills, Calif., 1978); Michael Gordon, ed., *The American Family in Social-Historical Perspective* (New York, 1983); Carol Groneman and Mary Beth Norton, eds., *"To Toil the Livelong Day": America's Women at Work, 1780-1980* (Ithaca, N. Y., 1987); Steven Mintz and Susan Kellogg, *Domestic Revolutions. A Social History of American Family Life* (New York, 1988); and Linda Gordon, *Heroes of Their Own Lives: The Politics and History of Family Violence* (New York, 1989).
23. See, e.g., Sara M. Evans, *Personal Politics: The Roots of Women's Liberation in the Civil Rights Movement and the New Left* (New York, 1979); Susan D. Becker, *The Origins of the Equal Rights Amendment: American Feminism Between the Wars* (Westport, Conn., 1981); Mary Frances Berry, *Why the ERA Failed: Politics, Women's Rights, and the Amending Process of the Constitution* (Bloomington, Ind., 1988); Linda Gordon, *Woman's Body, Woman's Right: A Social History of Birth Control in America* (New York, 1990); Herman Belz, *Equality Transformed: A Quarter-Century of Affirmative Action* (New Brunswick, N. J., 1991);

and Flora Davis, *Moving the Mountain: The Woman's Movement since 1960* (New York, 1991).

24. Lawrence Douglas, "Wartime Lies: Securing the Holocaust in Law and Literature," *Yale Journal of Law and the Humanities,* 7 (1995), 368. See also Theodore Y. Blumoff, "The Third Best Choice: An Essay on Law and History," *Hastings Law Journal,* 41 (1990), 537.
25. Richard J. Ross, "The Legal Past of Early New England: Notes for the Study of Law, Legal Culture, and Intellectual History," *WMQ,* 50 (1993), 33, 34.
26. Ibid., 34.
27. R. Richard Banks, "The Political Economy of Racial Discourse," *Yale J. Law and Hum.,* 9 (1997), 217.
28. See, e.g., Kathryn Abrams, "Hearing the Call of Stories," *California Law Review,* 79 (1991), 971, which summarizes the use of narratives in Critical Feminist legal scholarship.
29. See, e.g., Richard Delgado, *The Rodrigo Chronicles: Conversations about America and Race* (New York, 1995), and *The Coming Race War? And Other Apocalyptic Tales of America After Affirmative Action and Welfare* (New York, 1996); Stephen L. Carter, *Reflections of an Affirmative Action Baby* (New York, 1991); Judy Scales-Trent, *Notes of a White Black Woman: Race, Color, Community* (University Park, Pa., 1995); and Gregory H. Williams, *Life on the Color Line: The True Story of a White Boy Who Discovered He Was Black* (New York, 1995).
30. Robin Williams, "Communities, Texts, and Law: Reflections on the Law and Literature Movement," *Yale J. Law and Hum.,* 1 (1988), 155.
31. Bruce L. Rockwood, "The Good, the Bad, and the Ironic: Two Views on Law and Literature," ibid., 8 (1996), 533 n. 1.
32. Robert Weisberg, "Law-Literature Enterprise," ibid., 1 (1988), 1.
33. Ibid., 5.
34. See, e.g., James Boyd White, *The Legal Imagination: Studies in the Nature of Legal Thought and Expression* (Boston, 1973), *When Words Lose Their Meaning: Constitutions and Reconstitutions of Language, Character, and Community* (Chicago, 1984) and *Heracles' Bow: Essays on the Rhetoric and Poetics of Law* (Madison, Wis., 1985).
35. Posner, *Law and Literature: A Misunderstood Relation* (Cambridge, Mass., 1988), 8-9.
36. Ibid., 353. This educative ambition of law and literature, and the perceived limitation of the traditional casebook method is something most participants agree on. It is interesting to note in this connection that a comparison may be made between Turow, *One L,* and more recent accounts of experiences with legal education in Chris Goodrich, *Anarchy and Elegance: Confessions of a Journalist at Yale Law School* (Boston, 1991), and Richard D. Kahlenberg, *Broken Contract: A Memoir of Harvard Law School* (New York, 1992). Much like Turow, Goodrich and Kahlenberg relate personal stories about the loss of a moral vision of learning or service. There are 25 years between Turow's and Goodrich's and Kahlenberg's stories. Yet the initial amazement followed by resent-

ment at discovering that learning to think like a lawyer means losing one's soul, described by Goodrich and Kahlenberg, are very similar to that recalled by Turow. The high expectations Goodrich and Kahlenberg had, even in the early 1990s, on entering law school are remarkable.
37. In *Overcoming Law,* Posner does mention one particular way in which the study of literature may be of professional use to lawyers. Inspired by Thomas C. Grey, *The Wallace Stevens Case: Law and the Practice of Poetry* (Cambridge, Mass., 1991), 480-81, he comments, "I now see with the aid of my own interpretive struggles with the poems of Wallace Stevens discussed by Grey that there is another and more favorable light in which to regard [the principle that the reader of a statute or contract or other legal rule or instrument should assume that every meaning was placed there for a purpose]. It is an antidote to hasty, careless, lazy reading. If we assume that every word is there for a purpose, we are made to read and ponder – every word, as we would surely be led to do by a good teacher of poetry. It is only when that principle of interpretation is transformed from a discipline to an algorithm that it is aptly criticized as unrealistic and misleading. At some level, then, law and literature do converge."
38. Robert Weisberg's contribution to law and literature consists of his survey on the "Law and Literature Enterprise" and *Literary Criticisms of Law* (Princeton, 2000). In addition to *Failure of the Word,* Richard Weisberg has written "Text into Theory: A Literary Approach to the Constitution," *Georgia Law Review,* 20 (1986), 846-79; "Coming of Age Some More: 'Law and Literature' Beyond the Cradle," *Nova Law Review,* 13 (1988), 107; and *Poethics: And Other Strategies of Law and Literature* (New York, 1992). For James Boyd White, see note 34. His latest are *Justice as Translation: An Essay in Cultural and Legal Criticism* (Chicago, 1990), *Acts of Hope: Creating Authority in Literature, Law and Politics* (Chicago, 1995), and *From Expectation to Experience: Essays on Law and Legal Education* (Michigan, 2000).
39. This may have something to do with the fact that they were all three trained in literary studies before turning to law.
40. Ian Ward sees James Boyd White as a kind of transitional figure, whose interests span both parts of the law-literature enterprise. See Ward, *Law and Literature: Possibilities and Perspectives* (Cambridge, 1995), chap. 1.
41. Ibid., 16.
42. For Stanley Fish, see *Doing What Comes Naturally: Change, Rhetoric, and the Practice and Theory in Literary and Legal Studies* (Durham, N. C., 1989), and *There's No Such Thing as Free Speech, and It's a Good Thing Too* (New York, 1994). For Ronald Dworkin, see "Law As Interpretation," *Texas Law Review,* 60 (1982), 527-50. Since *Law's Empire* (Cambridge, Mass., 1986), in which he affirmed his commitment to the chain novel model as discussed in "Law As Interpretation," Dworkin has added little to this model of adjudication. In *Life's Dominion: An Argument about Abortion, Euthanasia, and Individual Freedom* (New York,

1993), for example, he focuses on the constitutional questions of legalized abortion and euthanasia. For Owen M. Fiss, see "Objectivity and Interpretation," *Stanford Law Review,* 34 (1982), 739.

43. Gerald Frug, "Argument as Character," *Stanford Law Review,* 40 (1988), 871.
44. Victoria Kahn, "Rhetoric and the Law," *diacritics,* 19 (1989), 26.
45. See Robin West, "Adjudication is Not Interpretation," in her *Narrative, Authority, and Law* (Ann Arbor, Mich., 1993).
46. West, "Communities, Texts, and Law," 143.
47. See, e.g., "Symposium: Popular Legal Culture," *Yale Law Journal,* 98 (1989), 1545-58.
48. Richard K. Sherwin, "Picturing Justice: Images of Law and Lawyers in the Visual Media," *University of San Francisco Law Review,* 30 (1996), 897.
49. Sherwin, "Picturing Justice," 898.
50. Steve Redhead, *Unpopular Cultures: The Birth of Law and Popular Culture* (Manchester, Eng., 1995), 3.
51. Ibid., 9-10. What makes the study of law and popular culture especially pertinent, according to Redhead, is that in our "media-saturated, self-referential culture," we are witnessing the disappearance of law into popular culture: "Put simply, the claim is that a legal (high) modernism (defined historically as the rule of law, the legal subject, legal rights) is currently fragmenting in such a way that what could be said to be an authority, or power, to regulate and discipline the boundaries of certain social discourses and practices (for example, 'popular culture,' 'postmodernism') which law once seemed to have had in modernist jurisprudential theory is now fast disappearing" (ibid., 6-7).
52. Stewart Macauley, "Images of Law in Everyday Life: The Lessons of School, Entertainment, and Spectator Sports," 21 *Law and Society Review,* 21 (1987), 185.
53. Papke, "Law in American Culture: An Overview," 4.
54. See Papke, "The Advocate's Malaise: Contemporary American Lawyer Novels," *Journal of Legal Education,* 38 (1988), 413, "The Courtroom Trial as American Cultural Convention," *Popular Culture in Libraries,* 2:4 (1994), 53, *Heretics in the Temple: Americans Who Reject the Nation's Legal Faith* (New York, 1998), and *The Pullman Case: The Clash of Capital and Labor in Industrial America* (Kansas City, Mo., 1999).
55. John Denvir, "Legal Reelism: The Hollywood Film As Legal Text," *Legal Studies Forum,* 15 (1991), 196. See also Denvir, ed., *Legal Reelism: Movies as Legal Texts* (Urbana, Ill., 1996). On the topic of law and movies, see Paul Bergman and Michael Asimov, *Reel Justice: The Courtroom Goes to the Movies* (Kansas City, Mo., 1996), and David A. Black, *Law in Film: Resonance and Interpretation* (Urbana, Ill., 1999).
56. See, e.g., Donald G. Baker, "The Lawyer in Popular Fiction," *Journal of Popular Culture,* 3 (1969), 493; Robert C. Post, "On the Popular Image of the Lawyer: Reflections in a Dark Glass," *California Law Review,* 75 (1987), 379; James W. Gordon, "The Popular Image of the American Lawyer: Some Thoughts on Its Nineteenth Century Intellectual Bases,"

Washington and Lee Law Review, 46 (1989), 763; Diane M. Glass, "Portia in Primetime: Women Lawyers, Television, and L.A. Law," *Yale Journal of Law and Feminism,* 2 (1990), 371; Suzanne Frentz, "T.V. Law: Image Versus Reality," *Focus on Law Studies,* 7 (1991), 1; Judith Grant, "Prime Time Crime; Television Portrayals of Law Enforcement," *Journal of American Culture,* 15 (1992), 57; Michael Asimow, "When Lawyers Were Heroes," 30 *U. San Francisco Law Rev.,* 30 (1996), 1131; Ralph Berets, "Changing Images of Justice in American Films," *Legal Studies Forum,* 20 (1996), 473; Justin P. Brooks, "Will Boys Just Be Boyz N the Hood? African-American Directors Portray a Crumbling Justice System in Urban America," *Oklahoma City University Law Review,* 22 (1997), 1; Randall Coyne, "Images of Lawyers and the Three Stooges," ibid., 247; Laura Krugman, "Judicial Fictions: Images of Supreme Court Justices in the Novel, Drama, and Film," *Arizona Law Review,* 39 (1997), 151; Peter Brooks and Paul Gewirtz, eds. *Law's Stories: Narrative and Rhetoric in the Law* (New Haven, 1996); Robert M. Jarvis and Paul R. Josephs, eds., *Prime Time Law: Fictional Television as Legal Narrative* (Carolina Academic Pr., 1998); Austin Sarat and Thomas R. Kearns, eds., *Law in the Domains of Culture* (Michigan, 1998); and Richard K. Sherwin, *When Law Goes Pop: The Vanishing Line Between Law and Popular Culture* (Chicago, 2000).

1
Plantation Economy and Legal Safeguards of Sexual Discipline in Early Tobacco Colonies

Irmina Wawrzyczek

When in 1984 Stanley N. Katz challenged the young generation of American historians to invigorate the somewhat neglected field of colonial legal history, he emphasized the significance of law for the better appreciation of colonial culture and pointed to the urgent need to develop theory helpful in a more systematic understanding of how law relates to society.[1] He did not anticipate how the virtual explosion of critical theory would soon complicate, rather than systematize, the conceptual landscape of historical studies in general and how various theoretical perspectives would compete for legitimacy in the historiography of early America.[2] Yet his sense of future direction in colonial legal history – the interest in the importance of law as a cultural factor – proved correct. During the last decade, a number of articles and books on the American colonial period, which would hardly pass as legal history by the standards of the older generation of lawyer-historians, have made innovative use of the evidence of courts and legislatures to determine how the first generations of white Americans used the law and with what cultural consequences.[3]

Virginia and Maryland, the two British settlements launched on the Chesapeake Bay in the early seventeenth century, quickly acquired the name of tobacco colonies. Both adopted the cultivation of the tobacco plant as their main economic activity; both began to prosper commercially and expand territorially thanks to tobacco. In both, the plantation economy constituted the framework determining social, political, and cultural development. The present microhistorical study of the legal behavior of the settlers in the region in the seventeenth century aspires to be a cultural project situated at the convergence of the once separate fields of social, economic, and legal history. Its aim is to inquire into the select aspect of colonial law and the legal system concerning the regulation of sexual activities and to relate their evolution to the plantation system in order to highlight a parallel between the legal and socioeconomic growth of the tobacco communities. It is argued here that the white male planter-lawmakers and law officers used the legal apparatus and discourse to install new, seemingly natural, and morally sound norms of sexual conduct that, at the same time, served as effective controls over the scarce and most valuable resource of the time – plantation labor.

Studies of the transfer of English law to the Chesapeake settlements often note that the novice colonial lawmakers, mostly men from middling ranks in England, lacked formal legal education and had, at best, a working understanding of certain parts of English law and procedure. They responded eclectically to the requirements of the growing colonies by borrowing, adapting, and creating statutory provisions.[4] This is exactly how they proceeded when the need to tighten sexual discipline emerged. A closer examination of seventeenth-century colonial statutes and court records shows that, when creating legal mechanisms of sexual regulation in the name of social order and Christian morality, the early colonial legislators and judges imposed rules ultimately benefiting the planter class they themselves belonged to.

A unique combination of economic and demographic factors made sexual discipline an important concern to the colonial authorities in the early Chesapeake. Virginia and Maryland experienced the same unforeseen consequences of the plantation system: the sustained imbalance in the sex composition of the population characterized by a severe shortage of women.

Immigration to both tobacco colonies was predominantly male. The demographic asymmetry resulted from the great demand for men as agricultural laborers, to which English transatlantic traders responded by recruiting and transporting male servants.[5] The available population estimates differ in numerical, temporal, and regional details but show the same overall sex ratio. In Virginia, the initial ratio of six men to every woman was first reduced to an average of four to one and then to about three men to every woman; nevertheless women remained scarce into the early decades of the eighteenth century.[6] Moreover, between 70 and 85 percent of the seventeenth-century immigrants to the Chesapeake were servants, most of them single, young, and representing social ranks from quasi-criminal to gentry.[7] Similarly, plantation labor needs were responsible for the preponderance of men among black slaves brought and sold to the Chesapeake in growing numbers since the 1680s.[8]

Indentured servants and African slaves constituted a costly investment for planters, who intended to extract maximum profit from the labor of the dearly purchased hands. At the same time the laborers remained young men and women (typically aged 15 to 24) whose sexual drive, naturally strong at that age – or rather the potential consequences of engaging in sexual activities – posed a threat to this goal. Moreover, the demographic imbalance seriously frustrated the chances of free male colonists for marriage and family formation, which in turn encouraged alternative sexual arrangements often involving maidservants. These practices – illegal, sinful, or criminal – quickly surface in the court records as several recognizable patterns: a male planter exploiting sexually his female servant, with her consent or by coercion; a single planter meddling sexually with a maidservant owned by another; sexual interaction between servants on the same or neighboring plantations, often resulting in pregnancy and illegitimate birth; and attempts at abortion or infanticide by fornicating women who became pregnant.[9]

The behavior of the colonists in courtship and marriage also exhibited the morally unsettling influence of the disturbed demography. Some men treated the seduction of a woman as a way of winning her consent to marriage. Women, often former servants, entered marriage when already pregnant by men other than the newly wed husbands. Wives, left alone for too long by spouses traveling on business, committed adultery or lived as concubines with available men. Some married women eloped with single men ready to cohabit with and support them.[10]

The presence of men and women of different races constituted another element disrupting the sexual discipline of the colonists. Whereas the early exclusion of Native Americans from the colonial societies prevented their admission as sexual partners of any white group, except for incidental episodes, it was not the case with the Africans, who permanently lived among the whites and were available also for sexual interaction.[11] This situation further constrained the colonists in their sexual choices when the official policy of racial segregation made miscegenation intolerable. Meanwhile, white men successfully sought sexual opportunities with black women, and white maidservants entered intimate relationships with black men.[12] None of these nonmarital or marital irregularities was pervasive, yet the evidence the unruly individuals left behind during the century indicates a drift of colonial sexual mores toward slackness and opportunism.

At the same time, powerful cultural and institutional forces were at work to prevent the tobacco colonies from becoming the scene of social disorder and moral collapse. By far the most effective mechanisms of sexual regulation were the law and law courts. The English-born Chesapeake colonists were accustomed to the interpretation and enforcement of moral order by ecclesiastical tribunals. However, logistical difficulties – mainly the absence of bishops and archdeacons trained in the rules and procedures of canon law – prevented them from re-creating ecclesiastical courts in America. Consequently, the task of ordering people's sexual lives and moral conduct passed irreversibly to the lay legislatures and judiciaries.

The Virginia assembly quickly recognized and assumed responsibility in this area and included sex regulation in its comprehensive code of moral conduct. In the section of the laws devoted to "every man's private conceit," the first colonial representatives convened in 1619 legislated against several "ungodly disorders," among them "suspicions of whoredomes, dishonest company – keeping with women and suchlike."[13] The criminal nature of transgressions against the sexual code was subsequently validated by several reenactments of increasing stylistic and technical sophistication. Such statutory developments as the 1632 oath for churchwardens, the 1662 specification of churchwardens' duties, the 1691 "act for more effectual suppressing the several sins and offences," and the 1705 provision against adultery and fornication tightened the grip of secular law on sexual relations among Virginians.[14]

The assembly of Maryland practically replicated the legislation of its southern neighbor, starting in 1650 with an "Act for punishment of certain Offences as Swearing, cursing, Adultery & c." Its first sentence stated that "Every person or persons that shalbe found or proved by confession of either party to haue comited Adultery, or fornicacon, such Offender or Offenders shalbe censured or punished."[15] Further laws to the same effect appeared repeatedly afterward, as the assembly developed and perfected its body of statutes, for example, an "Act Concerning Adultery & Fornication" of 1654, repeated in 1676, or the "Act for the Punishment of Blasphemy, Fornication & Adultery" of 1694, repeated in 1699.[16]

Parallel with the statutory regulation of the colonists at large, a series of laws was introduced specifically concerning the sexual conduct of servants, with the emphasis on bastardy and fornication committed by females. The amount of legislation devoted to the suppression of these offenses indicates important concerns of the planter lawmakers, concerns other than the mere sense of Christian responsibility for the moral condition of laboring people. The wording of the preambles to the acts and the punishments they prescribed reflect the practical secular motives behind this stream of legislation. In March 1643 the Virginia assembly expressed concern that "many great abuses and much detriment have been found to arise both against the law of God and likewise to the service of manye masters of families in the collony occasioned through secret marriages of servants ... and also by committing fornication."[17] The secular emphasis also appears in a 1658 Maryland law aimed against unmarried women servants "gotten with child in the tyme of their servitude to the great dishonour of God and the apparent damage to the Masters, or Owners of such Servants."[18]

The preoccupation with servants' sexuality sprang from the investment value of the laborers and the desire to recoup the cost of their purchase by maximum exploitation, goals threatened by the sexual activity of servants. Each sexual act was viewed as a potential act of procreation affecting, first of all, the strength and health of the woman, reducing her utility, keeping her out of work in the period surrounding birth, and adding a new dependent to the household. In extreme situations, not so rare in those times, a woman servant could die in childbirth, thus wasting the money invested in her. The planters' awareness of the direct connection between servants' sexual contacts, their capacity to work, and undesirable financial consequences is conveyed in the judicial justifications of punishments for bastardy with phrases such as "recompence of loss of service," "loss of service time," "great Trouble and Charge for keeping of the [bastard] Child," and "satisfaction of charges" expended by a female servant's "lieing in."

The development of the criminal law sector dealing with sexual offenses illustrates this awareness even better. The legislative initiatives in both colonies indicate a growing desire of the planter class for statutory safeguards against losses incurred by individuals and communities owing to the violation of these sexual norms. In Virginia, excommunication and penance were never enacted after 1619 and were replaced with a system of money or labor compensations or both. The act of 1643 constituted the first legal step in this direction:

> And it is also further enacted and confirmed by the authority of this Grand Assembly that if any man servant shall comit the act of fornication with any mayd or woman servant, he shall for his offence, beside the punishment by the law appointed in like cases, give satisfaction for the losse of her service, by one whole year's service, when he shall be free from his master according to his indentures, And if it so fall out that a freeman offend as formerly he shall be compelled to make satisfaction to the master or mistris of the said woman servant by his service for one complete year.[19]

All subsequent enactments in the seventeenth century progressed along the same line and perfected the system of converting sexual offenses into the amounts of tobacco and labor time owed by the culprits to the suffering parties. The "price" of proven fornication settled at the rate of 500 lb. of tobacco, a fine payable to the parish, and of adultery at 1,000 lb. The additional fine for a servant bearing a bastard was first set at 2,000 lb. tobacco or two years of service, later lowered to 1,000 lb. or one year of service. Fathers of bastards were obliged to put up security for the upkeep of the children, and free sexual offenders of both sexes had to pay security for good behavior. Unpayable fines were converted into whipping at the rate of twenty to twenty- five lashes for every 500 lb. of tobacco or into imprisonment.[20]

These provisions, hard on all individuals guilty of sexual crimes, affected servants with special severity. Rarely able to pay the high fines, they could not escape whipping unless their master bought them out. Only in exceptional situations did they manage to avoid an extended term of service, always longer for female than for male servants. In fact, during the first codification task undertaken in October 1705, the Virginia assembly definitely separated the sexual discipline of servants and slaves from the rest of the population, making it a part of the comprehensive labor law of the colony, "An Act concerning Servants and Slaves."

The laws of early Maryland set servants apart as a special category of sexual offenders even more decisively. Bastardy committed by female servants preoccupied the lawmakers most, and acts "concearning Servants that haue Bastards" were enacted at least five times in the period 1658-1694.[21] The law for servant bastard bearers elaborated on the procedure and punishment:

> Every such Mother of a Bastard Child not able sufficiently to proue the party charged to be the begetter of such child, in every such case The mother of such Child shall onely be lyable to satisfie the damages soe sustained by Servitude, or other wayes as the Court before whom such matter is brought shall see convenient. Provided that where the mother of any such Child as aforesaid shalbe able to prove her charge either by sufficient testimony of wittnesses or confession Then the party charged, if a Servant to satisfie halfe the said damage, if a freeman

then the whole damages by Servitude or otherwise as aforesaid.[22]

In Maryland, as in Virginia, evidently more importance was attached to the sexual discipline of servants than of free colonists; moreover, the sexual abstinence of unmarried servants ceased to be an absolute moral value even nominally and became a part of the colonial labor regulations.

A number of servant fornication and bastardy cases would have never entered the court agenda if marriage had been permitted to those wanting to legalize their sexual unions and illicit conceptions. Yet this simple solution, routinely allowed in similar situations in England, ran strongly against the labor claims and needs of the planters. Thus the colonial law never so much as recommended marriage to servants guilty of illegitimate pregnancy. On the contrary, special acts were passed against secret marriages of servants, which in practice allowed the masters of fornicating individuals to profit from the culprits' additional service time.[23] For women found guilty of sexual transgressions the system offered a prospect of living with the stigma of "whoredom," often for quite a long portion of the remaining contractual term and the extra penal period of bondage.

The gradual introduction of slavery to the plantations directed the attention of the lawmakers to the sexual activity of blacks and the possible complications it might cause to the racial divisions on which the system relied. In the 1660s, intensive efforts began in both colonies to bring statute law into conformity with labor employment customs, and to end the confusion of who was and who was not a slave. Until that time, the institution of slavery had been growing without much statutory sustenance, but as colonial practice made blacks valuable capital assets in financial and property settlements, the stability of the staple economy required an unequivocal regulation of their status. The new laws equated slavery with the black race, and thus black sexuality had also to be kept within racial boundaries. Consequently, not only did the sexual regulation of the blacks become a part of the slavery codes, but it also focused on the prevention of interracial sex. Out of these needs and considerations, a whole section of antimiscegenation provisions grew, a novel development with no precedent in the laws of England.[24]

The antimiscegenation legislation in Virginia and Maryland proceeded piecemeal, from decisions about the status of mixed-race children to the delegalization of all interracial sexual relationships. The Virginia assembly took the initiative in 1662 in response to doubts about the status of children "got by any Englishman upon a negro woman" and declared that "all children borne in this country shalbe held bond or free only according to the condition of the mother."[25] There followed a series of laws severely punishing and eventually forbidding altogether interracial nonmarital and marital sexual unions. The law of Maryland passed in 1664 and reenacted in 1671 discouraged such unions by prescribing life slavery for children of interracial marriages and servitude of the white wife to her slave husband's master "during the life of her husband."[26] In 1681, the Maryland assembly imposed high fines on masters permitting interracial marriages and on ministers performing them.[27] Ten years later, the Virginia assembly introduced an even more radical sanction against free whites who wed nonwhites of any status. "Be it enacted," the new law read, "that for the time to come, whatsoever English or other white man or woman being free shall intermarry with a negroe, mulatto, or Indian man or woman bond or free, shall within three months after such marriage be banished and removed from this dominion for ever." As in Maryland, a bastard child of a free English woman by "any negroe or mulatto" was to be bound as a servant until reaching thirty years of age, and the mother's fine was as much as £15 sterling. If the mother was a servant unable to pay, she was to be sold by the churchwardens of her parish for additional five years of service.[28] The crowning achievement of the seventeenth- century antimiscegenation legislation in the Chesapeake were the relevant sections of the 1705 Virginia slave code. They confirmed most of the earlier racial rules and supplemented them with a few novelties. For instance, the period of bondage for white women's illegitimate children by black fathers was raised from thirty to thirty-one years, and a white person of either sex who married "a negro or mulatto man or woman, bound or free" risked being "committed to prison, and there to remain, during the space of six months, without bail or mainprize" and paying a fine of "ten pounds current money of Virginia."[29]

The expanding network of secular courts in the Chesapeake energetically enforced the laws of sexual regulation. Each tobacco colony went through an initial period of searching for effective means of local government and judicial administration. After the experimental years 1617-1634 in Virginia and 1634-1644 in Maryland, there emerged from clouded and overlapping jurisdictions single systems of local and appellate courts, and the colonial legislatures laid down statutory foundations for the systems of county courts, of which there were twenty in Virginia and eleven in Maryland by the end of the seventeenth century. The general assemblies delegated most of their original jurisdiction to the local courts, and retained it – as provincial and general courts at Jamestown and St. Mary's City – for crimes for which the penalty was loss of life or limb and in civil suits over a certain value set by statutes. In all other cases they functioned as courts of appeal against local judicial decisions. The adaptation of the complex English divisions into a single system of local and appellate courts gave the county courts an amalgamated jurisdiction over administrative, civil, criminal, and ecclesiastical matters. Within the system, the trial of all noncapital criminal sexual acts and sex-related civil suits was assigned to the county jurisdictions, while appeals and capital offences, such as infanticide, went before the provincial courts.[30]

Parallel to the formation of the judicial institutions, procedures of detecting and prosecuting sexual irregularities were delineated and improved. These involved a whole range of local government officers and laymen. On the parish level in Virginia, the enforcement of the moral code was the duty of Anglican ministers and churchwardens, who performed it with apparent diligence. Symon Hancrek, churchwarden of Linn Haven parish, presented to the court of Lower Norfolk "the person of James Blisse of the same parish for committing of a rape with the maid of Mr. Land, upon report from her own mouth."[31] Samuell Cole, minister, informed the court of Lancaster County that "Sarah the wife of Andrew Bowyer a long time had lived in whoredom & lewde [?] of life."[32] In Surry County, the minister and a churchwarden of Southwark parish "had made it appear that Abraham Sapcoate & Emelia Lee, Wife of Robert Lee doe live together in a very lewed manner."[33] Sampson Calvert, minister of Elizabeth River parish, showed an exceptional sense of duty when he presented himself to the court for having committed adultery with the wife of a local planter.[34] In Northumberland, the whole vestry of Wicomico parish sued the estate of John Kelly who "transported out of this County one Neale MacKenny guilty of begetting a bastard child."[35] In Maryland, where the church and secular administration operated separately, the primary responsibility for the supervision of sexual behavior in the communities was vested in constables. Some of them demonstrated great zeal in pursuing sexual offenders, like Thomas Gibson of Charles County, who on November 14, 1665, presented two women servants "illegitimately got with child," a man for "hauing transported a young woaman out of this Prouince that hath had a bastard," and accused another woman of cohabiting with Gils Tomkinson and being pregnant by him. Another constable, Alexander Smith, presented to the same court one woman for "hauing a bastard."[36]

The colonial justices of the peace, alternatively called commissioners, selected by the governors from among the most prominent men of the counties, also participated directly in the enforcement of the sexual conduct rules. Witnesses to sexual crimes, victims of sexual abuse, and persons suffering damages due to the sexual transgressions of others could complain to the justices, who were authorized to take depositions on the location of the crime and begin criminal action in the county courts. Thus, for example, Bridgett Johnson, a witness to an act of adultery, chose to make a complaint before "Mr William Coursey & Mr Philip Steeuenson his Lordshipps Justices of the Peace" in Talbot County.[37] Elsewhere, "Information hath beene given to some of the Comissioners of this County [Kent] that [unmarried] Hannah Jenkins ... hath beene deliuered of A man Childe."[38] In their judicial capacity, as a bench of at least three judges, the Commissioners tried sexual crimes and settled sex-related civil suits, mainly frequent suits for sexual slander.

The judicial apparatus for dealing with sexual crimes and misdemeanors at the local level also included a number of ordinary free men and women of good reputation serving as grand juries, juries of women, and midwives appointed to attend deliveries of illegitimate children. Although statutory provisions for the selection of grand juries (a group of twelve to twenty-four men acting as a prosecuting body in criminal cases) were made at a fairly early stage of the formation of the court system, the cost and practical difficulty of gathering so many jurors were responsible for rare and irregular conventions of such juries in the tobacco colonies throughout the 1660s. Closer to the end of the century, the grand jury – known also as the Jury of Inquest – participated more systematically in the procedure of initiating charges against sexual offenders in both Chesapeake colonies.[39] In Charles City County, Virginia, on April 20, 1663, Richard Smith and his wife Jane were "presented and convinced by the Grand Jury of Enquest for fornicacon before marriage." Henry Francis and Mrs. Dennis were presented in November 1681 to the court of Surry County "by the Grand jury for liveing together in Adultry." The county court of Westmoreland made regular use of the grand jury in the 1680s and 1690s. In January 1687/8, the "grand Jury did present Elizabeth Powell servant of Nicholas Spencer for haveing a bastard child," and a few years later, in 1691, the records mention four other female servants who appeared before the court "being presented by the Grand Jury" for the same offense.[40]

The Maryland evidence for the use of the grand jury in prosecuting sexual crimes is also more frequent in the documents from the late 1660s onward. The Somerset County court used this body in May 1667, when Elyzabeth Johnson "was presented by the Jury of Enquest for having a bastard Chilld."[41] While the Charles County court appears to have made no use of the instrument before 1666, several cases from the 1670s show its vital role in prosecutions. In March 1672, a panel of nineteen jurors returned presentments for Mary Warren and Margaret Greeden for bearing bastard children. Eight months later, a panel of fifteen grand jurors presented Elinor Warren "for breading and entertaineing Thomas Howell for the space of Six weeks in her house and not lawfully married to him." In January 1673, three other women were tried for bastardy, and one couple "for haveing a bastard child abortive and concealing it" upon the presentment of "the Grand Jury for the body of

Charles Countie."[42] In the court documents of another Maryland county, four bastardy cases were entered in November 1671 preceded by the formula: "Wee the Jury of Inquest for Talbott County Being agreed In our Inquest giue theses presentment folloing."[43]

Women, too, could officially be engaged in a legal or quasi-legal capacity in actions against sexual offenders. As in contemporary England, the opinion of respectable matrons experienced in the matter of procreation was sought in cases of suspected irregular pregnancy, secret delivery, abortion, or infanticide. In doubtful situations, a jury of women was appointed that, after examination of the female suspect, delivered its verdict to the court. In Kent County, Maryland, in June 1662 the court charged nine local women with the task of ascertaining whether servant Mary Stedhed "be with Child or not."[44] A few years later, the same court "ordered a Jury of women to be called to Search the boddy of Hannah [Jenkins] whether she was delivered of a Child or noe," Hannah being suspected of infanticide.[45] At almost the same time, the suspicion of abortion or infanticide made the justices of Accomack in Virginia's Eastern Shore summon "a Jury of the most grave creditable & Judicious Weomen ... to examine & informe themselves of the Manner of Eliza Carter proceedings in Child birth To give there verdict how the said Bastard child might come by its death."[46] Such juries, composed of up to twelve women, further enlarged the circle of people directly involved in the institutional control of sexual conduct.

The evolution of punishment for sexual irregularities constitutes a big topic. Broadly speaking, offenders found guilty by the courts were punished as systematically as they were tracked down. Surviving court orders show servant parents of bastards as the most frequently punished category of sexual criminals, just as they constituted the biggest group of colonists charged with sexual transgressions in general. Moreover, a comparison of a representative sample of the types of punishment handed down in servant bastardy cases in three Virginia counties reveals a significant departure from morally humiliating shaming rituals performed before church congregations in favor of economically valuable years of penal service and fines paid in pounds of tobacco.[47]

By the end of the century the legally defined standards of moral conduct diverged for men and women, masters and servants, whites and nonwhites, free and enslaved. Yet although socially divisive and potentially antagonizing, colonial laws governing sexual conduct were administered by county courts in the atmosphere of broad consensus. All groups of white colonists keenly participated in the detection and punishment of transgressions. No other cases, criminal or civil, held in the local and provincial courts gathered so many eager witnesses as those related to sexual misconduct. Twelve persons testified in connection with the extramarital child of Mary Taylor.[48] Ten witnesses spoke in the York County court when the paternity of Ann Roberts's bastard child was being established[49] and nine when Jacob Lumbrozo was tried for raping his maidservant and inducing her abortion.[50] Eight were heard in connection with Captain Dowse's abandoned wife and her financial settlement.[51] Anne Barbery's crime of bastardy and suspicion of infanticide produced seven testimonies, and the marital discord between Dorothy and Robert Holt six.[52] The court depositions and spontaneous actions undertaken by Chesapeake men and women show no trace of class or gender solidarity interfering with the diligent performance of statutory and customary duties.

Although sexual regulation was hardly the main preoccupation of the Chesapeake legislatures in the seventeenth century and sex-related misdemeanors constituted only a fraction of the cases heard by the county and provincial courts, the extensive legal interference with the norms of relationships between the sexes in contemporary Virginia and Maryland demonstrates an intimate link between law and society at the formative stage of the culture of the American South. The English arriving at the tobacco coast lost nothing of their historically rooted respect for law and justice. As pioneer Americans, they also demonstrated genuine legal inventiveness and the extraordinary capacity for pragmatic adaptations of older legal ideas and institutions to the frontier conditions. Their need for law was strongly enhanced by the economic development of the settlements in the direction of commercial agriculture, an entirely new system without any precedent in England. Fairly early in the seventeenth century, white colonists were united around one dominant goal: the increase of everyone's share in the tobacco profits. In the name of this goal, the obstacles in the path to plantation prosperity had to be removed by all available means. In the unique demographic and labor situation of the early Chesapeake, the sexual activity of individuals emerged as directly connected with economic success. As such, it became the target of strict institutional control. The same reason made the entire white society identify with the increasingly secular principles of conduct enforced by a network of secular courts and law officers. This popular consensus about the restrictive operation of law in sexual matters helped establish a cultural system legitimizing almost complete powerlessness of the economically dependent groups: servants, slaves, and women, whether free and bound. It also placed law at the service of the developing racist system.

James Willard Hurst, who opened the law and legal studies to the law-and-society approach, observed that in the United States "people generally have used law in a narrowly practical way" and "were concerned with law more as an instrument for desired immediate results than as a statement of carefully legitimated, long-range values."[53] He arrived at this conclusion mainly by studying American law from the late nineteenth century on, and he dismissed the colonial period as irrelevant for the understanding of truly American national law. Yet in the light of the evidence of the first Southern colonies examined here, his view seems to apply to British America long before the United States was created.

Notes

1. "The Problem of Colonial Legal History," in Jack P. Greene and J. R. Pole, eds., *Colonial British America: Essays in the New History of the Early Modern Era* (Baltimore and London, 1984), 457-89.
2. For a good discussion of how early Americanists grapple, somewhat reluctantly, with intellectual and theoretical challenges posed by post-structuralism see Saul Cornell, "Early American History in a Postmodern Age," *William and Mary Quarterly,* 3d Ser., 50 (1993), 329-41. A more recent presentation of the impact of post-structuralist interpretive strategies on history is in the collection of critical essays by Mark

Poster, *Cultural History and Postmodernity: Disciplinary Readings and Challenges* (New York, 1997).

3. See, for example, N.E.H. Hull, *Female Felons: Women and Serious Crime in Colonial Massachusetts* (Urbana, Ill., 1987); Mary Ann Jimenez, *Changing Faces of Madness: Early American Attitudes and Treatment of the Insane* (Hanover, N. H., 1987); Yasuhide Kawashima, *Puritan Justice and the Indian: White Man's Law in Massachusetts, 1630-1763* (Middletown, Conn., 1986); Mary Beth Norton, "Gender, Crime, and Community in Seventeenth-Century Maryland," in James Henretta et al., eds., *The Transformation of Early American History* (New York, 1991), 126-34, and *Founding Mothers and Fathers: Gendered Power and the Forming of American Society* (New York, 1996), Section 3; Marylynn Salmon, *Women and the Law of Property in Early America* (Chapel Hill and London, 1986); and Donna J. Spindel, *Crime and Society in North Carolina, 1663-1776* (Baton Rouge and London, 1989).

4. See George B. Curtis, "The Colonial County Court, Social Forum and Legislative Precedent: Accomack County, Virginia, 1633-1639," *Virginia Magazine of History and Biography,* 85 (1977), 274-88; Warren M. Billings, "The Transfer of English law to Virginia, 1606-50," in K.R. Andrews, N.P. Canny, and P.E.H. Hair, eds., *The Westward Enterprise: English Activities in Ireland, the Atlantic, and America, 1480-1650* (Detroit, 1979), 215-44; and J. Hall Pleasants, "Early Maryland County Courts," in William Hand Browne et al., eds, *Archives of Maryland,* 72 vols. (Baltimore, 1883-1972), (hereafter cited as *Md. Archives*), 53:xi-xxv.

5. Details on white servant trade and prices according to sex in Abbot Emerson Smith, *Colonists in Bondage: White Servitude and Convict Labor in Early America 1607-1776* (New York, 1971; orig. pub. 1947), chap. 2, and Richard B. Morris, *Government and Labor in Early America* (New York, 1965; orig. Pub. 1946), 319-20.

6. Herbert Moller, "Sex Composition of Colonial America," *WMQ,* 3d Ser., 2 (1945), 96; Edmund S. Morgan, *American Slavery, American Freedom: The Ordeal of Colonial Virginia* (New York and London, 1975), 407-10; Russell R. Menard, "Immigrants and Their Increase," in Aubrey C. Land, Lois Green Carr, and Edward C. Papenfuse, eds., *Law, Society, and Politics in Early Maryland* (Baltimore, 1977), 96; James Horn, "Servant Emigration to the Chesapeake in the Seventeenth Century," in Thad W. Tate and David L. Ammerman, eds., *The Chesapeake in the Seventeenth Century: Essays on Anglo-American Society and Politics* (New York, 1979), 63; Menard and Lorena S. Walsh, "The Demography of Somerset County, Maryland: A Progress Report," July 1981, unpublished typescript (the author is indebted to Dr. Walsh for making a copy of the report available).

7. Horn, "Servant Immigration to the Chesapeake in the Seventeenth Century," 51-95; Menard, "British Migration to the Chesapeake Colonies in the Seventeenth Century," in Carr, Philip D. Morgan, and Jean B. Russo, eds., *Colonial Chesapeake Society* (Chapel Hill, N. C., 1988), 126-28.

8. Alan Kulikoff, *Tobacco and Slaves: The Development of Southern Cul-*

tures in the Chesapeake, 1680-1800 (Chapel Hill, N. C., and London, 1986), 68, 70, 355-56; Menard, "The Maryland Slave Population, 1658 to 1730: A Demographic Profile of Blacks in Four Counties," *WMQ,* 3d Ser., 32 (1975), esp. 29-34; Edmund Morgan, *American Slavery, American Freedom,* 310, 421.

9. Irmina Wawrzyczek, *Planting and Loving: Popular Sexual Mores in the Seventeenth-Century Chesapeake* (Lublin, 1998), chap. 2.
10. Ibid., chap. 3.
11. W. Stitt Robinson, "Conflicting Views on Landholding: Lord Baltimore and the Experiences of Colonial Maryland with Native Americans," *Maryland Historical Magazine,* 83 (1988), 85-97; Michal Rozbicki, *Transformation of English Cultural Ethos in Colonial America: Maryland 1634-1720* (Warsaw, 1985), chap. 2; Frederick Fausz, "Patterns of Anglo-Indian Aggression and Accommodation along the Mid-Atlantic Coast, 1584-1634," in William W. Fitzhugh, ed., *Cultures in Contact. The Impact of European Contacts on Native American Cultural Institutions, A.D. 1000-1800* (Washington, D. C., 1985), 225-268; Karen O. Kupperman, *Settling with the Indians: The Meeting of English and Indian Cultures in America, 1580-1640* (Totowa, N. J., 1980), 58-60, 169-88; Edmund Morgan, *American Slavery, American Freedom,* 71-81, 98-101, 250-257; David D. Smits, " 'Abominable Mixture': Toward the Repudiation of Anglo-Indian Intermarriage in Seventeenth-Century Virginia, *VMHB,* 95 (1987), 158-166, Bernard W. Sheehan, *Savagism and Civility: Indians and Englishmen in Colonial Virginia* (Cambridge, 1980), 24-25.
12. Kathleen M. Brown calculated 237 interracial bastardy cases in three Virginia counties alone in 1660-1729 in Table 5, *Good Wives, Nasty Wenches, and Anxious Patriarchs: Gender, Race, and Power in Colonial Virginia* (Chapel Hill, N. C., and London, 1996), 199.
13. John Pory, "Proceedings of the First Assembly of Virginia, 1619", in H. R. McIlwaine, ed., *Journals of the House of Burgesses of Virginia, 1619-1658/9,* 2. vols.(Richmond, 1914-1915), 1:13.
14. William Waller Hening, ed., *The Statutes at Large; Being a Collection of All the Laws of Virginia,* 13 vols. (Richmond, Philadelphia, and New York, 1809-1823), (hereafter cited as Hening, *Statutes at Large*), 1:182, 2:51-52, 3:71-74, 361.
15. *Md. Archives,* 1:286.
16. Thomas Bacon, ed., *Laws of Maryland at Large* (Annapolis, Md., 1765), no pagination.
17. Hening, ed., *Statutes at Large,* 1:252-53.
18. Ibid., 373.
19. Hening, ed., Act XX, *Statutes at Large,* 1:253.
20. Ibid., 2:114-15, 168 (1662), 3:73-74, Act XI, c. 3 (1691), 139-40, Act I, c. 4, 361 (1705); 3:chap. 49, c. 17, c. 18 452-53 (1705).
21. Bacon, ed., *Laws of Maryland at Large,* 1658, chap. 6; 1662, chap. 4; 1674, chap. 7; 1692, chap. 49; 1694, chap. 52, no pagination.
22. *Md. Archives,* 1:373 (1658).

23. Hening, ed., *Statutes at Large,* 1:252-53, c. 20 (1642-1643); 2:114 (1661-1662).
24. For discussion of the law of slavery in colonial Virginia and Maryland see Joseph Boskin, *Into Slavery: Racial Decisions in the Virginia Colony* (Washington, D.C., 1979), 38-50, and William W. Wiecek, "The Statutory Law of Slavery and Race in the Thirteen Mainland Colonies of British America," *WMQ,* 3d Ser., 34 (1977), 258-80.
25. Hening, ed., December 1662, *Statutes at Large,* 2:170.
26. *Md. Archives,* 1:533-34, 2:272.
27. Ibid., 7:203-04.
28. Hening, ed., *Statutes at Large,* 3:86-88 (1691).
29. Ibid., 453-54.
30. For details of the early institutional development of the Virginia and Maryland system of justice see Curtis, "Colonial County Court"; Martha W. Hiden, *How Justice Grew: Virginia Counties: An Abstract of Their Formation* (Charlottesville, Va., 1957), 1-21; Pleasants, "Early Maryland County Courts," xi-xv; Carr, "The Foundations of Social Order: Local Government in Colonial Maryland," in Bruce C. Daniels, ed., *Town and County: Essays on the Structure of Local Government in the American Colonies* (Middletown, Conn., 1978), 79-91; Robert Wheeler, "The County Court in Colonial Virginia," ibid., 111-25; and Warren M. Billings, John E. Selby, and Tate, *Colonial Virginia: A History* (White Plains, N. Y., 1986), 69-74.
31. Entry for Apr. 23, 1943, Norfolk [Va.] Deed Book A, 1637-1646, 220.
32. Entry for Sept. 29, 1658, Lancaster County [Va.] Orders, Etc., 1655-1665, 56.
33. Entry for Sept. 7, 1674, Surry County [Va.] Orders, 1690-1698, part I, 67. Other presentations by a minister (May 24, 1648) and a churchwarden (July 25, 1648) together in York County [Va.] Wills and Deeds, No. 2, 1645-1649, 350, 387.
34. Entry for Nov. 20, 1649, Norfolk [Va.] Wills and Deeds B, fols. 129, 129a.
35. Entry for Jan. 17, 1693/4, Northumberland County [Va.] Order Book, 1678-1698, part 1, 639.
36. *Md. Archives,* 53:599. For other presentments with the names of constables given see ibid., LX(1672):439; LIV (1656): 78; LIV (1670), 292; LIV (1675), 324; (1665), 385; (1665/6), 391; (1671), 486.
37. Ibid., 54 1672), 534.
38. Ibid. (1668), 250.
39. For relevant colonial legislation see ibid., 1(1638/9), 49, (1662), 37-438; 2 (1666), 141-42; and Hening, ed., *Statutes at Large,* 1:304 (1645), 315 (1645/6), 397-98 (1655/6), 2:74 (1661/2), 407-08 (1677).
40. Charles City County [Va.] Deeds, Wills, Orders, Etc., 1655-1665, 377; Surry County [Va.] Orders, 1671-1691, part I, 621; Westmoreland County [Va.] Orders, 1690-1698, fols. 24, 24a, 25.
41. *Md. Archives,* 54:671.
42. Ibid., 60:373, 439, 518-19.
43. Ibid., 54:513-14.

44. Entry for June 7, 1662, ibid., 233. Another example of six women jurors in action is Jan. 1, 1658, ibid., 41:20.
45. Entry for Oct. 13, 1668, ibid., 54:250.
46. Accomack County [Va.] Order Book, 1666-1670, fol. 65.
47. Brown, *Good Wives, Nasty Wenches, and Anxious Patriarchs,* 188-92.
48. *Md. Archives,* 10:280-90.
49. York County [Va.] Deeds, Orders, Wills, Etc., No. 3, 1657-1662, 168-70.
50. *Md. Archives,* 53:387-91.
51. McIlwaine, ed., *Minutes of the Council and General Court of Colonial Virginia, 1622-1632, 1670-1676* (Richmond, Va., 1924), 113.
52. *Md. Archives,* 51:329-31, 10:109-12.
53. James Willard Hurst, *Law and Order in the United States* (Ithaca, N. Y., 1977), 23.

2

The Irony of Progressive Historiography: A Critical Comment on the Revival of Anti-Federalism in Contemporary Constitutional Thought

Saul Cornell

American constitutionalism has been defined by a distinctive set of canonical texts that have shaped the content and structure of legal scholarship and jurisprudence. In addition to the complex body of case law that defines American constitutional thought, a select group of texts from the original debate over the Constitution have entered the canon. The most important of these founding documents, *The Federalist,* has become the most important source for reconstructing the thought of the founders.[1]

Although Publius remains the most frequently cited source from the founding era, other authors have attracted considerable attention in recent years. One of the most important and least appreciated transformations in the structure of the contemporary constitutional canon is the inclusion of a set of voices once consigned to the margins of American constitutional law. The rediscovery of the Anti-Federalists is one of the most profound changes in modern constitutional thought. Although once maligned as "men of little faith," they have now joined the canon alongside Publius.[2]

The revival of interest in Anti-Federalism has cut across

disciplinary boundaries. Historians and political scientists have lavished new attention on Anti-Federalist thought. Editions of Anti-Federalist writings are now widely available. Supreme Court opinions that once restricted themselves to citations from *The Federalist,* now also cite Anti-Federalist sources. If the content of law reviews can be taken as an accurate barometer of the thinking of the legal academy, it seems clear that over the last decade the Anti-Federalists have been accorded a status nearly comparable to that of the Federalists. Even more significant is the way in which Anti-Federalist ideas have entered popular legal culture. Elements of the far right have gravitated toward Anti-Federalist thought. The home page of the Michigan militia boasts several quotes from leading Anti-Federalists.[3]

The terms of scholarly discussion about the Anti-Federalists have been structured by the claim first put forward by Progressive historians such as Orrin Grant Libby that Anti-Federalism was essentially agrarian and populist in spirit. This insight was developed by later scholars including the neo-Progressive scholar Jackson Turner Main. Although he explicitly eschewed the materialism of both Progressive and neo-Progressive historians, Gordon S. Wood's account of Anti-Federalism in both *The Creation of the American Republic* and in his more recent work, *The Radicalism of the American Revolution* embraced an essentially Progressive view of Anti-Federalism.[4]

In the hundred years since Libby first characterized the Anti-Federalists as populist democrats, Progressive historiography has become one of the dominant metanarratives in American constitutional history. The notion of metanarrative is a useful means of analyzing the way in which scholarship has treated Anti-Federalism. Metanarratives organize the selection of evidence and the interpretation of texts. As Robert Berkhofer, Jr., notes in *Beyond the Great Story,* two metanarratives have shaped much of American historiography. Declension narratives frame history in terms of decline, and whig narratives focus on the theme of progress. In the case of the Progressive meta-narrative, elements of each of these powerful stories are united. The notion that Anti-Federalists were the true heirs of the Revolution and were defeated by Federalist conservatives appeals to the power of declension as a theme in American history. The eventual triumph of Anti-Federalist ideas during the Jeffersonian and Jacksonian periods draws on a countervailing whig narrative about progress. In more conventional terms, scholars have been sympathetic to the idea that Anti-Federalist may have lost the battle over the Constitution, but they won the war to define the character of American political culture. The Progressive paradigm thus manages to join aspects of the two most important metanarratives in American history: declension and progress.[5]

The belief that Anti-Federalism represented a lost populist heritage worth recovering has gained considerable currency both within and outside the academy. Many popular calls for constitutional reform have a distinctly Anti-Federalist tone. In a recent neo-Federalist manifesto, Kathleen Sullivan, Nelson Polsby, and Alan Brinkley describe Anti-Federalism in terms drawn from Progressive historiography. The opponents of the Constitution were, in their view, the group in post-Revolutionary America that favored "pure democracy." The authors of this collection of *New Federalist Papers* see evidence of a revival of a populist Anti-Federalist strain in recent attacks on federal power. Proposals for term limits, a balanced budget amendment, and calls for a radical decentralization of authority have, they argue, been cast in terms reminiscent of the original Anti-Federalist critique of the Constitution. For these neo-Federalists, the return of Anti-Federalism is a cause for alarm. As Sullivan notes, "the anti-Federalists lost the constitutional battle at the end of the eighteenth century." "Nothing," she emphatically declares, "has changed in two centuries to make them right at this stage."[6]

Evidence of the influence of Progressive scholarship in contemporary legal theory is also easy to locate. In an influential essay on "The Bill of Rights as Constitution," legal scholar Akhil Amar grounds much of his revisionist constitutional thought in ideas articulated by Anti-Federalist authors. This revival of the Progressive paradigm among legal scholars has spawned a rich and complicated literature on several neglected elements of the Bill of Rights. Anti-Federalist populism has been summoned to testify on behalf of the "standard model of the Second Amendment," a view of the right to bear arms that stresses an individual's right to own guns.[7] Jeffery Abramson, a leading advocate of an expansion of jury power, also grounds his ideal of deliberative democracy in Anti-Federalist populism. His ideas have been appropriated by more radical proponents of jury nullification. Thus, Anti-Federalist ideas have been summoned to provide a historical justification for anchoring a radical call for a reform of the jury system.[8]

The categories of Progressive scholarship have made it especially difficult to understand the complexity of Anti-Federalist political thought. Ironically, Progressive historiography has contributed to the homogenization of Anti-Federalist thought, making it impossible to see the tensions in the opposition to the Constitution. The thought of elite Anti-Federalists is difficult to accommodate in the Progressive model. Equally problematic is the way that Progressive ideas obscure the presence of an even more radical and genuinely popular variant of democratic ideology among the opponents of the Constitution.[9]

Consider such leading Anti-Federalists as Elbridge Gerry, George Mason, and Richard Henry Lee. Although these men authored texts that were among the most widely reprinted of any published during ratification, their ideas are discounted as unrepresentative of grass-roots opposition to the Constitution. Unless we treat the Anti-Federalist elite as victims of false consciousness, it is difficult to understand why such men opposed the Constitution. Rather than consider the thought of the Anti-Federalist elite as distinctive, most scholars usually cull quotations from their various writings and cobble them together as part of a single, coherent Anti-Federalist ideology. The common tendency to cut and paste statements with little concern to preserve the integrity of a particular author's work only exacerbates this homogenizing tendency.[10]

Populism does not adequately capture all the nuances of Anti-Federalist democratic thought. There was more than one variant of democracy associated with Anti-Federalism. Many of the most frequently cited Anti-Federalist texts were written by a newly empowered group of state politicians who were spokesmen for a moderate, middling, democratic ethos. Their ideal, tempered by a classically liberal approach to the market economy, was incompatible with the radical majoritarian ideal of localist democracy championed by plebeian populists in the backcountry. The differences separating plebeian Anti-Federalists from the elite or the middling sort were in many instances at least as great as those dividing Federalists from Anti-Federalists.[11]

Deconstructing the false dichotomies posited by Progressive historiography is a necessary prelude to formulating a more subtle understanding of Anti-Federalism. The categories of Progressive history have made it difficult to appreciate the distinctive class-based constitutional visions that divided Anti-Federalists from each other.[12] Part of the problem with the Progressive model stems from an ambiguity in Anti-Federalist discourse. At various moments, some Anti-Federalists spoke as if the struggle over the Constitution was a battle between the few and the many. At other times, Anti-Federalists described American society as divided among the lower, middling, and better sorts. Although this language is not identical to the modern language of social class, there are important affinities between these two discourses. Recasting Anti-Federalist constitutionalism in terms of distinctive elite, middling, and plebeian ideologies makes sense. Anti-Federalism was a complex movement that drew together members of the planter elite, commercial-minded democrats and plebeian farmers in the backcountry. While these different groups often drew on a common rhetoric, they espoused distinctive constitutional visions. A better understanding of Anti-Federalism must abandon the notion of a monolithic ideology and recover the chorus of voices that rose in opposition to the Constitution.[13]

One of the most frequently cited Anti-Federalist texts in contemporary constitutional scholarship is the *Letters of a Federal Farmer*.[14] In recent constitutional thought, Federal Farmer has been cast as the quintessential Anti-Federalist populist. Most legal scholars attribute the essay to the eminent Virginian politician Richard Henry Lee. If Lee, a conservative Virginia aristocrat, was forced to cast his arguments in democratic terms, surely Anti-Federalism fits the Progressive notion of a movement driven by a democratic ideology. The problem with this model is that most historians reject this attribution. The consensus among historians is that Federal

Farmer was not a Virginian, but was most probably a New Yorker, and may well have been the merchant Melancton Smith, a prominent moderate voice in the New York State Ratification convention.[15]

The ideas of Federal Farmer reflected those of an important group within the Anti-Federalist coalition, the middling democrats who formed the core of New York's Clintonian faction. John Lamb, a leading Clintonian, felt that Federal Farmer ably summarized the views of New York Anti-Federalists. Lamb wrote to Richard Henry Lee that "it would far exceed the Bounds of a Letter to detail to you our Objections to the proposed Constitution. And it is less necessary that we should do it, as they are well stated in a Publication, which we take the Liberty of transmitting you in a series of Letters from the Federal Farmer to the Republican."[16]

In Federal Farmer's essay is ample evidence to support the notion that he was not an agrarian populist but a commercial-minded democrat of much more moderate views. Federal Farmer made explicit his identification with "men of middling property, men not in debt on the one hand, and men, on the other content with republican government, and not aiming at immense fortunes, offices, or power." His authority to speak on the Constitution was contingent, he noted, on his being a member of the middling sort. "My opinion" he wrote, was "only the opinion of an individual, and so far only as it corresponds with the opinions of the honest and substantial part of the community, it is entitled to consideration."[17]

The suggestion that this important Anti-Federalist author may have been a commercial-minded New Yorker presents a serious problem for the Progressive model of Anti-Federalism. The claim that Anti-Federalists were populist democrats is difficult to reconcile with the Federal Farmer's own efforts to cast himself as a man of the middling sort who opposed Shays's Rebellion and the other populist excesses of post-Revolutionary America. He explicitly condemned "levellers" and "little insurgents, men in debt, who want no law, and who want a share of the property of others." In contrast to the extreme economic egalitarianism championed by more radical voices, Federal Farmer espoused a more liberal vision of the role of government and the economy.[18]

For neo-Progressive scholars, Anti-Federalism was a movement inspired by an agrarian democratic ideology. It is difficult to account for the ideology of Anti-Federalists such as Federal Farmer who were procommerce in matters regarding political economy and moderate on issues of democracy. Federal Farmer showed great sympathy with the impact of the Confederation government on commercial interests, for the plight of "commercial and monied men, who are uneasy," noting that their concerns were "not without just cause." While a number of Anti-Federalists excoriated a corrupt and sordid financial interest, Federal Farmer sought to assuage the concerns of commercial men. Federal Farmer also attacked paper money and tender laws explicitly. In economic matters middling democrats such as Federal Farmer were decidedly liberal. He asserted that "liberty, in its genuine sense, is security to enjoy the effects of our honest industry and labours, in a free and mild government, and personal security from all illegal restraint." Free governments, in Federal Farmer's view, were not activists in economic matters. Federal Farmer believed that people ought to "follow their private pursuits, and enjoy the fruits of their labor with very small deductions for the public use." While Federal Farmer espoused a democratic ethos, his view of economic matters was decidedly liberal, not egalitarian in spirit.[19]

If Federal Farmer opposed the populism of Daniel Shays, he was no less critical of the aristocratic temper of men at the opposite extreme of the social order. He showed little sympathy for the claims of self-styled natural aristocrats. These men were equally dangerous and constituted a group "unfriendly to republican equality." When set against the conservative views of elites on both sides of the struggle over the Constitution, Federal Farmer's ideas, at least on political questions, seem democratic. Yet Federal Farmer's vision of democracy stopped well short of the most radical ideology in the ranks of Anti-Federalists, that of plebeians who were the genuine populist democrats. On economic matters, Federal Farmer's liberalism also set him apart from plebeians.[20]

Although Federal Farmer had little confidence in either natural aristocrats or plebeians, both of these groups were crucial to the cause of Anti-Federalism. Opponents of the Constitution included men such as George Mason, a wealthy Virginia planter, and, at the other end of the spectrum, backcountry farmers such as the Carlisle rioters. To understand the complex dynamics that shaped the original debate over the Constitution it is important to accord all these different voices a place in historical accounts of Anti-Federalism.[21]

How does recognition of the diversity of Anti-Federalism, particularly the different class-based constitutional visions associated with the opposition to the Constitution, alter our understanding of important legal questions? One good illustration of how the Progressive paradigm has skewed recent constitutional theorizing may be found in efforts to rethink the nature of the jury. Many of the calls to reinvent the jury invoke the lost populist legacy of Anti-Federalism. In its most radical guise, jury empowerment sanctions the idea of jury nullification and accepts that local norms of justice may override the weight of precedent and statutory enactments. The question that naturally arises is simple: how historically accurate is the populist interpretation of the jury?

It is only natural that scholars interested in reinventing the jury would turn to the writings of Federal Farmer. This Anti-Federalist equated the power of juries with that of the legislative branch. "Juries are constantly and frequently drawn from the body of the people, and freemen of the country; and by holding their jury's right to return a general verdict in all cases sacred, we secure to the people at large, their just and rightful controul in the judicial department." Expansive jury powers were not only necessary to control the judicial branch, but they were essential for democracy. "The body of the people, principally, bear the burdens of the community; they of right ought to have a controul in its important concerns." "It is true, the freemen of a country are not always minutely skilled in laws," he noted, "but they have common sense in its purity, which seldom or never errs in making and applying laws to the condition of the people." Federal Farmer conceded that there would always be a need to interpret the law. In those cases, Federal Farmer placed his faith in the jury, not the judiciary, to make those decisions.[22]

Jury service also provided an important form of civic education and insured that citizens remained vigilant about their rights. "This and the democratic branch in the legislature" were "the means by which the people are let into the knowledge of public affairs – and are enabled to stand as the guardians of each others rights." In this sense, the jury was another embodiment of the public sphere in which citizens engaged in reasoned debate on public matters. The jury served a double function- it expressed the popular will and educated citizens in constitutional principles.[23]

For Federal Farmer, the jury was not an expression of the locality but of class interest. "When I speak of the jury trial of vicinage," a concept Federal Farmer felt necessary to define for his readers as the "trial of the fact in the neighborhood," he did not "lay so much stress upon the circumstances of our being tried by our neighbors." It was far less important that juries be composed of local citizens than that they be composed of "the common people." In contrast to some Anti-Federalists who espoused a more localistic conception of the jury, Federal Farmer was concerned that the values and ideals of the middling sort dominate.[24]

Although Federal Farmer did not explore the limits of participation in juries, some sense of this can be seen in his discussion of the militia, another popular institution dealt with at great length in his essay. Federal Farmer was unequivocal about the need to bar propertyless individuals from militia service. His hostility to Shaysism and leveling suggests that he did not wish to see juries serve as agents of a populist economic ideology. He attacked paper money and steered clear of endorsing other populist economic policies. Federal Farmer was distinctly middle class in his thought on such matters. What modern commentators on jural rights have not addressed is the way in which Federal Farmer's vision of democracy excluded the lower sort and explicitly opposed the populist economic agenda associated with plebeians. In short, modern discussions of a more democratic ideal of the jury invoke the democratic legacy of Federal Farmer and ignore his commitment to a liberal economic ideal.[25]

One of the many ironies arising from the Progressive interpretation of Anti-Federalism is that it actually obscures a much more radical voice within the opposition to the Constitution. The most extreme wing of Anti-Federalism included a group of plebeian populists who embraced an ideology far more revolutionary than that described by Progressives. For those Anti-Federalists the voice of the people embodied in the jury was tantamount to a perpetual constitutional convention that not only interpreted the law but also created new law by its deliberations.

Whereas spokesmen for the middling sort such as Federal Farmer embraced a liberal vision of the economy, spokesmen for the lower sort articulated traditional notions of moral economy and viewed the jury as a means of securing justice and equity in economic relations. For plebeian populists the jury was a vital means of exercising some control over the marketplace and addressing the problem of economic equality.

While it is more difficult to locate constitutional texts expressing the point of view of plebeian Anti-Federalists, one important source for understanding this viewpoint can be gleaned from the writings produced in response to the Carlisle riot in Pennsylvania. The leader of the riot, William Petrikin, authored a scathing satire on Federalist thought under the pen name "Aristocrotis." As the high Federalist Aristocrotis, Petrikin denounced the power of juries as "a gross violation of common sense." The vast powers possessed by juries in Revolutionary America were foolish: "In the first place it is absurd, that twelve ignorant plebeians, should be constituted judges of a law, which passed through so many learned hands; – first a learned legislature," and then "learned writers have explained and commented on it – Third, learned lawyers twisted, turned and new modeled it – and lastly, a learned judge." It was preposterous, Aristocrotis asserted, that "after all these learned discussions, an illiterate jury" composed of men of no property "must determine whether it applies to the fact or not." When juries determined both the facts and the law, an "insignificant cottager" might successfully challenge a "learned gentlemen." Expansive jury powers would provide a counterweight to the power of society's existing elite. Under such a scheme it would be possible for a simple cottager to challenge the authority of a rich merchant or large landowner. Empowering juries not only diminished the power of judges, it also undermined the economic clout of lawyers whose services would be less essential in such a system.[26]

The notion that juries might act as agents of a populist economic agenda raises another issue about the radical democratic conception of the jury defended by plebeian populists. Violence in Carlisle had been precipitated by the decision of Federalists to celebrate their victory in the Pennsylvania ratification convention. The Anti-Federalist rioters who opposed them were never brought to trial. The legal process was circumvented by the intervention of the militia, which freed the prisoners from jail. Local militia units acted without state authority and followed the logic implicit in the plebeian ideal of the jury to its ultimate conclusion. The actions of the crowd became a spontaneous expression of the will of the people – a voice indistinguishable from the Constitution. While plebeian populists celebrated this ideal of democracy, many moderate Anti-Federalists and Federalists viewed this as mob rule – the antithesis of constitutional government.[27]

Plebeian Anti-Federalists rejected the moderation of middling democracy in favor of a more radical localist variant of direct democracy. It was the will of the local community, not the numerical majority in either the state or the nation, that they sought to empower. In contrast to the democratic vision of middling democrats such as Federal Farmer, plebeians were not especially interested in protecting the power of the state governments. Local institutions such as the jury, the militia, or even the crowd, were the true embodiments of the voice of the people.

When the thought of middling democrats and plebeians are dis-aggregated, it is possible to see the important divisions within the ranks of Anti-Federalism. Two rather different versions of democracy existed among opponents to the Constitution. The democratic ethos of plebeian populists was intensely localistic and egalitarian. It represented the most radical vision of majoritarian democracy present in the debate over the Constitution. Ultimately, the democratic vales of middling opposition were not compatible with those of plebeian populists. Middling democrats were far more sympathetic to the needs of an emerging commercial order. In place of the radical localist ideology of plebeians, middling democrats were supporters of a theory of federalism in which the states would retain the bulk of authority.[28]

Members of the Virginia gentry, such as William Grayson, defended a conception of the jury that set them apart from middling democrats and plebeian populists. For leading Anti-Federalists in the Old Dominion, the absence of specific protections for jury trial in civil cases could only be corrected when juries were drawn from the neighborhood. The underlying fears animating the concern were the danger that debt cases would be prosecuted in areas less sympathetic to planter interests. Grayson did not wish to give the impression that he sought unfair advantage for debtors. "I have ever been an advocate for paying the British Creditors." Conceding this point did not, however, lead Grayson to lessen his support for strong local jury system. "It is a maxim in law, that debts should be on the same original foundation they were on when contracted." Contracts in Virginia were drawn with an understanding that they would be adjudicated by "State Judiciaries only." Debtors and creditors were familiar with "The procrastination and delays of our Courts." Grayson believed that "trial by jury must have been in the contemplation of both parties, and the *venue* was in favor of the defendant." Removing debt cases from local courts would have disastrous results for Virginians. Grayson believed that local courts empaneling local juries were necessary to protect the interests of Virginians. Grayson was emphatic on that point, stressing that, when Virginians spoke of local juries, they meant "the idea which I call the true vicinage," a notion that required "that a man shall be tried by his neighbors." He not only feared the threat to the state judiciaries, but also worried that under the Constitution individuals "may be tried in any part of the state."[29]

While leading Virginia Anti-Federalists defended a state's rights conception of federalism on many issues, the jury was one area in which Virginia's elite defended a truly localist ideology. Localism in the case of Virginia Anti-Federalists was not animated by a democratic impulse, but rather served as a means of defending gentry interests. Protecting Virginia's elite from outside creditors was the goal of Virginians' defense of the ideal of local juries.[30]

Despite the profound social differences separating elite Virginians from backcountry plebeians, both groups shared a hostility to an unrestrained market economy. Gentry and plebeians each believed that the legal system could be used to check the potential destructive forces of the marketplace. In the case of debt-ridden planters, the jury could protect the local gentry against outside creditors. This prodebtor view of the legal system was not exactly the same as the ideal of moral economy espoused by the Carlisle rioters. Anti-Federalist localism could support a political and constitutional theory decidedly elitist and hierarchical in the South, and populist and egalitarian in the backcountry.

The ideal of the jury meant different things to elite, middling, and plebeian Anti-Federalists. The example of the jury provides further evidence that efforts to conceptualize early American politics in terms of monolithic ideologies, whether liberalism, republicanism, localism, or populism, fail to capture the elasticity of political language during the post-Revolutionary period. It is important for scholars to recognize the multiple contexts in which the same language might function in radically different ways.[31]

Scholarship on Anti-Federalism has been largely shaped by a conceptual framework inherited from Progressive historiography. The terms of the debate inaugurated by Progressive historians make it difficult to understand the full range of Anti-Federalist thought. The tendency to identify opposition to the Constitution with an overwhelming populist ideology obscures the presence of an important conservative variant of Anti-Federalism and obscures the intensity of genuine populist radicalism.

In *The Liberal Tradition in America,* Louis Hartz noted that the consensual character of American politics derived from the absence of a true conservative ideology against which radicals could frame their opposition. Mainstream constitutional history replicates this Hartzian paradigm. When both ends of the Anti-Federalist spectrum are cut off, when there are no real conservatives or real radicals, it is difficult to understand the shifting process of accommodation that brought elite and middling democrats into a working alliance that ultimately led to the creation of a loyal opposition. The threat of plebeian radicalism was a crucial factor in the decision to accept the framework provided by the new Constitution.[32]

A number of interpretive problems inherent in Progressive historiography have been amplified in the work of legal scholars and political theorists. The notion that Anti-Federalists were populist localists blurs important distinctions among Anti-Federalists. Elite Anti-Federalists embraced a vision of localism that sought to preserve a hierarchical social order in which gentry domination would remain secure. Middling democrats were ardent champions of state power and feared the dangers of the majoritarianism championed by plebeians. The ideas of leveling democracy espoused by plebeians also ran counter to the liberal economic vision at the core of middling democracy. The radicalism of plebeian populism, by contrast, viewed the jury as a means of promoting a more egalitarian economic social order. The examples provided by elite Anti-Federalists and plebeian populists should also caution those eager to rediscover a lost Anti-Federalist heritage. As the example of William Grayson suggests, local juries could just as easily become the tools of powerful economic interests as they could serve the plebeian goal of economic equality. Similarly, the ideas of William Petrikin and the Carlisle rioters suggests that the simple majoritarian democracy embodied in plebeian populism was not always scrupulous about the rights of minorities.

Champions of an expansion of jury rights would do well to study these neglected Anti-Federalist voices. The rediscovery of Anti-Federalist ideas has greatly enriched contemporary discussion about the meaning of constitutionalism. An appreciation of the tensions and divisions among the Anti-Federalists will not only improve the quality of that discussion, but it may also alert scholars to dangers that they might otherwise not see.

Notes

1. On the critique of the canon in literary studies see Paul Lauter, *Canons and Contexts* (New York, 1991), and John Guillory, *Cultural Capital: The Problem of Literary Canon Formation* (Chicago, 1993). On the notion of a canon in constitutional law see J. M. Balkin and Sanford Levinson, "The Canons of Constitutional Law," *Harvard Law Review,* 111

(1998), 963-1024. On the problem of excluding non-elite voices from the constitutional canon see Saul A. Cornell, "Moving Beyond the Canon of Traditional Constitutional History: Anti-Federalists, the Bill of Rights, and the Promise of Post-Modern Historiography." *Law and History Review,* 12 (1994), 1-28. On the centrality of *The Federalist* to constitutional adjudication see James G. Wilson, "The Most Sacred Text: The Supreme Court's Use of the *Federalist Papers,"* *Brigham Young University Law Review,* 65 (1985), 65-135.

2. Cecelia Kenyon, "Men of Little Faith: The Anti-Federalists on the Nature of Representative Government." *William and Mary Quarterly,* 3d Ser., 12 (1955), 3-43. Herbert J. Storing, ed., *The Complete Anti-Federalist,* 7 vols. (Chicago, 1981). For a discussion of the rebirth of Anti- Federalist ideas in recent years see Cornell, "The Changing Historical Fortunes of the Anti-Federalists," *Northwestern University Law Review,* 84 (1989), 39-74.

3. For examples of the revival of interest in Anti-Federalism among legal scholars see Gary L. McDowell, "Were the Anti-Federalists Right?: Judicial Activism and the Problem of Consolidated Government," *Publius,* 12 (1982), 99-108. Efforts to strengthen congressional oversight of foreign affairs have been characterized as Anti-Federalist by Lawrence J. Block and David B. Rivkin, Jr., "Legislative Power Grab: The Anti-Federalist Counter-Revolution in the Making," letter to the editor, *New York Review of Books,* May 17, 1990, and Block and Rivkin, "The Battle to Control the Conduct of Foreign Intelligence and Covert Operations: The Ultra-Whig Counterrevolution Revisited," *Harvard Journal of Law and Public Policy,* 12 (1989), 303- 55. The movement for term limits has also been characterized as Anti-Federalist by Garry Wills, "Undemocratic Vistas," *NYRB,* Nov. 19, 1992, 28-34, and Troy A. Eid and Jim Kolbe, "The New Anti-Federalism: The Constitutionality of State-Imposed Term Limits on Congressional Terms of Office," *Denver University Law Review,* 69 (1992), 1-56. Justice William Rehnquist's jurisprudence has also been described as essentially Anti-Federalist/Jeffersonian in H. Jefferson Powell, "The Complete Jeffersonian: Justice Rehnquist and Federalism," *Yale Law Journal,* 91 (1982), 1317-70. For examples of recent Supreme Court opinions that have invoked the Anti-Federalists see Lewis Powell, dissent in *Garcia* v. *San Antonio Metropolitan Transit Authority et al.,* 469 US 569 (1984), and Clarence Thomas, concurrence in *McIntyre v. Ohio Elections Commission,* 514 U.S. 334 (1995). On the constitutional ideology of the militia movement see David C. Williams, "The Militia Movement and Second Amendment Revolution: Conjuring with the People," *Cornell Law Review,* 81 (1996), 879-952, and the web site <Mark Pitcavage, MILITIA - HISTORY AND LAW FAQ > Web Version 2.0, Sept. 1995.

4. Although the best-known work of Progressive history remains Charles A Beard, *An Economic Interpretation of the Constitution of the United States* (New York, 1913), the Progressive interpretation of Anti-Federalism owes much to Orrin Grant Libby, *The Geographical Distribution of*

the Vote of the Thirteen States on Ratification of the Federal Constitution, 1787-1788 (Madison, Wis.,1894). The most important neo-Progressive work on Anti-Federalism, Jackson Turner Main, *The Antifederalists: Critics of the Constitution, 1781-1788* (Chapel Hill, N. C., 1961), also influenced the interpretation of Gordon S. Wood, *The Creation of the American Republic, 1776- 1787* (Chapel Hill, N. C.,1969), and *The Radicalism of the American Revolution* (New York 1992). Wood's work has become the standard on the thought of the Federalists and Anti-Federalists.

5. Robert Berkhofer, Jr., *Beyond the Great Story: History as Text and Discourse* (Cambridge, Mass., 1995). For alternatives to the Progressive view of Anti-Federalism see Kenyon, "Men of Little Faith"; Storing, *The Complete Anti-Federalist;* and James H. Hutson, "Country, Court, and Constitution: Antifederalism and the Historians," *WMQ,* 38 (1981), 337-68. Although these alternatives eschew the materialism of the Progressive model and the notion that Anti-Federalists were populists, each approach replicates the Progressive historians' tendency to cast Anti-Federalism as a monolithic movement. See, for example, Richard E. Ellis, "The Persistence of Anti-Federalism after 1789," in Richard Beeman, Stephen Botein, and Edward C. Carter II, eds., *Beyond Confederation: Origins of the Constitution and American National Identity* (Chapel Hill, N. C., 1987), and Harry N. Scheiber, "Federalism and the Constitution: The Original Understanding," in Lawrence M. Friedman and Scheiber, *American Law and the Constitutional Order: Historical Perspectives* (Cambridge, Mass., 1978), 85-98. For legal scholars who argue that the Anti-Federalists may have been more right than wrong see Akhil Reed Amar, "Anti-Federalists, *The Federalist* Papers, and the Big Argument," *Harvard J. Law and Public Policy,* 16 (1993), 111-18, and Charles J. Cooper, "Independent of Heaven Itself: Different Federalist and Anti-Federalist Perspectives on the Centralizing Tendency of the Federal Judiciary," ibid., 119-28.

6. Alan Brinkley, Nelson Polsby, and Kathleen Sullivan, *New Federalist Papers: Essays in Defense of the Constitution* (New York, 1997). Sullivan, "The Contemporary Relevance of *The Federalist,"* ibid., 14.

7. Amar draws primarily on Wood for his analysis of the populist character of Anti-Federalist thought in "The Bill of Rights as Constitution," *Yale Law Journal,* 100 (1991), 1131-1210, esp., 1138, 1162, 1204. See also Williams, "Civic Republicanism and the Citizen Militia: The Terrifying Second Amendment," ibid., 551-615. The term Standard Model comes from Glenn Harlan Reynolds, "A Critical Guide to the Second Amendment," *Tennessee Law Review,* 62 (1995), 461-512. For a critique of this model see Wills "To Keep and Bear Arms" *NYRB,* Sept. 21, 1995, and the letters responding to Wills by Levinson, Williams, and Glen Harlan, ibid., Nov. 16, 1995.

8. On the move to expand the authority of juries see Jeffrey Abramson, *We, the Jury: The Jury System and the Ideal of Democracy* (New York, 1994). For an example of one radical defense of jury nullification see Paul But-

ler, "Racially Based Jury Nullification: Black Power in the Criminal Justice System," *Yale Law J.,* 105 (1995), 677-725. For discussions of the constitutional issues raised by jury nullification see Richard St. John, "License to Nullify: The Democratic and Constitutional Deficiencies of Authorized Jury Lawmaking," ibid., 106 (1997), 2563-97, and Nancy J. King, "Silencing Nullification Advocacy Inside the Jury Room and Outside the Courtroom," *University of Chicago Law Review,* 65 (1998), 433-500.
9. On the nature of Progressive historiography see Richard Hofstadter, *The Progressive Historians: Turner, Beard, Parrington* (New York, 1968); Gene Wise, *American Historical Explanations: A Strategy for Grounded Inquiry* (Minneapolis, 1980); and Peter Novick, *That Noble Dream: The "Objectivity Question" and the American Historical Profession* (Cambridge, 1988).
10. For a more elaborate treatment of this problem see Cornell, *The Other Founders: Anti-Federalism and the Dissenting Tradition in America, 1788-1828* (Chapel Hill, N. C., 1999), 1-15.
11. On the tensions within Anti-Federalism see ibid., 51-120.
12. See Jonathan Culler, *On Deconstruction: Theory and Criticism After Structuralism* (Ithaca, N. Y., 1982). On the promise and problems of deconstruction as a historical methodology see Cornell, "Early American History in a Post-Modern Age," *WMQ,* 3d Ser., 50 (1993), 329-42.
13. For a more elaborate discussion of differences among Anti-Federalists see Cornell, *Other Founders*. On the ambiguity of American ideas about class during this period see Martin J. Burke, *The Conundrum of Class: Public Discourse on the Social Order in America* (Chicago, 1995). Historians are split over the degree to which American society was divided by issues of class during ratification; see Wood, "Ideology and the Origins of Liberal America," *WMQ,* 3d Ser., 44 (1987), 628-40. For the opposing view, stressing the importance of class tensions, see Gary Nash, "Also There at the Creation: Going Beyond Gordon S. Wood," ibid., 602-11.
14. The centrality of "Federal Farmer" to contemporary legal scholarship is aptly illustrated by the observation of Amar that this author was one of "the leading Anti-Federalist essayist of the ratification period." The importance of this essay to contemporary scholarship is further evidenced by the frequency with which it has been reprinted in modern anthologies; Amar, "Bill of Rights as Constitution," 1187; Murray Dry, "The Debate over Ratification of the Constitution," in Jack P. Greene and J. R. Pole, eds., *The Blackwell Encyclopedia of the American Revolution* (London, 1991), 473. A good survey of recent documentary collections of Federalist and Anti-Federalist writings is Richard Bernstein, "Charting the Bicentennial." *Columbia Law Review,* 87 (1987): 1565-624. The most frequently repeated Anti-Federalist authors in the collections cited by Bernstein are Federal Farmer and Brutus.
15. The identity of the Federal Farmer is a subject of considerable controversy. The case against Lee is forcefully argued by Wood, "The Authorship of the *Letters from the Federal Farmer,*" *WMQ,* 3d Ser., 31 (1974),

299-308, and Robert H. Webking suggests that Federal Farmer may have been Melancton Smith in "Melancton Smith and the *Letters from the Federal Farmer,*" ibid.., 44 (1987), 510-28. For examples of legal scholars who have used the mistaken attribution see David T. Hardy, "The Second Amendment and the Historiography of the Bill of Rights," *Journal of Law and Politics* 4 (Summer 1987), 1-62; Robert J. Cottrol and Raymond T. Diamond, "The Second Amendment: Toward an Afro-Americanist Reconsideration," *Georgetown Law Journal,* 80 (1991), 309-61; Anthony J. Dennis, "Clearing the Smoke From the Right to Bear Arms and the Second Amendment," *Akron Law Review,* 29 (Summer 1995), 57-9; David B. Kopel, and Christopher C. Little, "Communitarians, Neorepublicans, and Guns: Assessing the Case for Firearms Prohibition," *Maryland Law Review,* 56 (1997), 438-554; and Williams, "Civic Republicanism and the Citizen Militia: the Terrifying Second Amendment," *Yale Law Journal,* 101 (1991), 551-615, and "The Militia Movement and Second Amendment Revolution: Conjuring With the People," *Cornell Law Review,* 81 (1996), 879-952.
16. Lamb to Lee, May 18, 1788; Merrill Jensen et al., eds., *The Documentary History of the Ratification of the Constitution,* 12 vols. to date (Madison, Wis., 1976-), 9:814 (hereafter cited as *DHRC*). For a discussion of the circulation and reception of Federal Farmer see ibid., 14:14- 18. On New York politics during this period see Edward Countryman, *A People in Revolution: The American Revolution and Political Society in New York, 1760-1790* (Baltimore, 1981).
17. [Melancton Smith?], "Federal Farmer," *DHRC,* 14:50.
18. Ibid., 19, 50-51. On the ideology of Shays and his followers see David Szatmary, *Shays' Rebellion: The Making of Agrarian Insurrection* (Amherst, Mass., 1980), and Robert A. Gross, ed., *In Debt to Shays: The Bicentennial of an Agrarian Rebellion* (Charlottesville, Va., 1993). On liberal thought in early America see Joyce Appleby, *Capitalism and the New Social Order: The Republican Vision of the 1790s* (New York, 1984).
19. *DHRC,* 14:20. "Federal Farmer: An Additional Number of Letters to a Federal Republican" ibid., 17:273, 277. Federal Farmer's sympathy for the plight of the commercial interests and his hostility to paper money place him outside the agrarian populist ideology at the core of Anti-Federalism described by Main in *Anti-Federalists.* A similar view informs the work of Ellis, *The Union at Risk: Jacksonian Democracy, States' Rights and the Nullification Crises* (New York, 1987). Federal Farmer more closely resembles the commercial variant of Anti-Federalism described by Cathy D. Matson and Peter S. Onuf, *A Union of Interests: Political and Economic Thought in Revolutionary America* (Lawrence, Kan., 1990).
20. [Melancton Smith?], "Federal Farmer," *DHRC,* 19, 50-51.
21. For a discussion of the Carlisle riot and the spectrum of Anti-Federalist thought see Cornell, "Aristocracy Assailed: The Ideology of Backcountry Anti-Federalism," *Journal of American History,* 76 (1990), 1148-72.
22. [Melancton Smith?] "Federal Farmer: An Additional Number of Letters

to a Federal Republican," *DHRC,* 17:339. On the notion of jural rights see Shannon C. Stimson, *The American Revolution in Law: Anglo-American Jurisprudence before John Marshall* (Princeton, N. J., 1990). On the representative character of the jury see Pole, "Reflections on American Law and the American Revolution," *WMQ,* 3d Ser., 50 (1993), 123-59. For criticisms of Pole's thesis see Peter Charles Hoffer, "Custom as Law: A Comment on J. R. Pole's 'Reflections,'" ibid., 160-67; Bruce H. Mann, "The Evolutionary Revolution in American Law: A Comment on J. R. Pole's 'Reflections'" ibid., 168-75; and James A. Henretta and James D. Rice, "Law as Litigation: An Agenda for Research," ibid., 176-80. A useful discussion of how juries could serve the interests of local elites is F. Thornton Miller, *Juries and Judges Versus the Law: Virginia's Provincial Legal Perspective, 1783-1828* (Charlottesville, Va., 1994).
23. [Melancton Smith?], "Federal Farmer: An Additional Number of Letters to a Federal Republican," *DHRC,* 17:339. On the notion of the public sphere see Jürgen Habermas, *The Structural Transformation of the Public Sphere: An Inquiry into a Category of Bourgeois Society,* trans. Thomas Burger and Frederick Lawrence (Cambridge, Mass., 1991).
24. [Melancton Smith?], "Federal Farmer," *DHRC,* 14:46.
25. Ibid., 20, 22.
26. "Aristocrotis" [William Petrikin], "The Government of Nature Delineated," in Storing, ed., *Complete Anti-Federalist,* 3:204. For a discussion of Petrikin's authorship see Cornell, "Aristocracy Assailed," 1166.
27. Cornell, "Aristocracy Assailed," 1150-56.
28. Popular traditions of social justice are discussed by E.P. Thompson in "The Moral Economy of the English Crowd in the Eighteenth Century," *Past and Present,* No. 50 (1971), 76-136, in "Eighteenth-Century Class English Society: Class Struggle without Class," *Social History,* 3 (1978), 133-65, and in "Patrician Society, Plebeian Culture," *Journal of Social History,* 7 (1974), 382-405. For a stimulating discussion of the transplantation of English traditions of popular justice to America in the same period see Alfred F. Young, "English Plebeian Culture and Eighteenth-Century American Radicalism," in Margaret C. Jacob and James R. Jacob, eds., *The Origins of Anglo-American Radicalism* (London, 1984), 185-212.
29. Grayson, "Speech in the Virginia State Convention," June 21, 1788, *DHRC,* 10:1447, 1449. Similar concerns were expressed by Richard Henry Lee to James Gordon, Jr., Feb 26, 1788, ibid., 7:418-19. On the culture of debt in Revolutionary Virginia, and its contribution to the mentality of the gentry see T. H. Breen *Tobacco Culture: The Mentality of the Great Tidewater Planters on the Eve of the Revolution* (Princeton, N. J. 1985).
30. Members of the Anti-Federalist elite believed that there was an identity of interests uniting individuals that cut across class; see Cornell, *Other Founders,* 73.
31. On the fate of the republican synthesis see Daniel T. Rodgers, "Republicanism: The Career of a Concept." *JAH,* 76 (1992), 11-38. On the impor-

tance of localism to constitutionalism in this period see Greene, "The Colonial Origins of American Constitutionalism," in Greene, ed., *Negotiated Authorities: Essays in Colonial Political and Constitutional History* (Charlottesville, Va., 1994), 25-42, and *Peripheries and Centers: Constitutional Development in the Extended Polities of the British Empire and the United States, 1607-1788* (Athens, Ga., 1986). In both accounts Greene tends to conflate localism and federalism. Most discussions of localism link it to a democratic or egalitarian political culture; see Robert E. Shalhope, "Republicanism, Liberalism, and Democracy: Political Culture in the New Nation," in Milton Klein et al., eds., *The Republican Synthesis Revisited: Essays in Honor of George Athan Billias* (Worcester, Mass., 1992), 37-90. A number of political theorists also equate localism with democracy; see Joshua Miller, *The Rise and Fall of Democracy in Early America, 1630-1789* (University Park, Pa., 1991), and Christopher M. Duncan, *The Anti-Federalists and Early American Political Thought* (DeKalb, Ill., 1995). A useful corrective to this view that explores the way localism could function to support hierarchy is Kenneth Lockridge, *Settlement and Unsettlement in Early America* (Cambridge, 1981).

32. Louis Hartz, *The Liberal Tradition in America: An Interpretation of American Political Thought Since the Revolution* (New York, 1955). On the role of plebeian violence in shaping the course of politics after ratification see Cornell, "Aristocracy Assailed."

3

"Hunting in the Pond Where the Ducks Are": Conservative Opposition to Civil Rights Legislation in the 1964 Election and Beyond

Niels Bjerre-Poulsen

Since its emergence in the late 1940s, the American conservative movement has been a shotgun marriage of widely different strains of thought; an attempted fusion of libertarians and traditionalists, an uneasy alliance between elitists and populists. The vital glue throughout most of this period has been a shared detestation of communism or "collectivism" in all its alleged forms. There have been other uniting bonds as well. Following the Supreme Court's 1954 landmark decision in *Brown* v. *Board of Education of Topeka,* a shared opposition to "judicial usurpation of power" has been among the most notable. Conservatives have reacted strongly to the role of the Supreme Court as a catalyst for social and cultural change in America. In their view, the court, in its attempt to create a more egalitarian society, has overstepped its boundaries and imposed the views of a liberal elite on the rest of the American public in the disguise of constitutional interpretation. Whether one finds such charges justified, it is evident that the Supreme Court has triggered dramatic changes in the American polity with its controversial decisions on such issues as voting rights, racial integration, affirmative action, school prayer, the rights of criminal defendants, freedom of speech, abortion, and gay rights. These changes have brought new groups into the conservative fold.

Since the late 1980s, when the appointments of conservative Supreme Court judges by Ronald Reagan truly began to take effect, many conservatives have changed their perception of the judiciary and have come to see it as a possible engine for their own cultural counterrevolution. Rather than complain about legal usurpation, they have entered the struggle over expressive dominance in the legal sphere by stating their political agenda in the form of "rights": the rights of the unborn, the right of women to stay in the home, the rights of the community to condemn homosexuality and obscenity.[1] Other conservatives have stuck by the theme of legal usurpation, maintaining that genuine conservatives on the Supreme Court are still a minority.

The Supreme Court's turn to the right and the expectations it has raised but not (yet) fulfilled have also exposed fundamental disagreements among conservatives.[2] Whereas they have previously been able to gloss over these disagreements and unite in a shared opposition to the social tinkering of an allegedly liberal Supreme Court, they do not always share a view of the proper role of the judiciary in the political process, nor do they necessarily agree on principles of constitutional interpretation. The nature of these disagreements is the subject of the last part of this essay. First, however, I will focus on how conservative attitudes toward constitutional interpretation in the crucial area of civil rights has changed since the 1960s, in order to accommodate the political needs of the movement.

The process that increasingly made race and racial attitudes the defining characteristics of partisanship began in 1964, when the conservative movement managed to win the Republican presidential nomination for Senator Barry Goldwater of Arizona. Since the early 1960s, Republicans had been cashing in on the growing tensions that the civil rights revolution had triggered within the New Deal coalition, but whether the GOP should actively exploit the Democratic split through a "Southern strategy" had for years been a controversial issue. Goldwater's nomination provided an affirmative answer. As Goldwater himself had put it a couple of years earlier, it was time to "go hunting in the pond where the ducks are."³

The defeat of the party's eastern establishment meant a rejection of the attempt to stress the legacy of Abraham Lincoln and compete with liberal Democrats in civil rights. The GOP would no longer cater to black constituencies who voted Democratic in overwhelming numbers anyway. Furthermore, the surprising strength demonstrated the same year by Alabama governor George C. Wallace in several Democratic primaries outside the South even suggested that the political gains of Goldwater's stand on civil rights would not necessarily be confined to Dixie.⁴

In the following decades, race would prove itself to be an effective "wedge issue" in the process of political realignment. In 1960, polls had indicated that American voters did not perceive any significant differences in the two major parties' attitudes toward racial issues. By 1968, the Republican Party had clearly shown itself as the party of racial conservatism, and by the 1970s the two parties were perceived to be at opposite extremes on the issue.⁵ Also during the 1960s, opposition to the interventionist role of the federal government in the process of racial integration provided the scattered forces of fiscal conservatism with an argument that transcended class divisions and addressed the concerns of many white working-class voters. Later they were joined by other groups of social conservatives, among them Protestant fundamentalists, who in the early 1970s were mobilized in large numbers when the Internal Revenue Service in the denied tax exemption to Christian schools on the grounds that they were de facto segregated and thus violated the Fourteenth Amendment.

Thus, since the early 1960s conservatives have been aware of the realignment potential in racial issues, and they have also been aware that racist arguments would kill the maturing movement's aspirations to intellectual respectability. The answer has been to stick with the legal grounds for continuing opposition to enforced integration. Without openly refuting the goal of racial equality, Goldwater Republicans marched under the banners of States Rights and Constitutionalism and argued that civil rights, good intentions notwithstanding, happened to be legal wrongs. The real threat to American democracy, they claimed, was not the political and social repression of black Americans in the South, but the encroachment of the federal government and the usurpation of power by the federal courts.

Many of the constitutional arguments that Goldwater adopted in his campaign had been in circulation for years. Among the leading conservative spokesmen in the field was James J. Kilpatrick, editor of the *Richmond [Va.] News Leader*. Kilpatrick was the author of *The Lasting South* and of *The Sovereign States,* and in 1957 he began writing for the country's leading conservative journal, the *National Review*. There readers were provided with constitutional arguments for the states' right to apply the principle of *interposition* in defiance of federal authority.[6] Kilpatrick had argued that the Civil Rights Act of 1957 deprived the states of their right to control voting requirements, just as it undermined property rights.

When new civil rights legislation was proposed in 1963, Kilpatrick objected once again. The right to vote, he stressed, was not an absolute right, because it did not apply to children or lunatics. He did not deny that willful intimidation of black voters might occur, for example, in the form of phony literacy tests, but he insisted that this was not a valid legal problem, because there was "abundant law on the books" and had been even prior to the Civil Rights Acts of 1957 and 1960 – to prevent and punish any such intimidation. As for the proposed ban on racial segregation, Kilpatrick argued, the bill would impose a "requirement to serve," which in his view was unconstitutional in any other field than public utilities such as power, water supply, and telephone services.[7] There was no adherence to any notion of moral law in Kilpatrick's argument. He insisted that he did not defend racial discrimination but merely citizens' constitutional right to discriminate, because nothing in the Constitution prevented such discrimination.[8] By the time Goldwater entered the race for the presidency, this had become the standard conservative argument against enforcement of civil rights in the South.

Goldwater was in a perfect position to use this argument. On the one hand, he consistently expressed his personal dislike of racism and segregation and frequently mentioned that he had been an active supporter of the NAACP in Arizona. He even told students at Phillips Academy that "if I were a Negro,

I don't think I would be very patient."[9] On the other hand, he defended states rights as an essential constitutional principle concerning the proper role of the federal government. The Supreme Court's decision in *Brown* v. *Board of Education* could not make him change his mind. While he agreed with the objectives of that decision, he did not think it was a matter for the Supreme Court to decide:

> It so happens that I am in agreement with the objectives of the Supreme Court, as stated in the Brown decision. I believe it is both wise and just for Negro children to attend the same school as whites, that to deny them this opportunity carries with it strong implications of inferiority. I am not prepared, however, to impose that judgment of mine on the people of Mississippi or South Carolina or tell them what methods should be adopted and what pace should be kept in striving toward that goal. That is their business, not mine.[10]

Goldwater thus presented the standard conservative argument against federal intervention on behalf of African-American citizens whose civil rights were blatantly violated in the South: Social justice and compassion had to make way for larger principles involved. Further legislation or, even worse, demands for strict enforcement of such legislation were not acceptable ways of ameliorating existing inequities. In any case, such violations remained "essentially local problems [that were] best dealt with by the people most directly concerned."[11]

Goldwater, who received special advice in the field from Robert H. Bork and William Rehnquist, two aspiring lawyers with a special interest in constitutional law, also gave voice to another recurring conservative theme in the debate over enforced integration, namely, that the judiciary did not have a monopoly on constitutional interpretation:

> The Constitution is what its authors intended it to be and said it was – not what the Supreme Court says it is. ... I therefore support all efforts by the States, excluding violence of course, to preserve their rightful powers over education.[12]

The senator did make one notable concession during his campaign. Urged by his advisor Denison Kitchel, he told the press on January 5, 1964, that he now believed the federal government had the authority to intervene in local desegregation disputes if a federal court order had been violated. Goldwater also maintained (albeit reluctantly) his support for possible federal intervention to secure the right to vote, even if it meant sending troops to the South.[13] Such concessions did not destroy his political support in the South, which increased even further on June 19, 1964, when he was one of the six Republican senators who voted against the Civil Rights Bill.

Despite Goldwater's rejection of the 1964 Civil Rights Bill, it would be difficult to claim that he opposed civil rights legislation as such. He had supported the civil rights bills that were enacted in 1957 and 1960, and he claimed to be sympathetic to most parts of the 1964 bill. At one point during the debate about President Kennedy's original proposal, he had even suggested a mandatory denial of federal funds for programs in which discrimination was practiced. Nor did he question the federal government's right to secure the voting rights of African Americans, "even if it means with troops."[14] What he objected to in the final bill were the provisions (Titles II and VII) that gave the federal government a regulatory capacity with regard to private enterprise in the areas of public accommodation and employment.

This was no minor objection. One can even argue that these provisions made all the difference. Goldwater was in a sense reviving the constitutional argument about the limits of the federal government's power to legislate on interstate commerce, although a broad interpretation of what "commerce" meant had not been seriously challenged since President Franklin D. Roosevelt's clash with the Supreme Court in 1937. Among recent laws based on a broad interpretation of the commerce clause was the Labor Reform Act of 1959, which Goldwater himself had voted for without any principal objections. Also, some three years before his "no" to the Civil Rights Act of 1964, Goldwater had discussed the so-called Freedom Rides in a private letter to Jack Bell, who at the time was writing a biography of him:

> I ... feel in relation to the Freedom Riders that while I think the N.A.A.C.P. or whoever is behind them is making a bad mistake in continuing them that under the Commerce Clause of the Constitution, bus companies, airlines, railroads, etc., engaged in interstate commerce cannot deny any citizen the right to their facilities.[15]

Apparently he had since changed his mind about the proper interpretation of the clause or did not think that the same principles also applied to employment and public accommodation.

Many southern supporters had hoped that Goldwater would make at least one speech that could be interpreted as a defense of segregation, but he did not. As a matter of fact, Goldwater hardly touched on the issue of civil rights while campaigning in Dixie. He was honoring an agreement made with President Lyndon Johnson, on July 24, that neither would attempt to exploit the sensitive issue in their speeches.[16] Although this was a noble gesture at a critical moment in history, one can also argue that the senator did not have to address the race issue openly. Given the widespread American custom of negative voting, he did not even have to declare opposition to the principles of civil rights and racial equality in order to win the segregationist vote as long as it remained clear that, unlike the current administration, he would not actively use the power of the federal government to enforce them.

On election day, 71 percent of the white voters in the South supported Goldwater.[17] In Mississippi, probably the most segregated state in the region, he received a stunning 87 percent of the white vote. Evidently, commitment to the New Deal coalition was disintegrating in many southern constituencies as racial politics were given higher priority than economic issues. "Volunteers for Goldwater" groups naturally stimulated this realignment process by attempting to convince voters that Republican conservatism could provide a respectable ideological framework for resistance to further racial integration and that the time had come to "forget meaningless party labels."[18]

The Republican use of racial integration as a wedge issue continued in the following years. Admittedly, President Richard Nixon's record on civil rights was better than Goldwater's, but he too clearly practiced a Southern Strategy of some sort, among other things by signaling to the voters that he would do only a minimum to comply with existing civil rights legislation.[19] His Supreme Court nomination of two judges, Clement F. Haynsworth and G. Harrold Carswell, both with dubious records in the field of civil rights and whose primary qualification seemed to be that they were southerners, is also difficult to explain in any other way.[20] In time, however, Republican conservatives abandoned the notion of states rights and turned their attention toward the increased use of affirmative action remedies. By the time Reagan moved into the White House, conservatives were no longer defending the constitutional right to discriminate, but instead calling for "equal opportunity" for white Americans allegedly subjected to "reverse discrimination."

The entire discourse on civil rights had been reversed. President Reagan could present himself as a true defender of equality by opposing the liberal conception of group rights and group remedies – a conception which had been expressed in the Burger Court's decisions in *Griggs* v. *Duke Power Co.* (1971) and *Fullilove* v. *Klutznick* (1980). What Reagan suggested was a formal racial neutrality based on the assumptions that racial discrimination was a thing of the past and that all past injustices that might justify group rights had long since been remedied. The law should be "color blind" and solely concerned with the rights of individuals. Rather than oppose the notion of civil rights, conservatives had now redefined its primary purpose as the protection of citizens from coercive social engineering by the courts and by the federal government.[21]

As the Reagan Administration realized the poor odds of making a Congress still dominated by Democrats carry out its "conservative revolution," it increasingly put its faith in the judiciary, where it was helped by historical circumstances. During Reagan's eight years in office, he had the chance to appoint 378 federal judges, and by 1991, he and his successor George Bush (also a former Goldwater activist who, like Reagan, had opposed the 1964 Civil Rights Act) had appointed more than half of the 837 judges in the federal judiciary.[22] To the Supreme Court the two presidents appointed Sandra Day O'Connor, Anthony Kennedy, Antonin Scalia, David Souter,

Clarence Thomas, and Chief Justice William H. Rehnquist, who could all be characterized as conservatives of some sort.

Rehnquist had been one of Goldwater's advisors on civil rights in 1964. When another member of Goldwater's "Arizona mafia," Richard Kleindienst, went to work in President Nixon's Justice Department, he recommended his legal advisor, Rehnquist, who became an assistant attorney general. In 1971, Rehnquist was named to the Supreme Court. By the time he was promoted to chief justice in 1986, his views on civil rights were pretty clear: he had voted against the plaintiffs in eighty-two of eighty-three cases concerning civil rights matters.[23]

The turn to the right in the Supreme Court became evident during 1989 in decisions such as *Richmond* v. *Croson* and *Wards Cove Packing Company* v. *Atonio,* in which the court affirmed a new standard of formal color blindness and shifted the burden of proof to the plaintiff. Statistics or other forms of social scientific evidence could no longer serve as evidence of any pattern of discrimination. Only as individuals could African Americans attempt to prove that conscious discrimination had taken place and that personal harm had been done to them. Scalia argued that remedies designed to overcome the effects of past discrimination simply sustained racism by creating a racial spoils system.[24]

Considering the reputations of Scalia and Rehnquist as conservatives who supposedly recognized both the blessings and the burdens of culture and history, there is something odd about their belief that the cumulative effects of racism could be removed by the enforcement of color-blind legislation. As Harry Blackmun expressed it in his dissent to *Wards Cove Packing Company* v. *Atonio:* "One wonders whether the majority still believes that race discrimination – or, more accurately, race discrimination against nonwhites – is a problem in our society, or even remembers that it ever was."[25]

In a sense, conservative arguments on civil rights had come full circle in the debate about affirmative action. No longer did conservatives argue for a constitutional right to discriminate – not even for white employers' right to voluntarily practice reverse discrimination in the hiring and promotion of minority workers. Instead they employed a literal reading of the Fourteenth Amendment when it came to racial relations. "Equal protection for any person," they argued, barred government programs that discriminated against white males. When it came to other issues, such as whether the Pentagon could discriminate against homosexuals, they were less willing to apply a literal reading.[26] The Civil Rights Act of 1964 had also become a major conservative argument against affirmative action. The irony is difficult to ignore: conservative judges such as Rehnquist and Bork, who had worked for Goldwater and helped him flesh out his opposition to the 1964 Civil Rights Act, now employed that same act in their attempt to strike down affirmative action.

Thus, many conservatives seem intent on having it both ways. On the one hand, they rally against the expansion of individual rights, particularly if the beneficiaries are homosexuals or belong to other minorities whose values or behavior are seen as an affront to "community values." In these matters, conservatives would like the courts to be more responsive to such values in their rulings. When it comes to affirmative action and other remedies designed to help groups who have historically suffered from discrimination, the same conservatives employ a different interpretation of the Constitution, stressing that it related solely to citizens on an individual basis.

How has the Supreme Court's turn to the right in recent years changed the perception of the institution among American conservatives? Not much. Many conservatives still seem to be arguing against the Warren Court. While they recognize that the Supreme Court has changed its position on some issues, they are disappointed that the court has not been able or willing to overturn *Roe* v. *Wade* and remove other thorns in the flesh of conservatives.

Some, like Bork, have given up the idea that the court can be reformed by changes in its membership. "Republican Presidents have used the nomination process in an effort to change the direction of the Court with almost zero results on the major issues," argues Bork, who favors an arrangement in which Congress has the ability to modify or reverse court decisions by majority vote.[27]

This majoritarian view was also the point of departure,

when the editors of *First Things* magazine held a symposium on "The End of Democracy" in fall 1996. Based on the notion that in the last fifty years a judicial oligarchy has taken over all the truly important questions that should have been handled by the country's representative political institutions, the editors presented the symposium as "an urgent call for the repoliticizing of the American regime."[28] What the symposium reveals, however, is that beneath the common theme of "keeping the judges in their place," conservatives are seriously divided in their views on constitutional interpretation and the proper role of the judiciary.

The most fundamental division is probably between majoritarians and those who adhere to the primacy of "moral law" or "natural law." The latter group argues that the courts are run by gnostics who have detached their deliberations from any reference to a basic framework of moral truth. To these conservatives, the struggle against abortion is a struggle for the soul of the nation. They see the notion of a disinterested public ethic as the basic problem with the judiciary. According to James C. Dobson of Focus on the Family: "Among the most elementary principles of Western Civilization is the truth that laws which violate the moral law are null and void and must in conscience be disobeyed."[29] To most proponents, this suggests that the Supreme Court has a moral obligation to ban abortion, condemn homosexuality, and take similar actions, regardless of its views on constitutional interpretation. On these matters, which the religious right particularly finds essential, notions of textualism, "original intent," and "original meaning" become irrelevant. This view, based on the idea of natural law, is a far cry from Goldwater's claim that on the issue of civil rights neither he nor the Supreme Court had the right to impose their morals on the people of the South.

Interestingly, several contributors to the symposium quote Martin Luther King, Jr.'s *Letter from a Birmingham Jail* in their justification of civil disobedience in case the government or the judiciary detaches itself from moral law: "A just law is a man-made code that squares with the moral law of God."[30] One contributor even uses the civil rights revolution as evidence that the United States is, after all, "a society of moralists," because the majority of Americans reject the notion of any constitutional right to discriminate.[31] Then why, he asks, is it not equally justified to let moral standards set by the community through public debate limit other individual "rights" as well? Even if the analogy is false, because segregation was not so much an expression of individual rights as it was of "community values" at their worst, the argument is nevertheless emblematic of how the conservative discourse on civil rights has changed since the 1960s.

On the other side of the argument one finds the majoritarians and the textualists. Majoritarians maintain the primacy of democracy and remind their opponents that the basic principle in democracy is majority rule. The Supreme Court may still invalidate positions held by the majority but "only because the people previously agreed to restraints on majority rule through the Bill of Rights and other constitutional provisions."[32] Among the leading conservative majoritarians are Bork and Justice Scalia, who despite his personal opposition to abortion has argued that the courts have no jurisdiction over the matter because the issue simply is outside the purview of constitutional law. "If the people want abortion," Scalia has argued, "the state should permit abortion in a democracy."[33]

To majoritarians, the real problem is not the right to abortion but that the Supreme Court represents a liberal elite that is imposing its political views on the majority of the American public in the disguise of constitutional interpretation. In their view, the courts have legalized issues that are properly political and thus usurped majoritarian democracy. Some majoritarian conservatives such as Bork are also firm believers in textualism or original intent (Chief Justice Rehnquist has expressed his sympathy for the idea). The Supreme Court, they argue, has not only expanded constitutional rights far beyond the original intentions of the Founding Fathers, it has invented new ones as well. The primary example of such an invention, originalists argue, is the "right of privacy" established in *Griswold* v. *Connecticut* and later used in *Roe* v. *Wade*.

But what if original intent conflicts with the principle of majority rule? One need not read much in the Federalist Papers to find arguments for James Madison's stern opposition to simple majority rule. Indeed, as former Supreme Court justice William J. Brennan has put it:

> It is the very purpose of a Constitution – and particularly the Bill of Rights – to declare certain values transcendent, beyond the reach of temporary political majorities. The majoritarian process cannot be expected to rectify claims of minority rights that arise as a response to the outcomes of that very majoritarian process.[34]

And what if original intent conflicts with moral law? In the words of Kermit L. Hall:

> History also teaches – as the fate of women and blacks reveal – that for all of the framers' genius, the Court must be prepared to shake free of the past when the only purpose of precedent is to perpetuate that which we know to be unjust.[35]

Which should be the more important principle: democracy or moral law? What if the majority of Americans does not agree with the moral law as it is interpreted by the religious right? By definition, democracy only reflects the will of the majority, not necessarily moral truth. One can only hope for a virtuous polity. Even so, proponents of majoritarian democracy and proponents of moral law have been able to join forces as long as they could argue that a liberal Supreme Court violated both. Now, with a Supreme Court that supposedly has a conservative majority, the conflict is out in the open.

As for conservative arguments in favor of original intent, the underlying assumption seems to be that full application (however one would conduct the required historical analysis) would generally validate conservative constitutional views on current issues, because conservatives generally are less engaged than their liberal counterparts in constitutional interpretation. The changing conservative views on civil rights legislation amply demonstrate that this has not been the case. To illustrate this point, one need look no further than the Supreme Court decision that started the discussion of legal usurpation, *Brown*. One would expect that this decision, with its inclusion of sociological evidence, is anathema to proponents of textualism. Yet few conservatives now dare touch it. They will argue, as Bork has done, that the judiciary was justified in stretching its authority when the other branches of government were paralyzed in the matter of segregation. Or, like Reagan's attorney general Edwin Meese, III, a firm believer in original intent, will find *Brown* "restoring the original principle of the Constitution to constitutional law":

> The *Brown* decision was correcting the damage done fifty years earlier, when in *Plessy* v. *Ferguson* an earlier Supreme Court had disregarded the clear intent of the Framers of the civil war amendments to eliminate the legal degradation of blacks, and had contrived a theory of the Constitution to support the charade of "separate but equal" discrimination.[36]

In addition to these arguments, majoritarian conservatives have added that the decision was approved by a majority of the American people. The revised views of the *Brown* decision illustrate how conservatives have adapted to the changing views of the American public in general or, if one is more cynical, to new political needs and interests. They also make it evident that, beneath the cloak of textualism, conservatives too are constantly engaged in constitutional interpretation. In that respect, they are still, just like their liberal counterparts, attempting to hunt where the ducks are.

Notes

1. For this struggle over expressive power, see Kenneth L. Karst, *Law's Promise, Law's Expression: Visions of Power in the Politics of Race, Gender, and Religion* (New Haven, 1993).
2. The conflicting conservative views of jurisprudence were highlighted in the 2000 presidential election, when the court's conservative majority – its leading proponents of states' rights and judicial restraint – decided to stop the recount of votes in Florida and thus secure the election for Republican nominee george W. Bush. However, most conservatives could take comfort in the fact that the new president would probably be granted the opportunity to nominate two or three new Supreme court judges,

and thus pave the way for a decisive shift to the right in constitutional interpretation.

3. Phillip E. Converse et al., "Electoral Myth and Reality: The 1964 Election," *American Political Science Review,* 59 (1965), 327. Republican attempts to make inroads in the once Solid South could actually be traced as far back as the election of 1952, when Dwight Eisenhower successfully carried Tennessee, Florida, Texas, and Virginia. Four years later he had managed to add Louisiana to the list, and in 1957 GOP National Chairman H. Meade Alcorn launched "Operation Dixie" as a sustained effort to gain a foothold in Southern politics.
4. George Wallace received about 34% of the vote in the Wisconsin primary, 30% in Indiana, and 43% in Maryland.
5. See Thomas Byrne Edsall and Mary D. Edsall, *Chain Reaction; The Impact of Race, Rights, and Taxes on American Politics* (New York, 1992), 55 ff.
6. Both books published by Henry Regnery Company, Chicago, 1957.
7. James J. Kilpatrick, "Civil Rights and Legal Wrongs," *National Review* (Sept. 24, 1963), 232.
8. Ibid., 234.
9. Quoted in Lee Edwards, *Goldwater: The Man Who Made a Revolution* (Washington, D. C., 1995), 231.
10. Barry Goldwater, *The Conscience of a Conservative* (New York, Inc., 1974; orig. pub. 1960), 38.
11. Ibid., 30.
12. Goldwater, *Conscience of a Conservative*, 37.
13. Edwards, *Goldwater,* 239. Rehnquist, who later became Chief Justice of the Supreme Court, was then working for Kitchel's law firm in Phoenix.
14. New York *Post,* May 11, 1961, quoted in Robert A. Goldberg, *Goldwater* (New Haven, 1995), 154.
15. Goldwater to Jack Bell, Aug. 8, 1961, in Barry M. Goldwater Papers, Arizona Historical Foundation, Tucson, Arizona.
16. Goldwater, *With No Apologies* (New York, 1979), 193.
17. Dewey W. Grantham, *The South In Modern America: A Region at Odds* (New York, 1994), 247. For evidence that race was the central issue in the Deep South see James L. Sundquist, *Dynamics of the Party System* (Washington, D. C., 1983), 352-53.
18. *Facts,* pamphlet distributed by Florida Volunteers for Goldwater (undated), Goldwater papers.
19. See Hugh Davis Graham, *The Civil Rights Era; Origins and Development of National Policy* (New York, 1990), 301 ff.. See also John Morton Blum, *Years of Discord; American Politics and Society, 1961-1974* (New York, 1992), 332-41.
20. Both candidates were rejected by the Senate, but Nixon basically got what he had hoped for from having nominated them in the first place. Afterward, he could tell the press that the nominees had really been rejected because of their belief in strict construction of the Constitution and "the fact that they had the misfortune of being born in the South. ...

I understand the bitter feeling of millions of Americans who live in the South about the act of regional discrimination that took place in the Senate yesterday"; quoted in Blum, *Years of Discord,* 339.
21. As Edsall and Edsall note, Reagan had an outspoken ability to use race-neutral language, which nevertheless "implicitly evoked submerged racial and cultural conflict"; *Chain Reaction,* 184.
22. David G. Savage, *Turning Right; The Making of the Rehnquist Court* (New York, 1993), 423.
23. Ibid., 21.
24. Scalia had come to the Supreme Court from the U.S. Court of Appeals for the District of Columbia, where he had been part of a group of conservative judges which also included Robert Bork, Kenneth Starr, James Buckley, and Laurence Silberman.
25. Quoted in Savage, *Turning Right,* 276.
26. Ibid., 220 ff.
27. Bork, "Our Judicial Oligarchy;" *First Things,* 67 (Nov. 1996), 23.
28. The editors, "The End of Democracy? The Judicial Usurpation of Politics," ibid., 18-20. As the word "regime" implies, the editors seemingly questioned the very legitimacy of the government of the United States, and several contributions to the symposium had contained implied threats ranging from civil disobedience to revolution.
29. James C. Dobson, in "The End of Democracy? – A Discussion Continued," ibid., 69 (Jan. 1997), 19-24. Such statements made four members of the journal's Editorial Board , among them Gertrude Himmelfarb and Walter Burns, resign in protest
30. Quoted in Charles W. Colson, "Kingdoms in Conflict," ibid., 67 (Nov. 1996), 34-38.
31. William J. Stuntz, "When Rights Are Wrong," ibid., 62 (Apr. 1996), 18.
32. Jon Mitchel, "Critique of the *First Things* Symposium (The End of Democracy?)," on Scalia Shrine Home Page: http://home.uchicago.edu/
33. Quoted in Robert P. George, "The Tyrant State," *First Things,* 67 (Nov. 1996), 40.
34. William J. Brennan, "On the Failure of the Doctrine of Original Intent," 1985, reprinted in Kermit L. Hall, ed., *Major Problems in American Constitutional History,* vol. 2: *From 1870 to the Present* (Lexington, Mass., 1992), 560.
35. Hall, ibid., 550.
36. Edwin Meese, "Address to the American Bar Association," Nov. 15, 1985, reprinted in Hall, *Major Problems in American Constitutional History,* 2:555.

4
Protection under United States Law?: It Depends on Who You Are, Where You Are, What Aspect of Your Job You Are Talking About, and Who Is Trying to Hurt You

Mark Gibney

One of the more popular cliches in the United States is that we live under the rule of law. Sounds nice. And for most of us this is true. In our day-to-day existence, law certainly guides much of our behavior and in a manner that few of us notice. The law often tells us what we can and cannot do: What drugs are we prohibited from taking? How fast can we drive? How old must we be before we can drink alcohol, if we are allowed to drink alcohol at all? But in addition to legal prohibitions, the law serves to protect us. Its protections can be found in a variety of sources: the United States Constitution, various state constitutions, federal law, state law, local ordinances, and the like.

For most of us there is a balance between the prohibitions of the law and the protections afforded under the law. To give one example, the law states that we cannot use cocaine. That is a prohibition. But the law (the Fourth Amendment, to be precise) also states that law enforcement agents cannot simply go around kicking in doors to look for drugs. Instead, they must first have probable cause for believing drugs are in a certain residence, and in addition, they must (in nearly all cases) obtain a search warrant from an independent magistrate before conducting the search.

This essay examines the intersection of citizenship and nationality, where the mixture of prohibition and protection of United States law is not what we experience in the domestic realm. I have broken it into two main sections. The first concerns how United States law treats "aliens," and the second covers how United States law treats American citizens who live and work in foreign countries.

For more than a quarter century the United States has waged a "war on drugs," and with it has come a surfeit of law. Most of this law comes in the form of a vast array of prohibitions against the sale and use of a myriad of drugs. There is a flip side to these prohibitions, which is that certain protections – particularly constitutional safeguards – are afforded by the law.

In the past decade or so, the war on drugs has inexorably moved beyond the territorial boundaries of the United States. To what extent does United States law apply outside the country's borders? Suffice to say that domestic prohibitions have been applied in the international realm with a vengeance. No country even comes close to approaching the United States in this regard.[1] No country applies its drug laws (and its criminal laws generally) abroad the way that the United States does. No country has anywhere near the number of drug enforcement agents posted overseas as does the United States. No country has anywhere near the number of military personnel stationed in other countries for purposes of fighting drug trafficking. In sum, no country in the world seems so intent on preventing its citizens from using drugs.[2]

Notwithstanding its decidedly military slant, in many respects overseas drug enforcement does not look all that different from its domestic version. Imagine if you will "Miami Vice" somewhere further south, only now with a battery of helicopters, the routine use of antiaircraft weapons, the massive deployment of defoliants, and so on. However, perhaps the real difference between the domestic and the international realms is in their legal protections or, more accurately, the lack thereof. Although the prohibitions of the law have been extended past America's borders, the protections afforded by the law – constitutional protections in particular – have stayed at home. In essence, the moment you cross the border this part of the law vanishes.

The leading case in this area is a 1990 decision by the United States Supreme Court.[3] Verdugo-Urquidez is a Mexican national who was arrested by Mexican authorities and handed over to officials of the United States for prosecution in this country for drug trafficking. Subsequent to this, United States Drug Enforcement Agency (DEA) agents searched his residence in Mexico and found incriminating evidence. The question in the case was whether the Fourth Amendment to the Constitution was applicable to this search and seizure.[4] The court held that it was not. In an opinion by Chief Justice William Rehnquist, the court held that Fourth Amendment protection is afforded to "the People" of the United States – which is to say, members of the governed. Note that Rehnquist did not insist that only American citizens, or even lawful permanent resident aliens, were protected. Instead, he defined "the People" as those with sufficient contacts with the United States. What does that mean? It is hard to say, but Rehnquist wrote that Verdugo-Urquidez, who had only been in the United States for a few days (in a jail, no less) before the search of his residence took place, did not have the requisite "sufficient connections."

Semantics aside, what seemed to be of utmost concern to the court was what the implications of an opposite holding would have on all "other" overseas operations, whether law enforcement or foreign policy related, or however one might begin to distinguish between the two.

> The result of accepting his [Verdugo-Urquidez's] claim would have significant and deleterious consequences for the United States in conducting activities beyond its boundaries. The rule adopted by the Court of Appeals would apply not only to law enforcement operations abroad, but also to other foreign policy operations which might result in "searches and seizures." The United States frequently employs Armed Forces outside this country. ... Application of the Fourth Amendment to those circumstances could significantly disrupt the ability of the political branches to respond to foreign situations involving our national interest. Were respondent to prevail, aliens with no attachment to this country might well bring ac-

tions for damages to remedy claimed violations of the Fourth Amendment in foreign countries or in international waters.[5]

A concurring opinion by Associate Justice Arthur Kennedy highlights even further some of the distinctions of where and to whom the protections of the law should apply. Kennedy rejected out of hand the notion that the language "the People" was in any way dispositive of the issue. In his view, the reason the Fourth Amendment should not apply in the search of Verdugo-Urquidez's home is that the warrant requirement would be "impracticable and anomalous" under the circumstances. Where would United States authorities go for a warrant? Kennedy lists some of the inherent logistical problems:

> The absence of local judges or magistrates available to issue warrants, the differing and perhaps unascertainable conceptions of reasonableness and privacy that prevail abroad, and the need to cooperate with foreign officials all indicate that the Fourth Amendment's warrant requirement should not apply in Mexico as it does in this country.[6]

Having taken this position, Kennedy goes on to point out that the "rights of a citizen, as to whom the United States has continuing obligations, are not presented by this case."[7] But what does that mean? It seems to suggest that the result would have been different had the home in Mexico been that of a United States citizen. It does not explain how DEA agents would apply to the same unreasonable Mexican judges with the same misperceptions regarding privacy?

The better-reasoned opinion is Associate Justice William Brennan's dissent. In his view, Verdugo-Urquidez became a member of the American community the moment that we applied our criminal laws against him. As such, Brennan argued, he is entitled to full constitutional protection. This sounds reasonable to me, particularly when considering the we/them dichotomy that the case creates. Under the court's holding, Verdugo-Urquidez is a man without a country or, perhaps more accurately, a man without a country to protect him.

Although the search occurred in Mexico (and although Mexico has laws governing searches and seizures), the protections of Mexican law carried absolutely no weight in an American criminal proceeding. Neither did United States law – or at least not the provisions of the Fourth Amendment.

Perhaps the most dangerous aspect of Verdugo-Urquidez is that it apparently gives license to American DEA agents that they are not bound by American rules. This is true not only with respect to searches of homes, such as the one conducted in Verdugo-Urquidez's home. The case could also be read (and apparently Chief Justice Rehnquist *wants* it to be read) so that those caught up in our "war on drugs" – drug lords, dealers, and pushers, but also innocent bystanders and simple farmers – will be without any legal protection whatsoever against the phalanx of American enforcement activities and officials.

The reader will soon discover, if s/he has not already, that the protections of the law are often premised on whether something occurs in the United States. Events taking place in the United States are afforded constitutional protection, while those done outside the country are not – unless we are dealing with a United States citizen. This sounds simple enough.

But if we look at the case law in the field of immigration law – a legal quagmire if there ever was one – we find that this nice neat distinction breaks down very quickly. Take one of the earliest cases, *Chae Chan Ping* v. *United States [Chinese Exclusion Case]*.[8] Chae, a Chinese national who had been living and working in the United States for several decades, decided to take a trip to China. Although United States law at that time prohibited further Chinese immigration into this country, it did allow a Chinese national to leave and come back to the United States, as long as the traveler had obtained a certificate of residence before leaving. This is exactly what Chae Chan Ping had done. After he left this country, however, the United States Congress changed the law: no further Chinese migration, period. A week after this law took effect, Chae Chan Ping arrived back in the San Francisco harbor. Too late, said the United States Supreme Court. In language that is frequently quoted, the court held that over no conceivable subject do the political branches exercise greater control than they do over the entry and exit of individuals.

A decade later the Supreme Court decided another immigration case that goes to show how serious it is about this proposition. Because the Chinese people in the United States refused to act on our various hints, in 1892 Congress passed a law requiring that all Chinese nationals in the United States prove that they were here lawfully. They had to do this within one year, by certification from a credible white witness. Failure to comply with these requirements could lead to deportation proceedings, brought before any judge in the United States.

In *Fong Yue Ting* v. *United States,* the Supreme Court was faced with a challenge to this law.[9] Three Chinese nationals, who had lived in the United States since 1879, 1877, and 1874, had not done what federal law required. That is, they did not obtain certification of their residence from a credible white witness. The government then moved to deport these individuals, and the Supreme Court held that there was nothing, including the Constitution, to prevent the government from doing exactly this. In fact, the court held that there would be nothing unlawful if Congress had decided simply to evict from the United States the entire race of Chinese people. Given this perceived power, in the court's view what Congress had done in this particular instance was relatively benign.

It is much too easy to write off the *Chinese Exclusion* case and *Fong Yue Ting* as products of their times, although there is some disturbing evidence of this.[10] Fast forward to the 1950s and we have a situation where a permanent resident alien, Ignatz Mezei, leaves his Buffalo home to say farewell to his dying mother in Romania.[11] Mezei never did get to his mother's bedside, and his return to the United States eventually took nineteen months, much of it behind the Iron Curtain. When he arrived back in the United States, he was told that he posed a security threat to the United States. Based on what evidence? The attorney general never told Mezei. In fact, the attorney general never told anyone, including the members of the United States Supreme Court. This, however, did not prevent them from upholding Mezei's exclusion order. The problem for Mezei, in addition to being separated from his family for reasons never explained to him, is that other countries began to be scared away by his reputation as a national security threat. Because the United States was so frightened of his presence, so was every other country. So Mezei's applications for admission to other countries were turned down, and he simply sat and waited on Ellis Island, free to leave – but only if he were an amphibian.[12]

Constitutional protection? No, the Supreme Court held. Notwithstanding two and a half decades of a life of "unrelieved insignificance" in Buffalo, New York, and despite his physical presence at that time on Ellis Island, the court held that Mezei was to be treated like a first time entrant, and for it "due process" is whatever Congress (but not the Constitution) says that it is.[13]

More recently, some of the harshness of this ruling has been removed, although it is still "good law." *Landon* v. *Plascencia* concerns a foreign national who, after five years' residence in the United States, left the country and took a trip to Mexico that lasted a couple of days.[14] When Ms. Plascencia attempted to return, she was caught smuggling in a group of aliens. She claimed constitutional protection, and the Supreme Court agreed that after an alien had lived for some period of time in the United States constitutional protection begins to accrue for this person. In other words, Ms. Plascencia is not to be treated like a first-time entrant. Her years in the United States stand for something, although perhaps not enough to have her removed from this country for her criminal activities.

Before we become too sanguine, it is important to note a group of aliens for whom the Constitution apparently offers no protection, notwithstanding the fact that in many instances they have been living among "us" (in a manner of speaking) for a number of years. These are "excludable" aliens, whose return cannot be effectuated by the United States government. This was the case with several thousand Cubans who were part of the Freedom Flotilla in 1980 but who were found to be excludable because of their criminal records back in Cuba. The problem was that Fidel Castro, having rid his country of a problem, was not willing to re-admit this problem. Does the Constitution offer any protection to these individuals? Again, the answer is that it does not, although one inventive judge found some protection for these inmates under international law.[15]

Limitations on the protection of the law are not restricted to provisions of the Constitution. Instead, protections under federal law have also been given a niggardly reading. Consider refugee protection. Under both international and domestic law, the United States is obligated by the principle of *nonrefoulement*, which means simply that we have pledged ourselves not to return an individual to another state if his life would be threatened there. This obligation exists even if the person is in the United States illegally. This is by no means a radical concept in international law, and the vast majority of states (including the United States) have bound themselves to this principle as signatories to the Refugee Convention.

The Haitian interdiction program added a novel twist. For some years Haitians had been leaving their country and sailing to the United States. That Cubans have been doing exactly the same thing for decades (and in much larger numbers) was never seen as a problem. But Haitian migration was seen as a problem, so the United States and Haiti reached an agreement whereby the United States Coast Guard would intercept boats leaving Haiti and return those boats and their passengers to their homeland. For several years, the United States government held asylum hearings aboard the Coast Guard cutters, but eventually this policy was abandoned. Given the minute number of Haitians who were ever granted asylum through such proceedings, this was a cruel exercise raising false hopes.[16] The political intent was clear enough: stop Haitian migration.

Still, the United States had legal obligations under international and domestic law, and the Haitian interdiction program was challenged as a violation of those standards. In particular, this policy arguably violated the principle of *nonrefoulement* because people were being returned to face persecution.

The executive branch argued in response that no individual was being returned to face persecution. But the Supreme Court's response made this a moot point.[17] The court held, quite simply (and erroneously, I think), that the *nonrefoulment* provisions of United States law only applied within the territorial boundaries of the country. The court spent an enormous amount of time examining what "return" means, and it concluded that in this context "return" only applies after a person was in the territorial jurisdiction of the United States.

The law here, then, is like a light switch. If a person had not yet arrived here – one can even imagine a person not quite straggling ashore but still being a few, cruel feet away – there is absolutely no protection afforded by the law. Added to that, for Haitians at least, the United States government will do nearly everything in its power to ensure that they do not arrive – no matter how badly they need protection. In fact, there would seem to be nothing unlawful (according to the Supreme Court) in a situation in which American agents would literally hand a person back over to her persecutors – here is the outspoken opponent of the military junta who had escaped from your prison! – knowing full well that she would be persecuted.

A host of other foreigners have become involved in our internationalized war on drugs, and one of these is Humberto Alvarez-Machain, a Mexican doctor who was living in Mexico and who was wanted by the United States government for the kidnapping and murder of DEA special agent Enrique Camarena-Salazar and of Alfredo Zavala-Avelar, a Mexican pilot working with Camarena. The DEA believed that Alvarez-Machain participated in the murder by prolonging Camarena's life so that others could torture and interrogate him. The Mexican authorities, however, were not cooperating with their American counterparts on this one. Not to be deterred, on April 2, 1990, DEA agents forcibly kidnapped Alvarez-Machain from his medical office in Guadalajara, Mexico, and flew him by private plane to El Paso, Texas, where he was placed under arrest. The Mexican government immediately protested this abduction as a violation of their national sovereignty and as being directly contrary to the provisions of the extradition treaty between the two countries. In the United States, Alvarez-Machain moved to dismiss his indictment, claiming that the abduction constituted outrageous government conduct and that United States courts lacked jurisdiction to try him because of the abduction.

The California District Court agreed with the defendant, a decision affirmed by the 9th Circuit Court of Appeals. The Supreme Court, however, overturned these decisions.[18] The court held, in a most imaginative fashion, that there is nothing in the extensive extradition treaty between Mexico and the United

States that specifically prohibits abductions. The majority is correct on this point, but as Associate Justice Sandra Day O'Connor pointed out in her dissent, the entire reason for having an extradition treaty is to avoid situations where one country decides to take the law into its own hands in another country. This is exactly what the United States government did, and neither the extradition treaty between the United States and Mexico nor international law (or at least Chief Justice Rehnquist's unique reading of international law) offered any protection to Alvarez-Machain.

Just when the reader might think that the American judiciary is completely callous toward aliens and the claims that they present in our courts, those courts produce a decision that has now come to represent an entire line of litigation – *Filartiga* v. *Pena-Irala*.[19] The facts of the case are as follows. A young boy, Joelito Filartiga, the son of a leading political dissident, was tortured and killed in Paraguay. No legal action against the perpetrators was taken in Paraguay. The family's attorney was imprisoned and later disbarred for his efforts. In short, this seemed like yet another case of violence with impunity in Latin America. When Pena-Irala, the police official who was behind the atrocities, made a trip to the United States, the Filartiga family brought suit against him in federal district court in New York City, under a previously obscure statute passed by the very first United States Congress: the Alien Tort Statute (ATS).[20] The federal district court dismissed the suit, but in a historic decision the Second Circuit Court of Appeals reversed. The court both held that personal jurisdiction had been obtained over the defendant during his brief stay in the United States and that the requisite subject matter jurisdiction was provided in that torture is a violation of the law of nations (in addition to being prohibited by both Paraguayan and American law).

In some ways we have become accustomed to the *Filartiga* line of cases. Since then, a number of foreign plaintiffs have successfully brought cases for human rights abuses suffered by them in their home country, and oftentimes these suits have been against high-ranking former or current foreign government officials, including presidents and cabinet ministers.[21] For the most part American courts have followed the holding in *Filartiga,* the most important exception being the decision of the Court of Appeals for the District of Columbia in *Tel- Oren* v. *Libyan Arab Republic.*[22]

But it is important to recognize how unusual *Filartiga* and its progeny are. Foreigners are able to use American courtrooms to seek some measure of justice against other foreigners for events occurring in a foreign country. No other judiciary in the world has ever attempted such a feat. And what is just as remarkable is that for a number of years aliens were treated more favorably than United States citizens, in the sense that, until the 1996 passage of the Torture Victim Protection Act there was no provision in United States law that allowed for comparable suits by American citizens.[23]

The *Filartiga* cases alleged human rights abuses by others. When foreigners have attempted to bring cases alleging human rights abuses by the United States government in American courts, their claims have been denied as a matter of course. The plaintiffs in *Sanchez-Espinoza* v. *Reagan* were Nicaraguan civilians who were suing nine present or former officials of the executive branch, including President Reagan, for providing support to the contra rebel forces, who were in turn committing terrorist raids in Nicaragua in violation of fundamental human rights established under international law and the fourth and fifth amendments of the United States Constitution.[24] Despite recognizing the "gravity and legal complexity of the plaintiffs' claims," the District Court of the District of Columbia dismissed the suit on the basis of the political question doctrine, holding that "in order to adjudicate the tort claims of the Nicaraguan plaintiffs, we would have to determine the precise nature of the United States Government's involvement in the affairs of several Central American nations, namely, Honduras, Costa Rica, El Salvador and Nicaragua."[25] The Court of Appeals for the District of Columbia affirmed this decision, but on the basis of sovereign immunity. In an opinion by then-Judge Scalia the court held:

> It would make a mockery of the doctrine of sovereign immunity if federal courts were authorized to sanction or enjoin, by judgments nominally against present or former

Executive officers, actions that are concededly and as jurisdictional necessity, official actions of the United States. Such judgments would necessarily interfere with the public administration, or restrain the government from acting, or ... compel it to act.[26]

Similarly, *Saltany v. Reagan* was a suit brought on behalf of fifty-five residents of Libya who were either killed or suffered personal injury or whose property was destroyed during the course of the United States air strikes on that country in retaliation for the deaths of two United States servicemen in a West Berlin disco.[27] The district court dismissed the case on the basis of the Act of State Doctrine, although it readily conceded that the alleged conduct would be "tortious" were it judged by any civil law standards. In this case, the court never applied any standards. Instead, it simply pointed out how United States servicemen were "following orders." The court noted that the defendants had exercised "discretion in a myriad of contexts of utmost complexity and gravity, not to mention danger. And each acted, as duty required, in accordance with the orders of the commander-in-chief or a superior order."[28] What seemed particularly upsetting to the court was simply that suit had been brought against the United States in the first place. The court held:

> The plaintiffs, purportedly citizens or residents of Libya, cannot be presumed to be familiar with the rules of the United States. It is otherwise, however, with their counsel [former Attorney General Ramsey Clark]. The case offered no hope whatsoever of success, and the plaintiffs' attorneys surely knew it.[29]

The court continued:

> The injuries for which suit is brought are not insubstantial. It cannot, therefore, be said that the case is frivolous so much as it is audacious. The Court surmises it was brought as a public statement of protest of Presidential action with which counsel (and, to be sure, their clients) were in profound disagreement.[30]

The United States invasion of Panama in 1991 and the resulting deaths (as many as 2,000 civilians were killed) and property claims were the basis of *McFarland* v. *Cheney*.[31] Unlike the invasion of Grenada in 1983, where civilians were compensated for their losses, the United States Army Claims Service rejected the claims presented by Panamanian civilians on the basis that the injuries had occurred during combat operations (as had the Grenada injuries). A district court upheld the administrative finding, and its decision was affirmed on appeal. Although Panama has received emergency assistance from the United States since the invasion, no funds have been set aside for the relief of the innocent victims of the combat.

The shooting down of Iran Air Flight 655 over the Persian Gulf by the USS Vincennes has also given rise to legal claims by foreigners. *Nejad* v. *United States* was dismissed on a rationale that we have seen before: following orders.[32]

> It is indubitably clear that plaintiffs' claim calls into question the Navy's decisions and actions in execution of those decisions. The conduct of such affairs are constitutionally committed to the President as Commander in Chief and to his military and naval subordinates.[33]

Another judgment arising from the same incident goes even further in its deference to the political branches and to the military. In *Koohi* v. *United States,* the 9th Circuit Court of Appeals held that the claims made by the families of Iranian civilians were barred by the "combatant activities" exception under the Federal Claims Tort Act.[34] What is more, the court held that the statute would mandate the same result, *even if the warship had purposely shot down the civilian aircraft.*[35]

One purpose of United States law is to protect the lives, property, and well-being of American citizens. This task, apparently, is not restricted to the territorial borders of this country but has been extended extraterritorially. Consider *Ramirez de Arellano* v. *Weinberger.*[36] The case centered around a meat packing plant in Honduras owned by Ramirez, a United States citizen. The plant was confiscated by the United States government for military training exercises in Latin America.

Ramirez brought suit in the United States, but the District Court of the District of Columbia dismissed the case on the same grounds that so many suits against the United States by foreigners have been dismissed: the issue in the case constituted a "political question" that was nonjusticiable. The Court of Appeals for the District of Columbia saw the case differently. It viewed the situation as little more than unlawful confiscation by the federal government, which the government cannot do, not when the property is owned by an American citizen. At one point the court held that "the Executive's power to conduct foreign relations free from unwarranted supervision of the Judiciary cannot give the Executive *carte blanche* to trample on the most fundamental liberty and property rights of this country's citizenry."[37] The court continued:

> The suggestion [by the United States government] that a United States citizen who is the sole beneficial owner of a viable business operation does not have constitutional rights against United States government officials' threatened complete destruction of corporate assets is preposterous. If adopted by this court, the proposition would obliterate the constitutional property rights of many United States citizens abroad and would make a mockery of decades of United States policy on transnational investments.[38]

Justice, it seems, was served in this case. But would it have been served if the meat packing plant had been owned by a Honduran citizen instead? That seems unlikely.

Sometimes United States citizens are treated badly by other governments. Under the provisions of the Torture Victim Protection Act, alluded to earlier, American citizens (or their heirs) can now bring suit against the individuals responsible for carrying out these acts.[39] In order to do so, however, these agents must be physically present in the United States.

What about suing the government rather than the individual agents? Suing governments is no easy matter. In the not too distant past, states used to enjoy absolute, sovereign immunity. The king could do no wrong. But things have changed, or so we would like to think. We now recognize and understand that states can in fact do wrong, and some countries now have laws to guard against abuses by the government. For example, people in the United States enjoy what have been termed "Bivens-style" remedies for constitutional violations committed by American law enforcement agents.[40] The same remedy would also seem to result if an American citizen were tortured by United States agents abroad. Recall Justice Kennedy's concurrence in *Verdugo-Urquidez* about the importance of being an American citizen.

What about suing foreign governments? Here things get more complicated. First consider the case of Scott Nelson, an American citizen who had been working in a state-run hospital in Saudi Arabia. Nelson saw deficiencies in hospital safety and reported them. He was told by the hospital staff, essentially, to mind his own business. Then one day Nelson was summoned to the hospital's security office, where agents of the Saudi government arrested him. He was then shackled, tortured, and held without water [and presumably no food] for four days. Although he did not understand Arabic, Nelson was forced to sign a confession written in that language and was thrown into a rat-infested cell in the Al Sijan prison to await trial. Nelson was taken out just once a week for exercise and fresh air. After thirty-nine days Nelson was released owing to the intercession of a United States senator.

On his return, Nelson attempted to seek redress under the law. But the Nelson suit was against Saudi Arabia, and nation-states protect one another. Some states continue to provide "absolute" sovereign immunity to themselves as well as to other states. But under United States law – the Foreign Sovereign Immunities Act – foreign states enjoy only limited liability.[41] The way the law reads, another state may enjoy sovereign immunity with certain, enumerated, exceptions, none of which could be applied to Scott Nelson's circumstances. The only possible exception was the so-called commercial activity exception, and Nelson argued that when the Saudi government recruited him in the United States it was thereby engaging in a commercial activity in this country. The Supreme Court did not accept this argument, holding instead that the basis of Nelson's suit was torts committed in Saudi Arabia, not the commercial activities that preceded their commission.[42]

The disposition of Nelson's case seems cruel, and in many respects it is. A United States citizen who was recruited in this country to work in Saudi Arabia ended up being tortured and imprisoned in a nightmarish episode. He eventually came home only to find that his government had given him no recourse. But Nelson's problem was that he was in the wrong place at the wrong time – and I do not say this to be clever. If Scott Nelson had been tortured somewhere else, his suit might well have been successful.

The *Nelson* case did not sit well in many quarters in this country, and there was a cry heard on Capitol Hill to do something. In 1996, Congress responded by amending the Foreign Sovereign Immunity Act to allow American citizens to sue foreign governments for their involvement in acts of political terrorism. According to the amendment, a claim must contain the following statutory elements:

- that personal injury or death resulted from an act of torture, extrajudicial killing, aircraft sabotage, or hostage taking; and
- the act was either perpetrated by the foreign state directly or by a non-state actor which receives material support or resources from the foreign state defendant; and
- the foreign state be designated as a state sponsor of terrorism either at the time the incident complained of occurred or was later so designated as a result of such act.[43]

The new law was put to good use in *Flatlow* v. *Islamic Republic of Iran*.[44] The case concerned Alisa Flatlow, an American on a study abroad program in Israel, who was killed in that country by a suicide-bomb attack carried out by the Shaqaqi faction of the Palestine Islamic Jihad group. The United States Department of State gave the dead woman's family evidence that each year the Iranian government provides the Palestine Islamic Jihad group with $2 million. For the court, this amounted to "material support" from a "foreign state defendant" that had previously been designated by the State Department as a "state sponsor of terrorism." This, in turn, allowed the Flatlows to sue the Iranian government and ultimately to obtain a default judgment against it.

We come to the situation of employees of United States-based transnational corporations. What protection, if any, does American law provide? Perhaps the whole notion of applying United States law to overseas business operations might seem like a strange proposition. This was the case the first time the Supreme Court was asked to address the matter. In *American Banana Co.* v. *United Fruit Co.,* the matter before the court was whether the provisions of the Sherman Antitrust Act applied to business operations in Central America.[45] Writing the majority opinion, Associate Justice Oliver Wendell Holmes seemed puzzled that the case was before the court in the first place:

> It is obvious that, however stated, the plaintiff's case depends on several rather startling propositions. In the first place, the acts causing the damage were done, so far as it appears, outside the jurisdiction of the United States and within that of other states. It is surprising to hear it argued that they were governed by the act of Congress.[46]

The reason, Holmes went on to say, is "the general and almost universal rule is that the character of an act as lawful or unlawful must be determined wholly by the law of the country where the act is done."[47]

Notwithstanding the decision in *American Banana Co.,* in a short period of time United States regulatory law began to be applied to businesses – American or foreign – operating overseas that had some kind of "effect" on business operations in the United States. In this way, United States law could reach activities (such as counterfeiting) in other countries that threatened the well-being of American corporations.

Allow me to sum up nearly a century of law-making. At the present time, United States anticompetitive laws are applied extraterritorially almost as a matter of course. The Supreme Court has said that it is simply following congressional intent, but it is difficult to discern this intent from the language of any of the statutes. Instead, one gets the distinct impression that Congress has not even considered the issue.[48] In contrast to the ready extraterritorial application of regulatory measures, for instance, no United States health and safety laws and no United States environmental laws have been applied extraterritorially. In such matters, in their overseas operations American corporations are bound by the laws of the foreign state. If another country does not have any law in this area – as is often the case – then it is not bound by any law whatsoever.

What about workers? Here things become uncertain. At one point certain United States labor laws were given an extraterritorial application. In *Vermilya-Brown Co. v. Connell* the question before the court was whether the Fair Labor Standards Act (FLSA) applied to employees on a Bermuda military base that the United States had leased from Great Britain.[49] The FLSA covers commerce "among the several States or from any State to any place outside thereof." State is defined as "any State of the United States or any Territory or possession of the United States." Certain employees of contractors who had contracts for work with the United States government on the Bermuda base brought suit for overtime compensation. No distinction was made between employees who were American citizens and those who were not. Thus, if a military base constituted a "possession" of the United States, the FLSA would be applied to all employees working for the United States government, not just those who were American citizens. The court had no trouble accepting this position. It held that there was no conflict with Bermuda law on this question, and it also noted that "citizens of this country [United States] would be numerous among employees on the bases."[50]

In a dissenting opinion, Associate Justice Robert Jackson displayed enormous discomfort at the prospect of treating foreign employees the same as United States citizens. He noted, for example, that what would be "apparent to anyone even casually traveled in those islands was the great disparity of social, economic and labor conditions between the islands and our own Continent."[51] He continues this line of argument by pointing out the "different customs and institutions prevailing there, particularly the [race relations and assimilation difficulties]."[52] Thus, Jackson argued, "we should acquire no such responsibilities as would require us to import to those islands our laws, institutions, and social conditions beyond the necessities of controlling a military base and its garrison, dependents and incidental personnel."[53]

Within months, *Vermilya-Brown* was overturned, and *Foley Brothers* v. *Filardo* became controlling American law.[54] Foley was an American citizen who worked as a cook at United States public works projects in Iran and Iraq. The issue was whether the Eight Hour Law applied to this employment contract. One of the central issues relied on in Justice Reed's majority opinion is that the act does not distinguish between United States citizens and noncitizens.

> Unless we were to read such a distinction into the statute we should not be forced to conclude ... that Congress intended to regulate the working hours of a citizen of Iran who chanced to be employed on a public work of the United States in that foreign land. Such a conclusion would be logically inescapable although labor conditions in Iran were known to be wholly dissimilar to those in the United States and wholly beyond the control of this nation.[55]

Most recently, in *EEOC* v. *Arabian American Oil Co.*, the Supreme Court held that an American citizen working abroad for a United States corporation is not covered by the antidiscrimination provisions in the 1964 Civil Rights Act, a ruling consistent with *Foley Brothers*.[56] Congress responded a short time thereafter by specifically extending the Civil Rights Act extraterritorially with respect to American citizens. The law as it stands at present is that a United States-based corporation cannot discriminate against American citizens. There is no similar protection under United States law for foreigners working for American corporations. They are not protected by any other United States labor laws, such as the Occupational Health and Safety Act (OSHA), the Fair Labor Standards Act, or the Family Leave and Medical Act of 1993. Foreign employees working for either the United States government or American corporations receive no protection under United States law whatsoever.

Protection under United States law? What has been examined here are the quirky intersections between citizenship and territoriality and the implications of these quirks for American law. In a host of ways United States citizens are protected by American law even when they are outside the country. This result was strongly suggested in *Verdugo-Urquidez* and served as the basis of the court's holding in *Ramirez de Arellano*. In addition, certain aspects of United States law protect American workers abroad. And, finally, United States law offers some redress to American citizens who have been harmed by other governments.

We have seen how many of these protections are incomplete. For example, the only protection American workers receive abroad is not to be discriminated against. All other protections – minimum wage laws, child labor laws, parental leave, and the like – do not apply. We have also seen the limitations on the ability to seek redress for human rights abuses in other countries. Scott Nelson was unable to sue the Saudi government for the torture he suffered at the hands of agents of that country; although Alisa Flatlow's family was allowed to bring suit against the Iranian government because of its support for international terrorism. The difference in the two cases? Iran is a country that has been designated as supporting political terror, while our ally Saudi Arabia simply practices political terror.

We have also seen how noncitizens receive very little protection under United States law. Although *Verdugo-Urquidez* was tried in the United States, he was not protected by the Fourth Amendment from a search of his home in Mexico. The Supreme Court determined that his connection with this country was not strong enough to make him one of "the People" for purposes of constitutional protection. Individuals harmed during the course of United States military/security/law enforcement activities abroad get even less protection than this. *Koohi* went so far as to say that American servicemen could *deliberately* harm innocent civilians and there would still be no redress under United States law.

This is not to say that foreigners receive no protection under American law. The *Filartiga* line of cases provides a unique opportunity for foreign nationals to sue individuals (but not governments) who have harmed them in their country of origin. As a signatory to the Refugee Convention, the United States has bound itself by the *nonrefoulement* provisions under international law. But what we have also seen in *Sale* is just how niggardly United States protection is. According to the view taken by our government, the obligation to protect refugees only begins after refugees are (somehow) within the territorial jurisdiction of this country. Apparently there is nothing unlawful in doing everything in our power to prevent them from being here in the first place.

In many ways American citizens receive substantial protections from United States law when they are outside the country's borders, particularly for acts committed by the United States government. Foreigners, on the other hand, receive very little protection from United States law. This is true whether they are the targets of American criminal investigations or they are merely innocent bystanders somehow caught up in (and harmed by) the pursuit of American military or security or law enforcement activities. To invoke the motto of the American Express Corporation: membership has its privileges. And one of the most important privileges of United States citizenship is protection by American law.

Notes

1. Ethan A. Nadelmann, "The Role of the United States in the International Enforcement of Human Rights," *Harvard International Law Journal*, 31 (1990), 37-76.
2. Although it may also be said that no country in the world has less success in acheiving this goal than the United States. But that is a different matter altogether.
3. *United States v. Verdugo-Urquidez*, 494 U. S. 259 (1990).
4. The Fourth Amendment reads: "The right of the people to be secure in their persons, houses, papers, and effects, against unreasonable searches and seizures, shall not be violated, and no Warrants shall issue, but upon probable cause, supported by Oath or affirmation, and particularly describing the place to be searched, and the persons or things to be seized."
5. 494 U. S. 273.

6. Ibid., 278.
7. Ibid.
8. 130 U. S. 581 (1889).
9. *Fong Yue Ting* v. *United States,* 149 U. S. 698 (1893).
10. The racist tone and language to be found in the Supreme Court's opinion is jarring today. At one point in his dissenting opinion Justice Brewer wrote: "It is true that this statute is directed only against the obnoxious Chinese; but if the power exists, who shall say it will not be exercised against other classes and other people?".
11. *Shaughnessy* v. *Mezei,* 345 U. S. 206 (1953).
12. This is Justice Robert Jackson's colorful dissenting opinion describing Mezei's plight.
13. This is also from Justice Jackson.
14. 459 U. S. 21 (1982).
15. *Jean* v. *Nelson,* 727 F. 2d 957 (11th Cir. 1984); *Fernandez* v. *Wilkinson,* 505 F. Supp. 787 (D. Kan., 1980).
16. As of 1989, of the 20,000 Haitians who had been given a preliminary asylum hearing aboard Coast Guard ships, only six (this is not a typographical error) were deemed worthy to be taken to the United States for a full hearing.
17. *Sale* v. *Haitian Centers Council, Inc.,* 509 U. S. 155 (1993).
18. *United States* v. *Alvarez-Machain,* 504 U. S. 655 (1992).
19. *Filartiga* v. *Pena-Irala,* 630 F. 2d 876 (2d Cir., 1980).
20. The statute reads in its entirety: "The district court shall have original jurisdiction of any civil action by an alien for a tort only, committed in violation of the law of nations or a treaty of the United States"; 28 U. S. C. Sec. 1350 (1994).
21. *Forti* v. *Suarez-Mason,* 672 F. Supp. 1531 (N.D. Cal. 1987), *aff'd in part and rev'd in part,* 694 F. Supp. 707 (N.D. Cal. 1988); *Abebe-Jiri* v. *Negewo,* No. 1:90-CV-2010-GET, 1993 WL 814304 (N.D. Ga., Aug. 20, 1993), *aff'd* 72 F. 3d 844 (1996); *Paul* v. *Abril,* 812 F. Supp. 207 (S.D. Fla. 1993) *aff'd,* 901 F. Supp. 330 (1994); *Todd* v. *Panjaitan,* No. CIV.A.92-12255-PBS, 1994 WL 827111 (D. Mass. Oct. 26, 1994); *In re Marcos Litigation,* MDL no. 840 (D. Haw. Sept. 24, 1992); *Xuncax* v. *Gramajo* and *Ortiz* v. *Gramajo,* 886 F. Supp. 162 (1995); *Mushikiwabo* v. *Barayagwiza,* No. 94-3627, 1996 WL 164496 (S.D.N.Y Apr. 9, 1996); *Doe* v. *Karadzic* and *Kadac* v. *Karadzic,* 866 F. Supp. 734 (S.D.N.Y. 1994) *rev'd and rem'd,* 70 F. 3d 232 (1995), *reh'g denied,* 74 F. 3d 377 (2d Cir. 1996), *cert. denied,* 135 L. Ed. 2d 1048 (1996).
22. 726 F. 2d 774 (D.C. Cir. 1984).
23. The Act provides: "An individual who, under actual or apparent authority, or under color of state law, of any foreign nation, 1) subjects an individual to torture shall, in a civil action, be liable for damages to that individual; or 2) subjects an individual to extrajudicial killing shall, in a civil action, be liable for damages to the individual's representative or to any pursuant who may be a claimant in an action for wrongful death"; 28 U. S. C. 1350 (1996).

24. 568 F. Supp. 596 (D.D.C. 1983) *aff'd* 770 F. 2d, 202 (D.C. Cir. 1985).
25. 586 F. Supp. 601.
26. 770 F. 2d at 207 (citations and emphasis omitted).
27. 702 F. Supp. 319 (D.D.C. 1988). The Act of State Doctrine holds that an act of a sovereign power, as a sovereign power, or an act of its delegates cannot be questioned or made the subject of proceedings in a court of law.
28. Ibid., 322.
29. Ibid.
30. Ibid.
31. 1991 WL 43262 (D.D.C.) *aff'd* 971 F. 2d 766 (D.C. Cir. 1992) *cert. denied* 506 United States 1053 (1993).
32. 724 F. Supp. 753 (C.D. Cal. 1989).
33. Ibid., 755.
34. 976 F. 2d 1328 (9th Cir. 1992). 28 U. S. C. Sec. 1346(b) (1994).
35. The court held: "The result would be no different if the downing of the civilian plane had been deliberate rather than the result of error. The combatant activities exception applies whether United States military forces hit a prescribed or an intended target, whether those selecting the target act wisely or foolishly, whether the missiles we employ turn out to be "smart" or dumb, whether the target we choose performs the function we believe it does or whether our choice of an object for destruction is a result of error or miscalculation. In other words, it simply does not matter for purposes of the "time of war" exception whether the military makes or executes its decisions carefully or negligently, properly or improperly"; 976 F. 2d 1334-35.
36. 568 F. Supp. 1236 (D.D.C. 1983) rev'd 745 F. 2d 1500 (D.C. Cir. 1984) (en banc) vacated and rem'd. *Weinberger* v. *Ramirez,* 471 United States 1113 (1985) (remanded in light of the Foreign Assistance and Related Appropriations Act, 1985, and efforts by Honduras to make restitution) rev'd 788 F. 2d 762 (D.C. Cir. 1986) (withdrawal of all U. S. personnel fundamentally altered the balance of equities).
37. 745 F. 2d 1515.
38. Ibid., 1515-16.
39. See note 22 above.
40. The term comes from the Supreme Court case, *Bivens* v. *Six Unknown Named Agents of the Federal Bureau of Narcotics,* 403 U. S. 388 (1971), which established the principle that under certain circumstances citizens can sue government officials for violations of their constitutional rights.
41. 28 U. S. C. 1604 (1994).
42. *Saudi Arabia* v. *Nelson,* 507 U. S. s349 (1993).
43. Antiterrorism and Effective Death Penalty Act of 1996, U.S.C. Sec. 1605 (a) (7).
44. 999 F. Supp. 1 (D.D.C. 1998).
45. 213 U. S. 347 (1909).
46. Ibid., 355.
47. Ibid., 356.

48. See, generally, Mark Gibney, "The Extraterritorial Application of United States Law: The Perversion of Democratic Governance, the Reversal of Institutional Roles, and the Imperative of Establishing Normative Principles," *Boston College International and Comparative Law Review,* 19 (1996), 297-321.
49. 335 U. S. 377 (1948).
50. Ibid., 389.
51. Ibid., 393-94.
52. Ibid., 394.
53. Ibid.
54. 336 U. S. 281 (1949). Foley Brothers was the company name.
55. Ibid., 286.
56. 499 U. S. 244 (1991).

5
Recognizing the Law: Value and Identities in William Gaddis's *A Frolic of His Own*

Bosse Ekelund

In a defiant public statement after the humiliation of testifying to a grand jury about his "improper" relationship with Monica Lewinsky, President Bill Clinton asked the American people "to turn away from the spectacle of the past seven months, to repair the fabric of our national discourse, and to return our attention to all the challenges and all the promise of the next American century." The same day the giant computer corporation Microsoft urged a federal appeals court not to allow the public to watch the government's pretrial interviews with Bill Gates, saying it would create a "carnival atmosphere" and a "media circus" that would interfere with the company's pretrial preparations. There is an irony in the attempts by these two men, arguably the most powerful men in the United States, to ward off the volatile element of "spectacle" as it interacts with law, politics, and business: the power of spectacle created these two Bills, and the genie cannot simply be summoned back into its bottle. In American culture, spectacle and law have a presence that can hardly be exaggerated, and they must be understood as social forces with the power to constitute values and identities.

My argument in this essay is that William Gaddis's novel *A Frolic of His Own* can be read as an astute analysis of a cultural moment when law, art and politics are all affected by the forces of spectacle.[1] To my mind, *Frolic* belongs to the tradition of great realist novels, with an array of vivid characters who map out a space that represents, in its own specific medium, a real, social space. In this essay I treat Gaddis's novel accordingly, as a species of "cognitive mapping" of the complex relationship between law and literature in a society dominated by spectacle. The pivotal concept for my analysis and, I would argue, for Gaddis's literary project is the one of value, and it is my contention that Gaddis's literary analysis to some extent mirrors the sociological analysis of social fields that Pierre Bourdieu has developed over the years.[2] In this view, value and identity are effects created in separate social universes, and in the clash between such universes questions of value and identity are precipitated. I show how Gaddis produces a literary understanding of the conditions for a defense of the values of law and art from the forces of spectacle, seen in this novel as the combined power of the press, Hollywood, and populist politicians.

By dramatizing the power of diverse social fields to accomplish a translation of identities and messages, values and verdicts, Gaddis performs a literary analysis of the division of symbolic labor in modern American society, with special reference to law and culture. He offers a critical view of the people who practice law and art at the same time he suggests that the two enterprises may embody specific values that must be "rescued" by conscientious agents. The key notion of "rescuing the language" becomes a cornerstone for a fictional analysis that presents a saving grace in what I call "the refusal of spectacle": what is rescued are the specific principles of recognition that preserve the relative autonomy of a field, and what is refused is a wholesale travesty of the forms that make such recognition possible. To give a somewhat crude example, insofar as the political field has its own values, a president would like to be recognized for the policies he has advocated and carried out rather than for stains on an intern's dress, but it is clear that the values of politics and the persona of a president are partly determined by other factors, in this case a fascinating mix of media spectacle and a supposedly "independent" legal inquiry.

In the following I show how Gaddis's novel plots out different bids for recognition and how values and identities are translated and deformed as they are transported from one context to another, for example, from the realm of "literature" to the legal arena. After a brief plot summary, I discuss how *Frolic* presents two opposing principles of recognition, one that operates according to the logic of equivalency in its money form, the other one insisting on the incommensurability of certain values. Thereafter I analyze how the novel presents the forces of spectacle as a threat to the independent discourses of law and art. The following two sections deal with the novel's dramatization of the defense of that autonomy. Finally, I discuss how the operation of "travesty" must be understood as an inevitable principle of translation between different social fields. This analysis invites an understanding of the predicament of modernity as the interplay of recognition and travesty: recognition travestied and travesty recognized.

It will be necessary to give an outline of the main lines of the story, while conceding that it is too convoluted to allow full paraphrase. Gaddis does not deny the reader the time-honored literary convention of having the main themes and motifs introduced in the first scene of his narrative. The opposition between justice and law is given in the first sentence, spoken by Harry Lutz, promising junior partner of the respected law firm Swyne & Dour: "You get justice in the next world, in this world you have the law" (11). He is speaking to his wife, Christina, on their way to see her brother, Oscar Crease, who is the central character of the novel. At this point, Oscar is in the hospital after having been run over by his own car when hotwiring it, but for the remainder of the book he will be convalescent in his dilapidated country mansion on Long Island. To this house flock not just his sister and brother-in-law and his girlfriend Lily, but also sundry other characters including but not limited to lawyers, real estate agents, a New York socialite, a class of graduate students in American history, and a process server fond of quoting Shakespeare. Consistent with the logic of the law that dominates the action, most other characters figure only as absent parties to lawsuits. Most important among the absent characters is Oscar's father, Judge Thomas L. Crease, who is only present in the legal opinions that his law clerk sends to Oscar and in the media reports about the cases he is involved in, until his ashes finally come to rest on Oscar's mantlepiece toward the end of the novel.

The most important lawsuit among the host that occupy the narrative is the one filed by Oscar against the Hollywood production company Erebus Entertainment, Inc.[3] This agent of darkness produced a blockbuster spectacular about the American Civil War called "The Blood in the Red, White and Blue." Oscar holds that it is based on his unpublished play "Once at Antietam," which he once submitted to a television production company in New York. It was rejected, as it turns out, by the same man who has now directed the gory Hollywood movie. Oscar loses the lawsuit because of a "trap" set by Erebus's counsel, Madhar Pai of Harry's firm Swyne & Dour, but he wins on appeal, thanks to the unexpected intervention of his father. It would appear that this solution was orchestrated by Oscar's counsel, Harold Basie, an African-American lawyer who is actually a fraud or, better, a felicitous manifestation of the American confidence man. The reversal is given a further turn by the ensuing creative accounting work that effectively reduces Oscar's grandiose dreams of millions in damages to the reality of a pittance that may not even cover his costs. In the meanwhile, Harry has successfully managed a case of infringement brought by the Episcopal church against the Pepsi Cola company but at the cost of a near-breakdown that plays a part in a fatal car accident that sees him off. The novel ends with Oscar, Christina, and Lily left to lick their wounds.

In the course of this narrative, rich in incident while lacking in plot progression, the legal system is treated ungenerously for the most part. From the misogynist Judge C. J. Bone to the "white-shoe," "blue-ribbon" firm of Swyne & Dour to the ambulance chaser Jack Preswig, who is fired after being caught digging a pothole in a street where a client had been injured, we are treading Dickensian territory. The absurdity of the proliferating lawsuits extends the satire to include both the supply side and the demand for legal services, in short, to a society gone litigiously berserk. As a satire, the novel is a wonder of wit and exact targeting, but it gains its force from the fact that it finally takes its subject almost as seriously as the men of law take themselves.

This leads to the most explicit type of discussion of recognition that takes place in the novel, a motif that is introduced in the first paragraph. After broaching the unstable Trinity of justice, law, and order and bracketing justice for the moment, Harry and Christina introduce two opposing interpretations of what the law is about. The more cynical of the two, Harry claims that people go to court for "the money, Christina, it's always the money. The rest of it's nothing but opera" (11). It is crucial that this turn of phrase gives a metonymical label of art or culture to the class of things that are not money, but then Harry does not mean to specify a realm of other values, quite the opposite: saying that "the rest of it's nothing but opera" means that everything that is not money is simply trimming, money in disguise, or perhaps rather the disguise of money. Christina objects that "the money's just a yardstick isn't it. It's the only common reference people have for making other people take them as seriously as they take themselves, I mean that's all they're really asking for isn't it? Think about it, Harry" (11). With this admonition, which is casually disregarded by Harry, the reader is presented with the very problems that Gaddis seems to have set himself in this novel: how does the law work as a specific mediation and adjudication of antagonistic claims and is a mediation at bottom about money or about individual recognition?[4]

The entire legal system as we see it in *Frolic* pivots on money, but money has no fixed referent, and its position in modern societies as "the form of the socially recognized universal equivalent"[5] allows Gaddis to stage the structural ambivalence of legal claims in a capitalist society where even law is in the process of being commodified. Money in *Frolic* represents two entirely different principles; it is either a kind of tautology, money as money, the embodiment of greed that has no object but its own perpetuation, or it is a poor substitute for something that is radically unrepresentable in such an abstract form, in which case it works, to borrow from Oscar's dabbling in legal language, as the "necessary indispensable formal proper artificial" (546) standard for something that has a genuine value in itself, tied to notions of identity, integrity and cultural value, in short, use value. In the discourse and practice of identity politics, or a Charles Taylorian "politics of recognition," Christina's formulation seems apt as a characterization for political goals that go beyond the fair distribution of material goods.[6] If indeed all members of a society were taken as seriously by others as they take themselves, we might perhaps reach the kind of ideal state theorized by, for example, Axel Honneth: "To the extent to which every member of a society is in a position to esteem himself or herself, one can speak of a state of societal solidarity."[7] In Honneth's Hegelian scheme, solidarity is a third stage of recognition that goes beyond those universal rights that can be established by law, as well as the basic affective satisfaction, by means of love, offered within the family.

In *Frolic*, the most cynical view sees law and in-laws as vehicles of a greed that operates at every social level. The novel goes a long way toward entirely eroding the slim hope that there may be social room for a type of value that cannot be reduced to the operation of final, tautological equivalency in the mediation of money by the market or by legal institutions.[8] As Oscar's counsel tells him, the court "doesn't give a good God damn about desecrating these great poetic passions you've got" (259). What it is interested in is, in Judge Crease's words, "proof or reasonable assumption of special damage of a pecuniary character" (38). Everything else is beside the point. As Harry insists to Christina, the discourse of law amounts to "talking about millions of dollars, that's what this country's finally all about isn't it?" (236). The ferocious translation of use value and sentimental value, nationality and individuality into the language of money is seen here in its full territorializing force, as it reaches out into the proper realm of signification so that linguistic and symbolic exchange becomes monetary. Gaddis's novel hardly exaggerates the scope and intensity of this process: in the patenting of gene sequences, in attempts to create registered trademarks of expressions that have been spontaneously formulated (such as "The People's Princess"), in innumerable cases the law serves a strictly economic market to shrink the space of freedom. Thus, when money is spoken of as a language in *Frolic*, it is more than a turn of phrase, because it indicates a real tendency for money to stand in for this form of exchange, too. Toward the end even Christina gives up her insistence on the difference between money and the underlying wish to be recognized on one's own terms, remarking that "there's nothing more important than a dollar in the bank to make people take you seriously is there Oscar, it's language we all speak isn't it" (423). The questions turned into statements underline the bleakness of her assessment.

An apparently predominant function of the law, then, is to allow money to determine human relations by a formal mediation between the market and other social contexts of value. As we will learn late in the book, Harry is an artist manqué, who went from divinity school and a "consuming interest in poetry" (526) to plans of becoming a novelist in the Dickensian vein and then, with a fresh sense of injustice derived from his reading, he went into law. In that field he moved from public interest law firms to corporate law. It is this final move of Harry's "reconciliation under duress," to use Theodor Adorno's phrase, that provides the most eloquent commentary on the rule of money.[9] "[That is w]hy I went into corporate law in the first place where it's greed plain and simple. It's money from start to finish, it's I want what you've got, nobody out there with these grievances they expect you to share" (44). In Harry's view, corporate law is the pure form of law because it is transparent to the underlying principle of all law, which is money. Harry's trajectory forms an underlying pattern for the cultural critique of the novel as a whole, because his descent from religion to art, from idealist legal work to corporate wrangling, traces the dual process of a disenchantment that removes all illusions except those engendered by the commodity form, and then, as an insult added to the injury, stamps the world with the magical imprint of money.

The theme of law as a facilitator of the conversion of other values into exchange value is repeated with historical poignancy within Oscar's play, where his protagonist, Thomas, can buy himself free from conscription during the Civil War, or even buy a substitute for himself, which is what he ends up doing, on both sides of the secession in fact. His unscrupulous Pennsylvania coal mine manager Bagby comments that that is "what Section 13 of the enrollment act is for, you know, to provide for the better class of people like ourselves" (155). When Thomas's Union and Confederacy substitutes end up killing each other at Antietam this becomes, in the logic of tautological equivalency, an image of money liquidating itself. As we shall see, it also represents metaphorically the peculiar ability of law to create virtual identities for any individual who enters its domain.

In a number of ingeniously varied instances the novel renders in satirical form the strict coupling of legal production with the capitalist marketplace. This is the bottom line among the "principles of vision and division," to use Bourdieu's terminology, that structure the practices of law so as to distribute society's rewards according to the principles that rule the field of power generally.[10] In most respects *Frolic* weighs in behind Marx's observation that "the laws of a state are printed on its banknotes," but Gaddis is too encompassing an observer to focus only on the bottom line, the bluntest interpretation of the facts. The satire turns equally on the naive hopes and ambitions entertained by the consumers of law like Oscar. As Bourdieu puts it, the process of rationalization within the legal field is "ideal for constantly increasing the separation between judgments based upon the law and naive intuitions of fairness," and this is not a process that works to undermine the legitimacy of the law, as one might think.[11] Instead, this disengagement tends to make the dependence of the law upon other power relations less transparent. When Oscar laments that "it's a travesty, they make a movie that's a vulgar travesty and now they make a travesty of the whole judicial process" (533), we should latch on to the etymology of the word travesty and confirm that the cinematic adaptation of Oscar's play, as well as the judicial proceedings, are both field-specific disguises of a content that can only exist in particular forms, accepted as such in fields, which impose their own principles of formalization on any given content. Oscar should have heeded the advice he quotes from George Bernard Shaw, to "get drama and picture making separate in your mind, or you will make ruinous mistakes" (127). Separate as Oscar holds drama and film, he submitted them both to the law for comparison, as ruinous a mistake as he could possibly commit. Although Oscar is crushed when he realizes he will not be awarded the millions he had envisaged, we must take seriously his denial of having been motivated only by money. He defends himself against Basie's insinuation by explaining that he is suing for money since "that's the only damn language they understand! ... Steal poetry what do you sue them for, poetry? and the court sentences Kiester to two hundred hours of community service? Two hundred hours teaching Yeats to the fourth grade? Expect me to pay your legal bill with Maid Quiet?" (88). It seems fair to say that Oscar's original urge to be taken seriously is transformed, distorted, and indeed travestied in the course of the narrative by precisely the logic of final equivalence that the law imposes on all those who seek recognition through its offices.

The other party may understand no language other than money, but for an artist to have recourse to the law, the language of art and the language of integrity must be given a place in law, and it was with this hope that Oscar filed his suit. When he hesitates before specifying a sum for the damages he is seeking, he says: "It's very difficult for me to translate offense into money" (234). Knowing Oscar, this might only be the fear that he may underestimate what can be squeezed out of the film company, but it is nevertheless a statement of a principle of incommensurability, an unwillingness to join in the charmed circle of equivalency. The final verdict, however, mediates the two principles: while Judge Bone's opinion, which decides the case, underlines the aesthetic differences between the play and the film, it makes no moral concessions in its award of damages. The law here recognizes the different values and insists on originality as the proper standard rather than novelty, but proceeds to adjudicate between the two products on the basis of the market's logic (399-415).

By having the two worlds of art and law collide, Gaddis explores the adjudication between entirely different sorts of values and identity claims and poses questions about the labor of legal formalization that subsumes all such differences under its arbitrary but legitimate violence, which finally serves the dominant actors in a capitalist market. Rather than simply cast the law as villain, however, *Frolic* sets the two domains up as separate spheres of value and suggests that their respective languages and procedures protect the status of different types of value. Judge Bone's decision articulates the wrong done to Oscar and the value of Oscar's play in distinction to the movie, even as it hands the reckoning of damages over to a market-dominated process, and implies that the law, like art, retains at least a minimal degree of autonomy. The threat to them both comes from another social process. The autonomy of these fields of specific values is menaced by the forces of spectacle, which themselves add to the logic of final equivalency and constitute a clear and present danger to the precarious independence of law and art.[12]

The category of the spectacle is not narrowly defined by Gaddis's narrative but can be constructed from its various instantiations there and can be contrasted with Guy Debord's concept of the society of spectacle as a stage of the commodification process, and thus of spectacle as "a social relationship between people that is mediated by images."[13] Spectacle may be embodied in television news casting, newspapers, Hollywood movies, or more local forms of public performance, but from its first appearance in the novel as the "brilliant spectacle" of opera, which may or may not be the supplementary trimming on the money nexus, to the "ninety million extravaganza" of Kiester's movie and the commotion surrounding the Szyrk case, spectacle represents a force that makes culture consumable in the form of the represented and, often enough, recycled image. Gaddis's treatment captures the element of addiction emphasized by Fredric Jameson in this respect, "a whole historically original consumers' appetite for a world transformed into sheer images of itself and for pseudo-events and 'spectacles.'"[14]

Law, art, and spectacle become entangled in the case of *Szyrk v. Village of Tatamount* in Judge Crease's district court. In this lawsuit, the sculptor Szyrk claims artistic recognition in order to defend his creation Cyclone Seven from being violated by locals wishing to free a dog caught in its steel maze. Through Szyrk and the people of Tatamount, Gaddis is able to bring into play issues that would be less exhaustively engaged in the somewhat private atmosphere of Oscar's lawsuit. Incidentally, the fictitious Virginia village that is the site of the sculpture and becomes the arena for a struggle over first amendment rights and the various value standards of art, private property, and politics is named by Gaddis so as to encrypt the central problem of the novel. "Tatamount" is almost tantamount to "tantamount," so that, but for the verbal magic of the absconded letter *n,* the setting would spell out the inexorable logic of total convertibility.

In *Szyrk* v. *Village of Tatamount et al.* Gaddis stages claims for recognition on a larger scale, and it is given special emphasis by a foregrounded narrative device. For most of the book's almost 600 pages Gaddis sticks to unattributed dialogue to tell his story, but he mixes this orchestration of individual voices with a number of other speech and text genres, such as, for example, the legal opinions given in full, the first two acts of Oscar's play presented nearly *in extenso* as read aloud or silently, newscasts booming in Oscar's living room, and newspaper articles read more or less coherently.[15] The virtuoso mimicking of these everyday genres is infringed on only at rare intervals by the narrator stepping in, normally to transport us from the last words spoken one evening through the silent Long Island night overlooking the pond, to usher in the new day in mock-lyrical cadences. In a very few instances, however, this narratorial voice is used for other purposes, when in the manner of a nineteenth-century novel it addresses the reader so as to reveal some encompassing truth about the narrative as a whole. Perhaps most striking among these is the introduction of the Szyrk case, some twenty pages into the story, and it needs to be quoted at length:

> And so we may as well begin this sad story with the document that has set things off or, better, that merely paced the events that follow, spattered as it was all over the newspapers, since it had nothing directly to do with them, much less its remote participants, distant in every way but the historic embrace of the civil law in its majestic effort to impose order upon? or is it rather to rescue order from the demeaning chaos of everyday life in this abrupt opportunity ... to be taken seriously before the world, in an almost inverse proportion to their place in it, their very names in fact and the inconsequential nature of their original errands, like that woman intending no further than Far Rockaway suddenly lofted to landmark status

by Justice Cardozo in *Palsgraf* v. *Long Island Railroad,* or the mere passerby rendered eternal by Baron Pollack [sic!] in *Byrne* v. *Boadle* beaned by a barrel of flour. [29-30]

The opposition between anonymity and recognition, marked by the disproportion between the trivial beginnings and the ultimate schoolbook status of the major common law precedents, reminds us that the law has it in its power to make people real through the performativity of its language. It is the attainment of this virtual reality that Oscar covets, whereas Szyrk wants the instituted reality of his reputation to be confirmed and augmented by the law. Neither barrel nor scales have fallen on Oscar or Szyrk, whose sense of injury comes from the abuse, perpetrated or intended, of their artistic creations. Christina, Harry, and Basie try to tell Oscar that his case is only about whether someone else has profited from his work, yet for Oscar it is a matter of its integrity, but he fails to see that integrity is dependent on an identity that must be validated by a market. Thus the question of an established reputation is precisely what is at stake in the comparison between Oscar and Szyrk. As Judge Crease's opinion records, Szyrk is "a sculptor of some wide reputation in artistic circles" (30). As with any reputation, Szyrk's renown exists only in specific relations to an existing market, that of the art world. Such recognition, however, has an effect outside its circumscribed market when the law considers the case. As Basie tells Oscar, Szyrk has a better case because of this: "He could shit on a shingle and call it a protected statement under the First Amendment" (114). Oscar needs to prove first of all that anyone has ever read his play, while in the case of Szyrk, the law has only to recognize an already socially recognized identity that then can be legally constituted. In the process, however, that identity becomes a commodity on the marketplace of spectacular recognition.

The *Szyrk* case becomes a circus because, by inviting the law, it invites spectacle. In *Frolic,* the forces of spectacle are seen as increasingly capable of travestying the various languages of society by invading each site that gives rise to struggles for recognition.[16] Once Cyclone Seven has been constituted as a legal controversy it becomes the site for all kinds of manifestations that, in a self-regenerating cycle, attract the mass media. In Oscar's living room the TV screen displays crowds of people "marching around for animal rights, artists' rights, black rights, right to life, abortion, gun control, Jesus loves and the flags, Stars and Stripes, Stars and Bars" (48). Before long politicians enter the act. The involvement of Senator Orney Bilk, an "old times States' rights advocate" (272), provides Gaddis the opportunity for splendors of satire, as Bilk moves in to gain political recognition by further travestying the issues raised by Szyrk's sculpture.

The ornery *Kulturkampf* waged by antistatist politicians is Gaddis's satirical comment on the "culture wars" that were raging in the early 1990s. It strays into the plot, attracted by the commotion already established around the Cyclone Seven sculpture and, more particularly, by the involvement of the adversary artist on the one hand and the independent judge on the other. The expansive edifice of art draws not only mongrel dogs but also various human actors into its labyrinthine environs. Clearly, the existence of a particular work of art itself may be a provocation, but it is the presence of the law and the media that whets the political appetites, much as in the cases of the Robert Mapplethorpe exhibition, the 2 Live Crew infringement case and others in which the legal apparatus can be drawn in to adjudicate the claims of art. The added provocation of federal money supporting the arts has also played its role in this political discourse, and Gaddis is careful to add all the necessary ingredients to this fictional controversy in which the evocation of "hard earned Federal tax dollars" (294) is contrasted with the obscenity of contemporary arts.

The various actors who receive recognition here – artist, politicians, vested-interest groups with lobbying power, single-cause citizens, the judge – are all but one dependent for that recognition on the spectacularization of the original conflict, and that conflict could not have attained the heights of spectacle without the intercession of the law. The legal constitution of the various agents underwrites their importance, because it connects their destinies to those of the state, of legitimate power. The common weal embraces them, and from that basic granting of recognition the foremost agent of spectacle, the media, can reproduce and expand their travestied forms until the original substance is exhausted according to the accelerated rate of turnover for this kind of image goods.

In this light, the travesty of justice that Oscar complains about is merely a sign of a more thoroughgoing travesty operating on and through the social codes a society lives by. The spectacle distorts each event and refracts each identity, no matter what form it was originally given in its proper network of authority and genesis, so that it can be presented as a public sign that can be recognized or rather misrecognized as instantly accessible and meaningful. The basic critique that Gaddis is able to stage has to do with this process of translation – in Bourdieu's socio-Freudian model the work of euphemization – and how it may affect various autonomous languages and socially specific identities. When the travestied version gains acceptance as a "common language" it can be freely cannibalized by a manipulative political discourse or enter into circulation in a marketplace indifferent to its original meaning. The dangers inherent in this process of diffused distortion are analyzed in contrast with the much more distinct, because localized and formalized, travesty performed by the law. Moreover, it must be remembered that the novelistic analysis itself is carried out in a medium that operates on the principle of a full conversion, or even transmutation. Gaddis's novel presents a world that is recognizable and yet radically unfamiliar – defamiliarized as the Russian formalists had it – and the totalizing transformation of signs that it effects tends to conceal that transformation, at least within the field that is constituted by the recognition and misrecognition of this power of art. Paradoxically, in order to make his point about art and law, Gaddis has to incorporate, alongside the language of the law, a congealed version of literary language in his own flowing language, he has to insert a play, and a very serious one, in the general playfulness of *Frolic*. Oscar's old-fashioned play can be recognized as "literary" in Gaddis' own hyper literary discourse, and for all its weaknesses it can stand in for the real thing, as far as the defense of values is concerned.

In a situation where independent contexts of value are threatened by the logic of equivalency, the language of good law has everything in common with the language of the modernist drama that Oscar has written. Not as rival art forms but as independent refusals of spectacle do Judge Crease's opinions and Oscar's play earn their place in the novel. To some extent it is by virtue of an anachronistic stance that their refusals can be marshaled. Most clearly this is the case with Oscar, whose constant need to be filled in on most aspects of modern law and culture provides the reader with an ingénue reaction to contemporary life. His distaste for the movies and for Broadway is true to a 1950s highbrow perspective in its presumptions, and his elitist fulminations against them set out the starkest possible contrast between crude gratification and sophisticated sublimation, stupidity and intelligence, art and money. Thus the only worthwhile spectacle is the interior one, and the faithful production that Oscar dreamed about for his own play is the minimum of betrayal that those words on the page must be subjected to in order to gain for him the recognition he yearns for. Consequently, his work can find no place in the current marketplace, where the author must aim for maximum exposure and marketing, not even of his work, but of "the author in this whole revolting media circus turning the creative artist into a performer in this frenzy of publicity" (98).

A similar distaste at the tendency to mistake the author's, or here the judge's, creation with the spectacle that can be generated around his persona is expressed in Judge Crease's irascible comment, "Damn the public's right to know!" (241), which ironically, and predictably, becomes fuel for the media machine it was directed against. As Judge Crease's obituary notes, this unwillingness to be at the mercy of spectacular recognition was "carried through to the last in his stipulation ... for immediate cremation with no funeral service of any sort" (443-44).[17] This last provision gains full significance in view of the uses found for Judge Crease's person in the opportunist discourse of Senator Bilk. After Oscar wistfully expresses his regrets that his father will not get the big funeral he deserved, Harry points out what the baleful consequences would have been: "You'd get Bilk and the rest of the political trash with the media in there exercising their First Amendment rights to turn it into a public spectacle" (468).

What Judge Crease has done is to follow the logic of his particular professional ethos to its conclusion, by insisting on the integrity of his duties and his works. By preventing the spectacle that would distort his juristic practice, by abolishing the extra-legal performance elements of his life and death, he has worked to minimize the "travestying" that every public performance carries with it. The refusal to have a public burial, one of the great traditional moments for retrospective recognition, reduces the risk of having one's individually accumulated symbolic capital appropriated by the holders of various forms of degraded, spectacle-based capital, such as Senator Bilk and the media.

To sum up, we have seen how Gaddis, in the choices made by the narrative agents and in the satire of many of the set pieces in the novel, stages the refusal of spectacle as the necessary condition for a kind of recognition that is not spurious, that is aimed at its proper object rather than the travesty that is generated by the translation of various forms into the arenas of spectacle. The law has a special role to play in this problematic, because it has its own powers of translation, and particularly since spectacle has a presence in the law, in the form of the courtroom drama.

It is crucial for the novel's mapping of values that Gaddis's treatment of courtroom drama itself turns out to be an example of the refusal of spectacle. The circus of the Szyrk case proceeds in bits and pieces reported by the media but in an extended form it only reaches us in the guise of Judge Crease's acerbic opinions. A case of wrongful death is similarly reported based on media accounts and then by the judge's highly manipulative instructions to the hapless Virginia jury. The climactic moment of Oscar's lawsuit comes when the court of appeals hears the case, and Gaddis eliminates the actual performance of that moment by having it transacted offstage, as it were, and letting Harry report it beforehand, as a kind of best-case scenario of how Swyne & Dour's man on the case, Madhar Pai, may find courtroom reality inimical to his proclivity for performance: "[Judge Bone] comes right in ... , sums up the argument in a couple of sentences and asks counsel to sit down, poor bastard's got himself up for a real performance and the place, the whole atmosphere's like a theatre but they're not there for a matinee and his whole star goes out the window, a few more questions and down comes the curtain" (397). To cap this extraordinary moment in the undermining of the power of performance as ostentatious display, the next thing the reader finds out about the appeal is the abrupt insertion of Judge Bone's opinion reversing the decision of the court below, and then Harry gets to repeat his prophetic description, but now in the past tense, describing how the behind-the-scenes action of Judge Crease had actually settled the case before Madhar Pai got the chance to say a word: "One look at that appeal brief they didn't doubt for a second it had come from a colleague, never prove it of course but I think they knew where it came from, turned [Madhar Pai]'s performance upside down on its face and left him out in the cold" (450).

What has happened here is of importance to my underlying argument that Gaddis gives the coordinates for a sociological analysis of field-specific recognition. That Oscar's father finally writes the appeal brief and has it filed so that the protracted lawsuit comes to an unexpectedly "happy" ending has all the marks of the comedy plot, although highly ironic in this case. Above and beyond its role in the plot, however, the spark of recognition that briefly leaps across the space between those "remote participants," the judges Bone and Crease, illustrates one principle of hierarchization in the juridical field.

Like any social field, the juridical field displays a tension between two poles, one where its own type of symbolic capital is dominant and one where the market or political power dominates. In the figures of the two old judges is embodied the principle of specific competence that is opposed to the principle of economic capital. Harry points out the irony of a "Federal judge [earning] a hundred thousand [a year] with this stream of hotshot lawyers pulling down half a million, a million shouting at him showing off to the client sitting there guilty as hell he collects win or lose" (488). Gaddis includes both poles of the juridical field, one drawing on economic capital for its adjudication of status, as in the reputation of the high-price, "fancy blue ribbon white shoe outfit" exemplified by Swyne & Dour, the other richer in the specific juridical capital constitutive of this field. The seeming paradox of a First Amendment champion who scorns the public's "right to know" articulates the specific juridical interest in a principle that can best be upheld as such if the forces of spectacle do not encroach on the "field of restricted production" of law. This squares with Bourdieu's model, which predicts that those agents in a given field who hold the greatest amount of field-specific capital will put up the fiercest struggle for the autonomy of the field. The big New York law firms must work within the rules of the field, but they have a clear, if delimited, interest in visibility outside it, because they base their strategies on reputations that can be broadcast in dignified forms. Even at Swyne & Dour there is a certain scorn for too crude a form of visibility, as seen in the young lawyer's distaste for how the media has portrayed the infringement case between the Episcopal church and the Pepsi Cola company: the "Pop and Glow" label is "just their vulgar shorthand for bringing a landmark case in the hundreds of millions down to the harried level of the general public who delight in trivializing anything they cannot understand" (579). Note that from the field position of Swyne & Dour juridical values are shared out between the specific juridical principle of vision ("landmark case") and the economic principle ("in the hundreds of millions"). Lower down in the hierarchy determined by an aggregate dominance of economic capital we find the law firm whose phone number Oscar comes across on a matchbook cover, and more or less bereft of economic capital and near the bottom of the ladder of juridical capital we might note the legal aid lawyer who helplessly watches Madhar Pai deprive his client of the money left to her in a will. In this last case, money immediately translates into money, whereas in the opinions written by Judge Bone and Judge Crease the law is treated less instrumentally.

While *Frolic* parades instance after instance demonstrating the truth of the proposition that all is money, Gaddis has the main plot device, Oscar's infringement suit, hinge on the crucial mutual recognition of the old judges, who can be judged equally intent on "rescuing the language" of judgment and for this reason will pay to each other the respect of a specific recognition that also, *en passant,* resists the simple conversion of money into law. It is then beside the point that the creative accounting of the manipulators of money and spectacle, the Hollywood producers, "cheats" Oscar out of the millions of dollars he has set his heart on. That is to be expected and no less than what the law in the last instance will guarantee to the dominant fraction of the dominant class.

On a general level, the quasi-analysis set out in *Frolic* can subtend a Marxist commodification critique, because the relationship between spectacle and the reification effected by exchange value is everywhere on the novel's pages. Spectacle confirms the logic of market-imposed equivalency, as the news parades images of distended bellies from one African country one day, from a neighboring one the next, in both cases followed by identical commercials for laxatives and antacids. Gaddis's civilization critique comes from a conservative position, however, and it suggest the defense of a highly specialized professional and class ethos as a precarious bulwark against commodification. It is from a highly ambivalent and ambiguous position that Harry recognizes the value of Judge Crease's dedication to the language of the law. If the words on paper constitute the internal performance – legal or literary – that stands opposed to the travesty of public performance in the novel, they are also the signs of a threatened autonomy in each social institution.

To protect that autonomy is to "rescue the language," in Harry's phrase. Not only does the law, like every profession, "[protect] itself with a language of its own" (284), but this principle of separation is also the guarantor of its value. Judge Crease's mission to rescue the language returns us to the narrator's early and fundamental vacillation when describing the task of the civil law to "impose order *upon?* or is it rather to rescue order *from* the demeaning chaos of everyday life" (29, emphasis added). The distinction between the two questions is important. To impose order on would be to exercise constraints on that "chaos" and make the whole of it conform to the rationality of the law, while to rescue order from the social space as a whole would imply seizing the notion of order from its ineffectual state in an inimical environment and confining it to a framework that affirms it. Implicit in Gaddis's depiction of the Judge who devotes his life to the two loves of law and language is the principle of a social autonomy of highly restricted mutual recognition, possible in the present only within the confines of the edifice of law. In the case of the dog Spot caught in Cyclone

Seven, Judge Crease pointed out that there were "no facts alleged to support recovery of the chattel safe and unharmed upon or during removal of the vehicle of its detention" (292). Similarly, the narrator announces the concern that the principle of order might not survive being removed from the juridical apparatus and its inherited constraints.

This reasoning can readily be applied to the autonomy of art, it seems to me, and not only in order simply to celebrate that relative independence, because it is invariably gained at the cost of substantial social efficacy. Language and visual forms can produce aesthetic joy, intimations of immortality, redemptive constellations, and so on, but such power is purchased on condition of their isolation in the order of art. In this respect, however, the nonlanguage of Szyrk's sculpture and the overly discursive play that Oscar has written present two very different "languages," each, furthermore, distinct from the narrative in which they figure as heteroglossic rivals. The expert witnesses attest to the reputation of Szyrk, yet Oscar cannot adduce that sort of evidence to his case, which can finally only be formally affirmed as "new and useful" (408) by the court of law, even though the previous recognition of its usefulness as story by Erebus Entertainment, Inc., shows that the language of modernist art runs the risk of surviving only in its spectacularized form. Travesty is becoming the norm in a field of cultural production that cannot defend its own principles of autonomy. Cyclone Seven must be seen as an instance of that autonomy, but the drift of Gaddis's *mise-en-scène* puts under suspicion a collective enterprise that has been driven to embrace an absolute refusal of meaning as its *raison d'être*. Szyrk denies "any intention of meaning to be construed in his sculptural works beyond the raw arrangement of their actual materials in which any meaning, if there were such, resided in this very meaninglessness hence the vacuous site specificity of Cyclone Seven" (280). In a brilliant mimicking of art babble, Gaddis then shows the vacuity of the brand of art discourse that will stake its claims only on the grounds of a purely formal autonomy. Again, Harry gets to expound the principle of a confusion of tongues inherent in a society with separate fields of values, where art criticism is "simply another language, art theory referring only to itself" (281). Szyrk's ritualistic refusal of meaning is the dead-end logic of the professionalization of languages, the exaggerated belief in the saving grace of restricting communication to those who command the specific code of a field; there will be little left for external forces to grab, but this last measure of a purely formal independence closes the door on a substantial social role for the arts.

The accidental invasion of the "meaningless" sculpture by an unknowing carrier of socially recognized, sentimental value, in the shape of a mongrel dog, makes the work come alive. Only when the community perceives it as the container of something meaningful does it come to participate in a social dialogue, even as this dialogue immediately degrades into a spectacular confusion of tongues. The task of the artist, if it is to have any resemblance to the rescuing of the language that the judge is (ideally) seen to perform, must be to insist on the specificity of the literary or artistic forms while preserving some core of common meaning to be communicated or performed. The discourse of art as a domain of products that, by virtue of their formal complexity, are inaccessible to the forces of commodification and mass mediation is given the lie in *Frolic,* where Cyclone Seven is from its very beginning dependent on various forms of federal, state, and corporate sponsorship and becomes immediately available as a commodity once it has been given cultural meaning by an entirely random set of events.

The power of reconfiguration commanded by commercial and bureaucratic techniques for producing meaning on a mass scale can easily convert the arcane innovation into a mass-consumable good. As Raymond Williams has argued concerning the fate of modernist forms, the "painfully acquired techniques of significant disconnection are relocated, with the help of the special insensitivity of the trained and assured technicists, as the merely technical modes of advertising and the commercial cinema."[18] Significantly, Constantine Kiester's trajectory has taken him from the making of "quality television productions of American theatre classics ranging from Elmer Rice to Eugene O'Neill and Tennessee Williams" to the making of "special effects"-based cinema (121). The forces of spectacle draw on the autonomous forms that are developed in the cultural field and have the further effect on the most autonomous producers to spur them toward making their works first inaccessible and then void of shared meaning. That elitist embrace of difficulty and the refusal to communicate meaning are as much a defeat as the reproduction of forms that can be more or less directly appropriated. The postmodernist show place for which the neighboring Long Island house is demolished and the self-referential language of art theory are equally removed from the search for forms with a capacity for taking people seriously. From the viewpoint of a claim for serious recognition, these forms are indeed "mere playthings" (284). Self-referentiality implies absolute incommensurability, and in that form art helps generate the commensurability guaranteed by the pure symbolic form of money; postmodern architecture, having learned its lesson from Las Vegas, is a more direct expression of the same equivalency.

In its formal autonomy the law mirrors the case of the arts, not by abstaining from a social role, but by turning social relations into formal ones. In the absence of all substantial connections, the law will at least afford individuals the formal embrace that will establish their identity, if only in an "artificial relationship." Lacking substantial forms of recognition, it is no wonder that individuals will turn to the law to have their being affirmed. As Madhar Pai cynically points out, sponsorship of art, like lawsuits, is an ersatz form of recognition, as there are "people all over the place with nothing to do and money they don't know what to do with, no act of their own so they buy their way into somebody else's like the ones who litigate because they don't know who they are and it makes them feel real, gives them an identity when they see their name on a docket" (363). The principles of a deficient autonomy that gives rise to travesty, to impersonation would seem to hold as true at the level of the individual as in the collective ensemble of practices that sustains a field of social production.

The novel demonstrates how the law serves to create counterfeit doubles as it translates identities generated in other fields. The most blatant example is when Oscar sues himself. The Pentecostal Insurance Company adjuster, Frank Gribble, sees the dilemma and repeats Harry's claim that the law has split and doubled Oscar. The law produces a formal identity for Oscar's fantasy of himself, and toward the end Oscar himself will support the idea with a reference to Montaigne "where he says it's a hard task to be always the same man?" (545). Harry, however, reveals the more acute predicament: the identity Oscar thinks is being defended in his lawsuit against Erebus Entertainment is a fantasy engendered by the original rejection of Oscar's play. Like so many other people in the novel, Oscar now turns to the law for a recognition that was not forthcoming in the field in which he had invested his own powers of recognition. In the same way that some people, blessed with money and nothing else, seek to become real by sponsoring culture, and like those other litigants who engage the law in order to become real to themselves, Oscar exemplifies the use of another field for a translation of one's own social being. Harry analyzes Oscar's predicament with a sense of intense frustration that is tied to his own trajectory, as he describes the writing of the play as the title's "frolic of one's own," an uncoerced, unbidden act. What then? "does [Oscar] keep at it? write another play? and another? No, no he splurges this one time and then lets it devour him year after year ... because it's safer to blame the world out there for rejecting who he thought he was" (398). The lawsuit then is a surrogate process for becoming "whole," as Harry's legal phrase has it: "to make him whole, restore someone" (310-11) after damages. The wholeness afforded by the law is based on a narrowly legal recognition and cannot in any real sense substitute for the literary recognition that has already passed Oscar by; more generally, the different social fields of legal and cultural production can produce recognition effects in the other field only as heteronomy, that is, by setting aside the rules by which the game normally rewards its players. As a consumer of the products created by the law, Oscar cannot have his status as a producer of literature recognized. It is different for Szyrk, whose "reputation" is already established.[19]

The idea, stated at the outset, that William Gaddis's *A Frolic of His Own* maps a social reality can be used to sum up the moves of my analysis. The universes of law and literature are represented by various characters and discourses in the novel, and Gaddis shows that in these spaces individuals can gain meaningful recognition. This recognition refers to both values and identities, and it follows that value and identity are strictly determined by these fields. When Oscar, the failed playwright, takes his work to the law, a process of translation takes place, and Oscar, who wanted literary and moral recognition for his play, can see only a travesty in the way the law treats it. The notion of travesty then becomes a general one, which can be said to operate whenever a value or an identity crosses from one field to another. Travesty implies a disguise, a new cover, under which an individual or a work can gain acceptance in a new space. On the other hand, the legal field is fairly directly subordinated to the economic field, which recognizes only the operation of equivalency that effectively erases all substantive differences so as to present values and identities in the denuded form of money. Moreover, the novel demonstrates how the logic of another space, that of spectacle, tends to invade the fields of art and law, reducing their autonomy and replacing their elaborate principles of recognition with the instantly consumable image. By contrasting the forces of money and spectacle, which I would like to bring together in the notion of commodification, with the values and identities produced by art and law, Gaddis sets up a defense of those field-specific principles for the creation of value. He does this mainly through a negative critique of various figures – Szyrk, Kiester, Bilk – who are complicit with the logic of equivalency and also in the shape of the old judges, Bone and Crease, who pay mutual recognition to each other's field-specific authority. In the choice between money and opera, Gaddis prefers to focus our attention on the *opus,* the work, in this case, of rescuing the language, whether of law or of art.

It seems to me that an understanding of the relation between literature and law must proceed from this perception of their workings as relatively autonomous fields of production. It follows from this division of domains for meaningful work that struggles for individual recognition are subject to the travestying involved as separate fields translate various claims into their formalized languages.[20] *Frolic* then helps describe a dilemma of modernity that directly affects the notions of value and identity: insufficient autonomy leaves a field open to the travestying force of marketplace spectacle, while excessive autonomy generates a power of form that travesties all content beyond recognition. Gaddis's own work is the difficult achievement of a form that travesties its materials so that we can more accurately recognize them.

Notes

1. I refer to the novel as *Frolic* and give page references in parentheses in the text. Note that William Gaddis's prose often does without normal punctuation, and I have not tried to emend this in my quotations. Gaddis, *A Frolic of His Own* (New York, 1994).
2. See especially the essays in Pierre Bourdieu, *Language and Symbolic Power,* ed. John B. Thompson (Cambridge, Mass., 1991).
3. The fictional case has several real-life parallels. One that Gaddis almost certainly knew of was filed by Art Buchwald against Paramount Pictures for its alleged "theft" of a Buchwald movie treatment for the making of the film *Coming to America*. The case brought to the public's attention the unorthodox accounting practices of Hollywood studios when Paramount claimed that the box-office hit had made no profit. See Pierce O'Donnell and Dennis McDougal, *Fatal Subtraction: The Inside Story of "Buchwald v. Paramount"* (New York, 1992), and Joseph F. Hart and Philip J. Hacker, "Less Than Zero: Studio Accounting Practices in Hollywood," Buchwald's comment on seeing the movie–"It was an awful movie, but it was my awful movie"–could have been made by Oscar Crease. I thank Ann Gross for telling me about this case. Another parallel is a suit brought by Barbara Chase-Riboud, who claimed that her novel *An Echo of Lions* was appropriated by Steven Spielberg's movie *Amistad*. Her 1997 counsel was the same used by Buchwald. In this case, as in Oscar's, one key issue was whether one can copyright history. See Claudia Eller, "Spielberg Lawsuit Pits Author vs. Auteur," Hollywood Online, Friday, Oct. 24, 1997, at www.hollywoodnetwork.com/Law/Hart/columns/index.html
4. Actually Harry's response, "I've thought about it" (11), is one of many examples of the novel's use of homonymy: on the surface level of this conversation seen as a speech act it is a way of dismissing Christina's question, but we shall see later that Harry has thought a great deal about this problem and has submitted to his apparent cynicism only after a long struggle. In his opposition between money and opera, Harry has effectively buried the root meaning of opera, in the sense of work and pain.
5. Karl Marx, *Capital,* vol. 1, trans. Samuel More and Edward Haveling (New York, 1967: orig. pub. 1867), 90.
6. See Charles Taylor, *Multiculturalism and "The Politics of Recognition"* (Princeton, N. J., 1992).
7. Axel Honneth, *The Struggle for Recognition: The Moral Grammar of Social Conflicts,* trans. Joel Anderson (Cambridge, 1995), 129.
8. I speak of tautological equivalency with a nod to Guy Debord's analysis of commodification in *The Society of the Spectacle,* trans. Donald Nicholson-Smith (New York, 1994; orig. pub. 1967), 15: "The spectacle is essentially tautological, for the simple reason that its means and its ends are identical."

9. Theodor Adorno, "Reconciliation under Duress," trans. Rodney Livingston, in Adorno, Walter Benjamin, Ernst Bloch, Bertolt Brecht, and Georg Lukács, *Aesthetics and Politics,* ed. and trans. Ronald Taylor (London, 1980; orig. pub. 1977), 151-76.
10. Bourdieu, "Force of Law," 829.
11. Bourdieu, "The Force of Law: Toward a Sociology of the Juridical Field," *Hastings Law Journal,* 38 (1987), 818.
12. Guy Debord goes further when he claims that "the spectacle is another facet of money, which is the abstract general equivalent of all commodities" in *Society of the Spectacle,* 32.
13. Ibid., 12.
14. Fredric Jameson, *Postmodernism* (London, 1991), 18.
15. *Frolic* fits a Bakhtinian conception of the novel as heteroglossia to an almost unlikely degree. As Michael Holquist, *Bakhtin and His World* (London, 1990), 69, puts it, heteroglossia "is a way of conceiving the world as made up of a rolling mass of languages."
16. Remember that Gaddis's perspective is a conservative one, able to grasp spectacle only in the limited sense that Debord, *Society of the Spectacle,* 19, 20, talks about: "If the spectacle – understood in the limited sense of those 'mass media' that are its most stultifying superficial manifestation – seems at times to be invading society in the shape of a mere apparatus, it should be remembered that this apparatus has nothing neutral about it, and that it answers precisely to the needs of the spectacle's internal dynamics." The way that spectacle in *Frolic* is connected to the general logic of equivalency, however, approaches the more profound understanding of the mass media as only the "general form of all social division."
17. This insistence on having the finished work speak for itself is also Gaddis's own, expressed in one of the few interviews he gave: "Writers in Conversation 13: William Gaddis with Malcolm Bradbury," Anthony Roland Collection of Films on Art, ICA Video.
18. Raymond Williams, *The Politics of Modernism: Against the New Conformists,* ed. Tony Pinkney (London, 1989), 35.
19. Szyrk's case can be compared with a lawsuit brought by Fredrick E. Hart against Warner Brothers for having infringed on his sculpture "Ex Nihilo" in the film *The Devil's Advocate*. This suit has nothing to do with gaining first-hand recognition for his work but only with ratification in another field of a fact produced in Hart's proper field of activity. See articles in the *Washington Post,* Dec. 5, 1997, and Feb. 7, 1998, and for the "amicable settlement" see Warner Bros release, Feb. 13, 1998.
20. This is Bourdieu's point with the notion of "censorship" in *The Political Ontology of Martin Heidegger* (Stanford, Calif., 1991), 70-87.

6

Dissenting Opinions: William Gaddis and Alan Dershowitz on the Spectacles of Justice

Peter Schneck

> No one ever lies – they just do everything to make you believe their story.
> – William Ginsburg

The following essay presents a comparative interpretation of two dissimilar texts, William Gaddis's *A Frolic of His Own* (1994) and Alan M. Dershowitz's *The Advocate's Devil* (1994). Using the term in its most general meaning, both texts can be described as "legal fictions," yet it is obvious that they differ remarkably in their perspectives on law and on literature. The first question, then, is do we have two cases that have to be argued separately or can both be put on the stand in a single court, as it were.

Although I am tempted to argue for the second option, I will restrain myself as far as possible from comparing the two novels directly. Rather, by way of indirection, I will first discuss what I think is their common concern, then make some short remarks about the definition of authorship and authority, and finally look at the two novels separately to highlight some of their interesting and significant similarities. This strategy is based on the assumption that Gaddis and Dershowitz are as much inspired as they appear to be troubled by some of the most important aspects of the cultural function of both law and literature, namely, the meditation and mediation of a common (cultural) sense of justice. This assumption is justified, I think, for several reasons. For one, despite the differences between the works and their authors, both novels are the result of a similar transgressive impulse since Gaddis as well as Dershowitz make a bold step beyond the field of their legitimate discursive authority. If the authority to speak in public and for the public is a claim that the authors share, these claims nevertheless are legitimized only by their distinct positions in two separate fields of social and cultural practice.[1] What separates literature from law most fundamentally, and especially in regard to their respective cultural significance, are precisely the different categories and assumptions according to which they are granted their legitimacy. Principally, the authority of a respected literary writer and that of a respected lawyer are based on the high level of performance in their respective fields, which is recognized and thus legitimized by such forms of public acknowledgment as the award of literary prizes or the award of professional law degrees and titles. In the cases at hand, the two authors use their authority to make inroads into the neighboring field: Gaddis acts as a lawyer in writing (fictitious) summaries and opinions, and Dershowitz assumes the role of an author of literary fiction that conforms to the rules of a specific genre – the courtroom drama.

The terms "acting" and "role" deliberately point to the performative nature of both transgressions, which means that neither author sheds his legitimate cloak of authority, he merely assumes another. Both thus meet in the most important area where law and literature as distinct modes of performative discourse overlap: the realm of public speech or rhetoric.

This introduces a second level of similarity, because both Gaddis and Dershowitz apparently share an obsession with the contemporary conditions of public speech, especially as it is concerned with the language of the law and its relation to justice. Rhetoric traditionally signified a mode of oral address that would elevate private, subjective utterances to the status of objective, commonly acceptable meaning. It thus addresses, not a concrete audience of individuals, but an abstract congregation of collective categories of understanding and communication, that is, a common sense.[2] And no matter whether rhetoric achieves its power by means of manipulation or persuasion or by reference to facts and truth, it always depends on the right – the just, the legitimate – choice of words.³ Both literature and the law share an intimate relation to rhetoric; although they may differ in their choice of words, their specific rhetorical strategies are aimed at the construction of a public audience that would grant them their legitimacy. Both thus rely on a specific use of language; for law and for literature language is the dominant medium of communication and legitimation.

Since the advent of modern mass media, however, the realm of public meaning and therefore of common sense has become less and less governed by language, that is, by verbal utterances and signs, and more and more by images, by visual signs.⁴ The transgressive impulse of both Gaddis's and Dershowitz's assumptions of authority thus must be seen as a reaction to the equally transgressive, or even aggressive, takeover of the public arena by the images of the media. This takeover affects both literature and the law, because their authority and legitimacy are deeply rooted in a specific understanding of the cultural relation – the symbolic hierarchy – that governs the opposition between words and images, between the verbal and the visual mediation of justice.

The opposition between words and images that dominates Western cultural history, as W.J.T. Mitchell convincingly argues, stands as the bedrock of commonsensical distinctions between idea and fact, between argument and evidence, between objective reality and subjective imagination. "The gulf between words and images," Mitchell states, is still seen to be "as wide as the one between words and things, between (in the largest sense) culture and nature," because, he explains:

> The image is the sign that pretends not to be a sign, masquerading as (or, for the believer, actually achieving) natural immediacy and presence. The word is its "other," the artificial, arbitrary production of human will that disrupts the natural presence by introducing unnatural elements into the world – time, consciousness, history, and the alienating intervention of symbolic mediation.⁵

The rift between image and word presents more than just a difference between two distinct modes of signification. In the face of the complex history of mediating technologies – technologies of telling and showing in public – the word-image opposition was and is a constant point of struggle between different media that in any specific historical situation characterizes the conditions of public rhetoric and common sense. It is precisely the specific hierarchy of the media as a system that essentially grounds the legitimacy of public speech in any given case.

"The law is a profession of words," David Mellinkoff's commonplace assertion in The *Language of the Law,* must be taken in its most ambivalent sense in order to point at *The* inherent particularity of the law's "professions."[6] The same words may be very different according to their mode of mediation: Spoken in private or public, in formal or informal contexts, pinned down in haste or printed after repeated and thorough revision, delivered in a theatre, a movie, a radio or a television broadcast, received by mail, by public announcement posters, in a textbook, a letter, or on a computer screen, scribbled down on a note sheet or engraved on a stone – the words may be the same but what they profess (to) may be very different. As Mellinkoff's seminal work implies, the language of the law itself owes its most significant transformations to the development of the media. The shift from oral to print culture also marks a decisive change in legal language; in fact, our own contemporary assumptions about the nature of the law and its relation to language rely heavily on this shift.

The most significant consequences of the transformation of the law concerned the rhetoric implicit in both its procedures and its concepts. The increasing dominance of the written/printed word gradually but inevitably redefined not only the rhetorical strategies of attorneys and counselors, but also the way juries made judgments and the reasoning of opinions and decisions by the judges. In other words, the shift from the spoken to the written word changed the role of both the audience and the speakers who addressed it:

> Important procedural changes determined the course of the law in its multiplied contact with the written word... As one consequence, the jury became courtroom *listeners*

instead of a forced muster of oath-swearers alert to neighborhood gossip. The serjeants changed from *oral pleaders* to *skilled examiners* of witnesses.[7]

Not only did the examination of witnesses and the record of evidence fall under the influence of the written word, but also the law itself relied more and more on writing as the source and legitimation for its profession(s). No longer exclusively represented by a person – the king, judges – and realized through specific, ritualistic procedures codified in writing, the law gradually turned into a more abstract entity – a body of texts:

> The changeover from oral to written pleadings also had more farreaching effects on the language of the law... The system of written pleading was intended to reduce decision to a single point. And this decision became – word of words – a *precedent*. The word (from the French for *preceding* in time) is not used in its law sense before the late sixteenth century... . It was a creature of the printed word... Printing combined with the system of written pleading to place form at ready call in both attack and defense. And the more that was recorded, the ... higher grew the mountain of precedent.[8]

By the seventeenth century, the growing number of precedents – of recorded decisions – became a source for lasting anxiety: the fear of an inevitable regress of legal language, endlessly returning to itself and reducing the idea of justice to the "letter of the law." At the same time, lawyers were also anxious to separate legal discourse and rhetoric from other specialized modes of public speech, which the advent of the printing press and the emergence of common literacy had helped to gain new authority. As a new kind of a public audience – a reading audience – emerged, the law took great pains to regulate the concept of authorship, that is, the authority over the written text, both in the realm of literature and in legal writing. As Martin Kayman and Mark Rose each suggest, legal definitions of literary authorship in the seventeenth and eighteenth centuries are the result of the redefinition of legal authority in regard to written language and rhetoric. Only by drawing a line between literary and legal authorship, was the law able to reassure the "mystical foundation" of its own authority.[9] The growing dominance of written law forced legal interpretation to acknowledge the rift between two concepts of justice, one based on custom, or unwritten law, and another, based on statutes, or written, recorded law.

Whereas "the Common Law ... based its authority precisely on the fact that these unwritten laws had no identifiable author, but had evolved through customary practices of the people," even the proponents of the Common Law asserted that "the law cannot be separated from its letters and its concrete historical occurrences, the precedents."[10] Thus, Lord Camden's demand that even the Common Law must be based "upon some solid written Authority" (772) has to be read in opposition to the legal definition of literary authority which was based on the laws of property and the concept of individual authorship. As Kayman comments:

> [The Common Law] is writing that is not writing because, it is claimed, it never creates; any recorded instance merely remembers an authority that always spoke before it wrote, and spoke with the nonindividuated wisdom of communal practical justice. For all its records, treatises, and codes ... the Common Law remains non scripta ... it belongs to no author, and its meanings are "literal," not "literary," held within its language, permanent and not contingent.[11]

The authority of the law as text thus became intrinsically bound up with a concept of authorship that transcends the personal identity of the author. Even today, the authority of written law rests on the idea of ideal authorship, as Joseph Vining insists:

> To put it concisely but paradoxically, if writers of legal texts ... were to speak for themselves, they would speak without authority. They speak for the law or for an entity – the *court,* the *agency,* the *legislature* – that in turn speaks for the law ... and even then there is an ostensible speaking for, for the "sovereign" if not "the law." The

late-twentieth-century sensibility might want to ignore these others, these authors beyond, as passé figments, but if one does ignore them one does so at the price of depriving speech of authority.[12]

The almost metaphysical reference to the "authors beyond" points to the law's desire for ideal and absolute authority beyond individual authorship – a desire that of course can also be sensed in Percy Bysshe Shelley's well-known claim that poets should be the "legislators of the world." In fact, literature gradually turned into the uncanny *Doppelgänger* of the law as a public discourse on justice and truth, claiming an equally exclusive, albeit different, intuitive access to higher laws, such as those of nature, of social reality, or of the human psyche. Because they both pretend to follow no law other than that embodied in their own texts, legal and literary writing almost always seem to be too close for comfort, and yet, at the same time they "appear perversely to need each other," because "each functions as a disavowal of the lack of autonomy that they denounce in each other."[13]

But if literature and law continue to compete for public attention and recognition in an ongoing struggle with the very medium they both rely on, the idea of justice as a common cultural property is not so easily confined to the realm of language alone, because justice is not merely an abstract concept that can be regulated and redefined solely by words and sentences. As the rapid development of visual media during the last two centuries indicates, justice as a common sense not only has been turned more and more into a highly visible presentation, it also depends largely on its visibility. In the "society of the spectacle" both literature and the law face severe competition from the visual media, which have become, as it were, both the legislators and the judges in the court of public opinion.[14]

Rhetoric is the source of the language of the law. The attempt of ancient lawyers to increase the effectiveness of litigation claims before the public in democratic courts, for instance, also gave birth to a concept of language as a medium of persuasion and performance. In *A Frolic of His Own* the rhetoric of litigation has spread far beyond the courts to become the universal mode of social intercourse. As Jonathan Raban remarks: "Almost everyone in the novel is suing almost everyone in sight for damages... For every suit there is a countersuit, for every judgement an appeal." It is no accident that the novel's main protagonist, part-time historian and amateur playwright Oscar L. Crease, the son and grandson of distinguished judges, ends up suing himself because he managed to run himself over with his own car. Oscar, naturally, "only wants justice, after all," but there is a self-destructive dimension to his claims. One of the many lawyers in the novel observes: "This is a suit between who you are and who you think you are" (*Frolic,* 474). This points at the unreconcilable antagonism between the ideal of justice and its reality, the system of the law. Obviously Oscar inherited the system but not the common wisdom of the judges who formed it. The system has become so intricate and complex that it leaves no room for justice, as Oscar's brother-in-law Harry, also a lawyer, exclaims in the novel's opening sentence: "Justice? – You get justice in the next world, in this world you have the law" (*Frolic,* 13). If they exist at all, the idea of justice and the authority of the law exist only in and as a (rather bad) piece of historical fiction, Oscar's ill-fated Civil War drama *Once at Antietam*. Even this attempt to reclaim the lost authority of the law with the help of literature fails, because the play is shamelessly plagiarized by a Hollywood producer and turned into a gory spectacle, aptly called "The Blood in the Red, White and Blue."[15]

In the social universe of *A Frolic of His Own,* Language is the weapon in what Deborah Tannen calls America's "argument culture," based on the "assumption that truth emerges when two polarized, warring extremes are set against each other."[16] People in the novel do not converse or communicate in the conventional sense of these terms; there is no orderly traffic of ideas or exchange of meanings. Instead, opinions and statements are regularly hurled against the opponent and hardly does anyone listen to anyone else. Misunderstandings abound and meanings collide and crash almost constantly. The persuasive force of verbal rhetoric and performance, as Marie Maclean writes, relies on a common frame of reference for both the speaker and the listeners: "a base of shared expectations, whereby power is granted to others, to the hearers as well as the teller." For Maclean, performance usually functions as a "metatext" for the audience.[17] In *A Frolic of His Own,* the metatext threatens to become the only text or, more precisely, a text whose only message is its performance – without the power of persuasion and without meaning. As Oscar notes in utter despair: "It's all just more words and more words until everything gets buried under words" (*Frolic,* 160).

Gaddis's formal strategies work against most of the conventional expectations of a reading audience and, more important, highlight the crucial function of performance in and for the text. Sentences flow into each other without punctuation, are left without closure, or are taken up by other speakers but with a very different meaning. There is an almost complete absence of formal order on the level of grammar and syntax in the dialogues that make up the most part of the novel.

This state of linguistic anarchy is complemented by a disturbing lack of personal naming and address. Often the identity of the speaker remains uncertain while the dialogue relentlessly rushes on, switching between its different sources and also between locations and time frames without warning or prior notice. In other words, Gaddis denies the marks of authorship and thus of authority to his characters, a crucial gesture that is reflected in the story itself in which the protagonists have to cope with the loss of authority in many different ways. What characterizes this loss most pertinently is the lack of control over language; where language appears to be independent of its sources, that is, of authorship and of control. Common frames of reference become increasingly unstable, and thus there can be no mutual recognition of meaning, no satisfaction of shared expectations. As Oscar's sister Christina suggests, this may well be the reason why the rhetoric of litigation has become so central: "It's the only common reference people have for making other people take them as seriously as they take themselves ... that's all they're asking for, isn't it?" (*Frolic,* 13). The law becomes the last resort for any claim of personal identity and authority.

If we move from the tale to the telling, we get an altogether different picture. Although the radical strategies Gaddis employs may leave his characters (and a number of his readers, to be sure) helplessly entangled in the gordian knots of (spoken) language, the medium itself – the written text of the novel – gains considerable weight as a means of authentic representation. It is an authoritative voice in its own right, a metavoice. Joseph Tabbi, for instance, states that, whereas "Gaddis suppresses his own personality and 'literate voice' to become a medium for other voices, a recorder of … multiple cultural quotations," he nevertheless "remains very much alive in the formal arrangement of the narrative." Raban adds: "Gaddis really listens to the way we speak now. The talk is brilliantly rendered, with a wicked fidelity to its flimsy grammar, its elisions and hiatuses, its rush-and-stumble rhythms." Again, it is obvious how the formal structure of the novel, with its technical control and performance, becomes the foundation of literary authority. Less obvious, yet probably more significant for the successful effect of this performance, is the sharp contrast of the anarchy of spoken language with other modes of written discourse and with the images of television and film. Paradoxically, the authenticity of spoken language as well as its loss of authority and persuasive power rest on its formal characteristics – the lack of order and structure that in turn point to the absence of a controlling source – and its inferior position in an entire system of different media of representation.[18]

Where everyday language has lost its authority, even the most simple commonsensical acts of discrimination must fail, as, for instance, in the burlesque conversations between Oscar and the insurance lawyer Frank Gribble, who is completely deaf to metaphors and literary allusions because he speaks and thinks only in legalese:

- Yes, it might be a little difficult, if we could dig up some similar cases and we need to examine the car, wouldn't we.
- Examine the car of course, I only want justice after all.
- It's garaged at your, at the place of the accident I can't find the, what kind of car is it.
- Sosumi.
- I'm being quite serious Mister Crease.
- So am I! It's a Japanese car, a Sosumi.

- Oh. Oh dear, yes I'm sorry, it's so hard to keep track of them all nowdays. We had a whole family killed in an Isuyu and I made a similar error [*Frolic,* 27-28].

The fine irony is that Gribble, like all the other lawyers in the novel, is obsessed with discrimination but only according to the *letter* of the law. For Gribble, "words always cause ... problems don't they when it becomes less a matter of their actual meaning than their interpretation" (*Frolic,* 473). Gribble's search for the actual meaning of words appears nostalgic compared to the linguistic zest of his colleague, Jawaharlal Madhar Pai, Esq. In a deposition, where Pai acts as the attorney for the film producer who allegedly plagiarized Oscar's play, he completely upsets Oscar's conventional belief in both the formal difference between idea and expression and their integrity in a work of art. While Oscar believes that "the idea executed is the idea expressed, transformed into a play, in other words it's definitely bound to the execution. So there are two things there to talk about" (*Frolic,* 183). He also insists that "you can't divide a work of art, the idea from the technique that expresses it." This is not the perspective of the law, Pai tells him, because to separate the idea from the execution is "exactly what you're going to have to do in a court of law. The idea is an abstract form and that's not what we're here to talk about" (*Frolic,* 200).

The law cannot talk about ideas because ideas, especially in literature, are not "actual thing[s]," that is, they cannot be defined according to form and so cannot be copyrighted. The basic form that allows the law to define the authorship as well as the identity of a work of literature is precisely the written, printed word. Even most of the deposition record is taken up by the objections of Oscar's attorney, Harold Basie, that are only allowed to "go on record" if they are to form, but not if they react to, the substance or content of Pai's questions. Gaddis's masterful exploitation of the very format of the deposition also demonstrates that the legal idea of form is completely shallow owing to the rigid formalization of its own language. The deposition stands as an obvious example of the law's obsession with the literal as against the literary use of language, an obsession clearly aimed at the regulation of public speech exclusively in terms of property rights. Language, Gaddis implies, only achieves power if it is allowed to go on record; everyday language, because it is always by nature "off the record" cannot claim any public authority. Thus there is no authority based on language apart from the law's definition of form and authorship.

Compared to the law's obsessive language of discrimination and literal definition, on the one hand, and the powerless chaos and ambivalence of everyday speech, on the other, the images of television and film represent two other modes of rhetoric, that seem to move across the boundaries between the private and the public realms with uncanny ease. In the novel, the television images present the only access to the world and its reality outside the run-down family estate where most of the action takes place. Oscar particularly seems to be as much addicted to the TV screen as he is to his Pinot Grigio, yet the reality presented by the TV images increases the chaos of indiscrimination beyond recognition, which common language desperately struggles to keep at bay:

> Scenes of mayhem from Londonderry to Chandigarh, an overweight family rowing down a main street in a freak flood in Ohio, a molasses truck overturned at the Jersey Turnpike, gunfire stabbings, flaming police cars and blazing ambulances celebrating a league basketball championship in Detroit interspersed with a decrepit grinning couple on a bed that warped and heaved at the touch of a button [*Frolic*, 237].

Television serves as a powerful source of dispersive images, a world without differences where any distinction between real and symbolic violence, between advertisement, info- and edutainment collapses into the overwhelming power of immediate emotional address – and distress. In a similar fashion, the detested movie spectacle, when it finally makes its appearance in the novel after more than 400 pages of spoken and written discourse, unfolds with a sweeping immediacy and presence of visible performance that even Oscar cannot resist:

> Suddenly the room shook with the sound of cannon fire, the screen with a tumult of plunging horses, flaring

rockets and the Stars and Bars and men, men – look! as **"The Blood in the Red White and Blue"** unfurled before them, going up in flames ... till the smoke cleared, the music died and now the room echoed with the clop, clop of a horse [*Frolic*, 411].

Just as during the deposition, when Oscar's play was reduced to its mere form and thus deprived of its authority by the definitions of the law, the movie transforms the text of the play into a spectacle, thereby reducing it to the performative power of the sensual – of sounds and images. Oscar's idea of justice embodied in a literary text is defeated on all fronts; while his authorial control over his own text is denied by the legal reduction to form, its emotional impact and public performance are superseded by the images of television and the movies. Oscar is the tragic figure of lost authorship, a living anachronism who still subscribes to an idea of authorial power and poetic justice magically emanating from the printed word:

> Because it's on the page! he suddenly erupted, – it's always been that way, the silent beautiful words coming off the page together to stop and listen to them to, to savour them without some vain fool in a costume prancing around up there just getting in their way, any of them [*Frolic*, 472].

The idea of justice is lost in its translation from text into image, from verbal rhetoric to visual performance: "Look at it it's travesty, they make a movie that's a vulgar travesty and now they make a travesty of the whole judicial process" (*Frolic*, 465).

For Gaddis, language has reached the zero point of its public and cultural authority. The logic of litigation, as the secret source of rhetoric and performance both in literature and in law, has completely given over to the latter and has reduced public speech to a meaningless spectacle – a spectacle where justice will not and cannot prevail. Oscar's stubborn and ultimately devastating litigation suits against himself and against the movie industry that form the central thread of the novel's various storylines are parables of the struggle for cultural authority between the word (in literature and in law) and the images of film and television.

The authority of both law and literature as modes of public speech is based on the specific construction of audiences and the regulation of authorship. The audience that the literary and legal texts address must possess a degree of competence in reading and interpreting such texts. The *common* sense of justice goes beyond the limits of literacy; it must also be made manifest as an experience. In other words, the idea of justice cannot be divorced from the concept of the public arena as a *space of collective experience*.[19] This also means that, as the conditions of collective experience change, the common sense of justice changes accordingly. The disturbing fact for both the law and literature is the threatened loss of control over the public sphere in the face of the enormous power of competing agencies of public discourse such as the newspaper and tabloid press, radio, and television. Thus the Warren Commission, for instance, after its investigation of President John F. Kennedy's assassination and the subsequent shooting of Lee Harvey Oswald in front of television cameras, stated that "part of the responsibility for the unfortunate circumstances ... must be borne by the news media." The commission also asserted that the media had completely upset the delicate balance between public judgment and judgment by the law, because the "experience in Dallas [was] a dramatic affirmation of the need for steps to bring about a proper balance between the right of the public to be kept informed and the right of the individual to a fair and impartial trial."[20]

Although the press claims that it only serves the strong public interest in the law and in justice, its "imperatives for newsworthiness, salability, speed, and excitement" work against the "solemn, dispassionate, calculated rules of evidence and the punctilious rules of court."[21] But television differs from written news in that the camera appears to be a much more impartial instrument of recording than the subjective descriptions of an individual observer. Television can document the rules of evidence and of the court with much more persuasiveness and truth than any other verbal medium. At least, that is what Friendly and Goldfarb could still assert in 1967:

> The dignity and integrity of trials depends on the participants, and not on television's portrayal of them. The

> performance of some attorneys at some trials is obnoxious, even without cameras; cameras would merely show it for what it is... . It is hardly an argument against the medium to assert that television may show a performance, good or bad, more vividly to more people.[22]

The idea of the transparency of the medium has always been the major argument for the defense of courtroom television by its proponents, even though it has developed from its early, experimental phase into a full-blown commercial enterprise. Celebrating television's "glass eye," Anna Quindlen of the *New York Times* enthusiastically remarked in 1991: "The raw material from which we reporters build stories on – most of it was there on screen. It was the first time ... that I could cover a story just as well from my living room as I could on the scene."[23] The problem, however, as Paul Thaler puts it, is that "television is hardly a glass eye, a benign and remote technology; rather, it is a powerful and active observer ... that narrowly frames the world ... to dictate 'meaning.'" For Thaler, a television trial "has added an entirely new dimension to the process [of justice]: a vast, mediated public, emotionally involved with the issues and controversy attached to a particular case."[24] Quindlen's assessment of the function of the camera suggests yet another predicament of legal rhetoric in the "age of the television trial." With the advent of courtroom television, the image has entered the inner sanctum of the word – of law and justice as a story – and turned it into yet another image. And this image threatens to become the transparent, the ideal, indeed, the "mystical" source of authority.

Abe Ringel, the protagonist of *The Advocate's Devil*, resembles his creator in obvious ways.[25] Both are defense lawyers from a Jewish, urban background who strongly believe in the principle of "innocent until proven guilty" and both are highly media conscious. In fact, the media have become such a decisive force in the legal system that no one involved can escape. Dershowitz describes Ringel's relation to the media in terms that most likely match his own:

> Abe was accessible to the media – most of the time. He had spent years building these relationships because

that was how the legal system worked – for better or for worse, press coverage was part of the game, and spin was the first rule [*Advocate's Devil,* 88].

Dershowitz, a professor at Harvard Law School, has been active in a number of the most spectacular and controversial trials in recent American legal history. He has defended, among others, Mike Tyson, Claus von Bülow, Michael Milken, and O. J. Simpson. In a book about the Simpson trial, Dershowitz explains why the lawyer has to observe the rules of the media game:

> Why should lawyers care about public relations? Their job is to persuade judges and jurors, not the public or the pundits. But the jurors come from the same public that would be watching [the case] on television: And judges, too, are human beings, who are influenced by public opinion.[26]

In the same book, he also notes that "many observers ... derived the wrong lessons from this case, largely because of the way much of the press, radio, and television treated it." Despite the intense media coverage of the trial, Dershowitz warns, crucial facts about it still remained invisible and therefore unintelligible to the larger public:

> Even those who watched the trial's live coverage saw only what went on in the courtroom itself, and not in the field, where investigation took place, or in the lawyers' offices, where many of the crucial decisions were made.[27]

The lawyer plays to two audiences at once, in two different courts: that of the law and that of the media public. Both games have rules that, though they may be similar in some respects, have to be distinguished carefully lest the difference between justice according to the law and justice according to public opinion break down. The major difference, as Dershowitz persistently points out, is that, while the public's judgment is mostly and almost inevitably based on belief – because people rely on "secondary sources," any juror's judgment and his or her decision must be based on doubt – reasonable doubt.

> The jurors in the Simpson case were not asked to vote on whether they believed "he did it." They were asked *whether the prosecution's evidence proved beyond a reasonable doubt that he did it*.[28]

As Dershowitz knows only too well, often enough such fine distinctions get blurred, especially in cases where the interests at stake reach far beyond those of the parties directly involved. As the modern media have gradually eroded the difference between the court of public opinion and that of the law judge and jury have been turned into public players, while the public audience is asked to sit on the bench. This also means that trials are no longer confined to a courtroom; before they can be decided in a court of law, they have already been argued in the public court of the media.

The confusion of the rules and the delicate relation between belief and doubt are at the center of *The Advocate's Devil*. When the famous basketball player Joe Campell asks Ringel to defend him against the charge of date rape, the lawyer accepts the case as a welcome opportunity to boost his public image with the successful defense of a celebrity client because "a victory in the Campell case would propel him into that small circle of lawyers whose names were immediately recognized around the country" (*Advocate's Devil,* 184). The problem is that Ringel wants to be both publicly known and professionally recognized, he wants to be on "the popular TV talk shows" as well as in "the casebooks that law students read" (*Advocate's Devil,* 183). In other words, the media-savvy lawyer's dream is to reconcile the image of justice with its exemplary text(s).

The Campell case turns into a lawyer's nightmare, however. The basketball star emerges as a pathological liar who is probably as guilty as hell, yet his competence in handling the media is of a superior order. Dershowitz gradually shows Campell as something of a law student himself; he checks out his dates by making his own little studies of the law's casebooks. Searching through electronic databases such as CompuLaw on the Internet, he looks for women who have claimed to be rape victims and whose claims have been denied in court and whose accused perpetrators are acquitted. Campell then sets up "chance" meetings with his victims, first to seduce and then to rape them. As Campell well knows, the women's credibility will prove to be severely damaged in the event of a trial. Campell thus uses the media to play off the law against itself, a cunning strategy that leads to the near-rape of Ringel's daughter, who is saved only in the very last minute. As a computer illiterate, Ringel for a long time remains blind to the immense power of this criminal use of information; his desire to get Campell acquitted for his own public profit proves stronger than his growing awareness of his client's guilt.

Campell is the "advocate's devil" precisely because he is able to use the power of the image against the text of the law and its rules in and out of court. He upsets the hierarchy that guarantees the authority of word over image, and in the trial he successfully introduces visual evidence that is not sworn and so cannot be recorded against the "stories," that is, the recorded testimony, of the prosecution witnesses. This is exactly the point where the authority of the law and of justice clashes with Campell's power over the image – his own image.

When Ringel first meets Campell, he is very careful about the story that his client tells him, because he knows that any changes in the story may shatter his defense:

> Don't let the client tell you his story before he understands the implications of what he is saying... If a client told one story at the outset and then changed it, this created big problems both for the lawyer and client. Most criminal defense lawyers had become ... cautious about letting their clients ramble on without some structure [*Advocate's Devil,* 36-37].

The facts of the case, from a defense lawyer's perspective, present a story that must appear structured, orderly, and consistent. Only then can the story, as told by the client, be used for his defense of his client. Defendant and attorney are thus both "authors," albeit in very different senses. The story allows for both the authorization and the control of the truth (or the lie) of the client's innocence by the lawyer, which is as much a means of power as of self-protection. Narrative consistency is not only the sign of truth, for the lawyer it is also the basis for the belief in the client's innocence. Ringel is thus afraid to hear his client's "untutored version of the facts" (*Advocate's Devil,* 37), because the "Supreme Court had recently ruled that if a lawyer knows his client is lying, he is not permitted to put him on the witness stand" (ibid., 36). Even when he finds out that Campell has been lying to him, Ringel sticks to this legal logic of narrative truth, unaware that his client tells his story with very different means. The problem is that Ringel's legal definition of knowledge (of the truth) is so completely tied to words that everything that escapes verbal description and definition cannot be accounted for. When his colleague argues that "you can't call Campell as a witness if you know he's going to lie about anything" (*Advocate's Devil,* 195), Ringel replies that his duty as a defense lawyer "is to separate the part of the truth that helps the client from the part that hurts" (ibid., 197). This separation, however, exists only through and for verbal discourse; it is made possible solely by the law's decision about what is being uttered and what has to remain silent. What does not get into the record does not exist as fact. To control the story is to control the facts.

Yet, despite Ringel's efforts to control the testimony of his client and to refuse to let him take the stand, Joe Campell manages to testify eloquently to his innocence:

> Jennifer [the rape victim] began to weep softly. Several of the jurors were looking at her as she sobbed. Ms. Scuba Diver's eyes [the forewoman of the jury, thought to be highly critical of Campell] were firmly on Campell's head, which was shaking gently back and forth. He must have been aware that the forewoman was observing him as he squinted slightly and formed a silent tsk, tsk sound. The effect of these subtle movements by Campell was to send a pained message of disappointment in Jennifer for finally crossing the line from truth to falsehood [*Advocate's Devil,* 227]

Nonverbal communication turns into an eloquent and devastating commentary on verbal testimony. The performance of the visual image of pained disappointment renders the story of the witness false; the image literally pushes the word across "the line from truth to falsehood." Campell thus uses the techniques of the public image – evoking belief, aiming at emotional response – to overturn the authority of verbal testimony and witnessing. Ringel only slowly becomes aware of what is actually happening:

> At first Abe didn't understand what Campell was trying to do. Then it hit him: Campell was testifying without taking the witness stand. He was having a ... private conversation with ... most important and dangerous member of the jury... And from the look on [her] face, Joe Campell seemed to be scoring, as usual [*Advocate's Devil*, 228]

What is so scandalous and upsetting for Ringel about Campell's behavior is that it turns the law court into a public court, dominated by strategies of the image. Because the way he singles out the forewoman through "eye-contact" to make her believe his image of disappointment and innocence is exactly the way Campell picks out one-night-stands from his audience at the basketball game. Even though he "used lust" (*Advocate's Devil*, 250) to communicate his innocence, Campell merely employs the image's excess of performative power, an excess that both addresses and satisfies the public's *desire to believe* in innocence or in guilt. The decisive gesture is the transformation of the courtroom and of the witness stand from spaces of the word and its professions into spaces, or better, screens for the image and its projections. This is where the image escapes the rules of legal discourse, where it successfully bypasses the control of the visual by the verbal in order to become an eloquent though silent proof, a piece of hard evidence always off the record.

Ringel, the media-conscious lawyer, thus becomes haunted by what Thaler calls the "Faustian Bargain": Once the image is allowed into the court of the law, which after all is still a court of verbal and written discourse, the rules of the game are changed forever. Campell, in a way, is Ringel's Mephistopheles. The promise of public recognition and professional acclaim has a sinister downside, as Ringel "had to worry about how to defend his client without losing his bar certificate – or his soul" (*Advocate's Devil*, 179).

Despite their differences, both novels give us as a central figure a man of the law who is also a man of letters. Both the older Judge Tnomas Crease in *Frolic* and Ringel's teacher Haskel Levine in *Advocate's Devil* live in the world of the word, are shut off from the public and the media, and die in the course of the novel. For Ringel, Haskel represents a bygone era, when it was possible "to emerge as the greatest and most respected lawyer in Boston without ever seeing the inside of a television or radio station." Haskel "never comment[s] about a legal matter outside of the courtroom" (*Advocate's Devil,* 185) and unlike his favorite pupil never had any difficulty finding the right balance between the desire for public recognition and the autonomy of the law. Haskel thus embodies Dershowitz's own criticism of the increasing impact of court television and public trials, while Ringel's acknowledgment of the important role of the media well reflects Dershowitz's own practices and appearances on television and radio. Ringel relies heavily on the wisdom of his teacher. Whenever he has a problem, he visits Haskel, hoping the old feeble man will give him advice. This advice usually takes obscure form, such as riddles, anecdotes, or fables, condensed quotes from the shared past of both law and literature, the past of oral and written tradition, or the verbal past. The authority of Haskel's "precedents," that is, the cases he uses as examples, relies exclusively on the authority of the word or, more precisely, on "stories" without authors that have already acquired the status of common wisdom or common sense.

The same can be said of Judge Crease, Oscar's father, who peppers his opinions with literary allusions and proverbs taken from literary and legal texts but already belonging to traditional lore. The old judge's texts stand in stark contrast to the sophistry of his younger colleagues, the indiscriminate dispersive images of television, and the desperate and mindless Babel of spoken discourse. In his opinions, the authority of the person and that of the text (of the words) converge and thus profess to each other's power. These are the only instances in the novel where the text acquires a body and where words are not merely uttered but embodied in a distinct and highly original style and voice.

Both Haskel and Judge Crease represent an almost archaic authority of legal and literary discourse that is bygone and about to be replaced by the authority of the image. They are the defenders of the dying word, who strictly separate the public from the court of the law. Their rhetoric is informed by rules, rules that come from language and are observed by language; a strictness of form that guards the word from the image and at the same time regulates it, controls it. William Gaddis and Alan Dershowitz seem to agree about the devastating effect of a totally commercialized production of images, yet Gaddis appears much more pessimistic about the possible resistance of legal and literary discourse. How can either survive the transformation into a travesty? Dershowitz, in contrast, believes in the power of the word, or, more precisely, in the authority of the author over the text. In the end, Ringel reads a letter aloud at his mentor's grave, arguing against the introduction of blanket rules and instead insists that "every lawyer will have to continue to struggle with the dilemma" (*Advocate's Devil,* 372), that there is no absolute security, no absolute justice in language. The common sense of justice, after all, cannot be ruled by words alone, because it will always be haunted by the desire for and the belief in the image.

Notes

1. As Pierre Bourdieu argues in *Language and Symbolic Power* (Cambridge, 1991), 230, authority is granted to individuals according to the specific power structure of a given partition of the entire field of social practices. These partitions are called fields by Bourdieu who insists that while any field may assume to be autonomous from other fields, its objective autonomy is always relative to the hierarchy of power between all fields. More important for the following argument is the fact that the autonomy of any field, while being more or less perfect in some respects, may be severely challenged where its regulating interest converges with those of other fields – as in the question of authorship and authority between law and literature. See also his remarks on the power of naming, ibid., 239-40, and on codification in *In Other Words* (Cambridge, 1990), 76-77.
2. The term "common sense" has been emphasized because it will be used in the following discussion in both its main connotation – as a lesser and more vague term for "meaning" or "significance" – and also as referring to a perceptual competence, meaning both "to be attentive or sensitive to" and "to be aware of," "to have a sense" for something.
3. On the thin line between rhetoric as referring to the truth and rhetoric as a means of deception, Richmond Y. Hathorn, "Rhetoric," in *Encyclope-*

dia Americana (Danbury, Conn., 1992), 466, remarks: "In ancient times attempts were made to specify that rhetoric is properly 'the lending of effectiveness to truth' and that an orator is 'a good man skilled in speaking,' but truth and goodness often seem to have been ignored by the Sophists. Hence ... ever since Plato the term 'rhetoric' has tended to suggest 'artful bombast and verbal chicanery.'"

4. For the changing structure of public opinion and the role of mass media see Jürgen Habermas, *The Structural Transformation of the Public Sphere,* trans. Thomas Burger with Frederick Lawrence (Cambridge, Mass., 1989); for the changing concepts of vision and visuality, see Donald Lowe, *The History of Bourgeois Perception* (Chicago, 1982).
5. W.I.T. Mitchell, *Iconology: Image, Text, Ideology* (Chicago, 1986), 43.
6. David Mellinkoff, *Language of the Law* (Boston, 1963), vii. Profession, according to *Webster's Third New International Dictionary of the English Language* (London 1971), 1811, is 2. "an act of openly declaring or publicly claiming a belief, faith, or opinion: an avowed statement or expression of intention or purpose." It is also 4a. "a calling requiring specialized knowledge and ... instruction in skills and methods as well as in the ... principles underlying such methods, maintaining by force of organization or concerted opinion high standards of achievement and conduct, and committing its members to continued study and to a kind of work which has for its prime purpose the rendering of public service." A profession, in other words, legitimately exists only in and through an act of publicly sanctioned speech that is binding on those who are allowed (or required) to utter it and excludes those who are unable (or prohibited) to do so.
7. Mellinkoff, *Language of the Law,* 138-39 (emphasis added).
8. Ibid., 139-40.
9. Martin Kayman, "Lawful Writing: Common Law, Statute, and the Properties of Literature," *New Literary History,* 27 (1996), 761-83; Mark Rose, "The Author as Proprietor: *Donaldson* v. *Becket* and the Genealogy of Modern Authorship," *Representations,* No. 23 (1988), 51-85. See Jacques Derrida's thorough discussion of the legitimation of the law's authority in his "Force of Law: The 'Mystical Foundation of Authority,'" in Drucilla Cornell et al., eds., *Deconstruction and the Possibility of Justice* (New York, 1992), 12, prompted by a passage from Pascal that puts the point succinctly: "Custom is the sole basis for equity, for the simple reason that it is received; it is the mystical foundation of its authority. Whoever traces it to its source annihilates it."
10. Kayman, "Lawful Writing," 768, 772.
11. Ibid., 773.
12. Joseph Vining, "Generalization in Interpretive Theory," *Representations,* No. 30, 1-12, quotation on 6.
13. Kayman, "Lawful Writing," 765; Shelley, " Defence of Poetry," in R. Ingpen and W. E. Peck, eds., *The Complete Works of Percy Bysshe Shelley,* vol. 7 (New York, 1965), 140. See also Bourdieu, *Language and Symbolic Power,* 42: "Legal discourse is ... speech which brings into existence that

which it utters... In other words, it is the divine word, the word of divine right, which, like the *intuitus originarius* which Kant ascribed to God., creates what it states, in contrast to all derived, observational statements, which simply record a pre-existent given. One should never forget that language, by virtue of the infinite generative but also *originative capacity* – in the Kantian sense – which it derives from its power to produce existence by producing the collectively recognized, and thus realized, representation of existence, is no doubt the principal support of the dream of absolute power."

14. Guy Debord, *The Society of the Spectacle* (New York, 1994), 3.
15. References to William Gaddis, *A Frolic of His Own* (New York, 1994). are cited in parentheses in the text of this essay. Jonathan Raban, "At Home in Babel," *New York Review of Books,* Feb. 17, 1994, 3. See George A. Kennedy, *The Art of Persuasion in Greece* (Princeton, 1963), 26-29, and *Classical Rhetoric and Its Christian and Secular Tradition from Ancient to Modern Times* (London, 1980), 18-21.
16. Deborah Tannen, *The Argument Culture* (New York, 1998), 131.
17. Marie Maclean, *Narrative as Performance: The Baudelairean Experiment* London, 1988), 7, 8.
18. Raban, "At Home in Babel," 3; Joseph Tabbi, *Postmodern Sublime: Technology and American Writing from Mailer to Cyberpunk* (Ithaca, N. Y., 1995), 180.
19. As Lance W. Bennett and Marta S. Feldman state in *Reconstructing Reality in the Courtroom: Justice and Judgment in American Culture* (New Brunswick, N. J., 1981), 20, "Even though justice procedures may vary, they have the common function of enabling members of society to understand ... the grounds for fair and just settlements of disputes. This implies that if the terms of justice are to make sense to the average members of society, the formal procedures of justice must somehow incorporate everyday means of communication and judgment." (New Brunswick, N. J., 1981), 20. Unfortunately, Bennett's and Feldman's important investigation of the crucial function of storytelling strategies in the courtroom almost exclusively relies on a concept of telling, a narratology. Written before the advent of Court TV, the book can offer only implicit suggestions as to how much "everyday means of communication and judgment" have changed under the growing influence of aggressive strategies of visualization; see esp. chap. 2.
20. Warren Commission, quoted in Alfred Friendly and Ronald L. Goldfarb, *Crime and Publicity: The Impact of News on the Administration of Justice* (New York, 1967), 10.
21. Ibid.
22. Ibid., 239.
23. Quindlen, quoted in Paul Thaler, *The Watchful Eye: American Justice in the Age of the Television Trial* (Westport, Conn., 1994), xxii.
24. Ibid., 12.
25. References to Alan Dershowitz, *The Advocate's Devil* (New York, 1994), are given in parentheses in the text of this essay.

26. Dershowitz, *Reasonable Doubts: The O. J. Simpson Case and the Criminal Justice System* (New York, 1996), 29.
27. Ibid., 29.
28. Ibid., 17, 38.

7

"The Promise of American Life": Derrick Bell, Critical Race Theory, and the American Jeremiad

Marcus Bruce

> The faith of Americans in their own country is religious, if not in its intensity, at any rate in its almost absolute and universal authority. It constitutes the kind of faith which is the implication, rather than the object, of thought, and consciously or unconsciously it enters largely into our personal lives as a formative influence. We may distrust and dislike much that is done in the name of our country by our fellow-country-men; but our country itself, its democratic system, and its prosperous future are above suspicion.
> – Herbert Croly, *The Promise of American Life*

During the last ten years, Derrick Bell, the civil rights lawyer, legal scholar, and law school professor, has published a series of provocative and rigorously argued books that challenge the governing concepts of American legal discourse and distinguish their author as a formidable legal scholar and critic of the law. Bell, whose career as a committed civil rights lawyer and staff attorney for the NAACP Legal Defense and Education Fund preceded his tenure as a law school professor, has been a vociferous, informed critic of both American legal discourse, especially in regard to race and gender, and American legal institutions, such as law schools and the Supreme Court, that play a fundamental role in defining the nature and scope of the law. Furthermore, Bell's recent scholarship and pedagogy, like his activist-scholar role, serve as points of a departure for a new, less traditional approach to legal scholarship.

Bell's particular approach to the relationship between race and the law has become so distinctive that many critics now identify him with, and many scholars consider him the founder of, a counter legal discourse known as "Critical Race Theory." More a collection of legal scholars and political activists at American law schools than a coherent movement, more a critique of the law than a set of guidelines for transforming the law, Critical Race Theory privileges the voices and concerns of African Americans and other people of color who traditionally have been excluded from conversations and contexts in which the law, both as it is theorized and practiced, is examined, shaped and institutionalized. Sometimes referred to as a "racial critique," Critical Race Theory serves as an advocate in the discussion and practice of the American law for underrepresented groups of Americans whose lives are profoundly shaped by the law.

To date, Bell's published work has sounded, and defined, many of the major topics of Critical Race Theory: the legacy of racism and its impact on American law and legal institutions, the limited impact of civil rights activism and legislation, the continued opposition of many Anglo-Americans to efforts at racial justice and equality, and the need to revise substantially the manner in which the law is studied, practiced, and written.

And We Are Not Saved (1987), less a detached analysis of racialist ideas implicit in the law than a series of lively discussions between Bell and a fictional black female lawyer, chronicles both the history of racially exclusionary legal practices and their social, political, and economic consequences. Bell critiques the methodology and format of legal analysis and reconstructs the history of race relations and the law. *Faces at the Bottom of the Well* (1992) begins with the bold and disturbing claim that racism is a powerful, pervasive, and permanent presence permeating American culture and its institutions and concludes that it is highly unlikely that African Americans will ever fully enjoy the rights and privileges of being American citizens, despite the alleged progress made through affirmative action and civil rights victories. In *Confronting Authority* (1994), an account of Bell's two-year protest at, and eventual resignation from, Harvard Law School over its failure to hire and tenure one woman of color, Bell adopts a more confessional and autobiographical approach, revealing the unusual degree to which his scholarship and academic career are integrated with his social and political commitments.[1]

Yet *The Gospel Choirs,* Bell's most recent book, moves beyond what many scholars and critics consider to be the radical edge of the Critical Race Theorists. Echoing the sobering prognosis of *Faces at the Bottom of the Well, Gospel Choirs* acknowledges that institutional racism and sexism are immune to the kind of legal reform advocated by Critical Race Theorists. This declaration notwithstanding, Bell does not believe this insight is reason for despair, as many of his readers have assumed. Rather, it compels activists to reconsider their motivations, commitments, and resources and so rediscover cultural traditions that have sustained and fortified them in the past. For Bell, African-American gospel music is such a tradition, one that provides a sense of hope in the midst of a desperate situation and becomes the occasion for renewing one's commitment to the struggle for freedom.[2]

In the following essay, I argue that to define Bell's work as primarily a "racial critique" is to miss his call for a profound spiritual transformation of American society. This message is both an extension of and departure from the stated agenda of Critical Race Theory. More important, *Gospel Choirs* revives and continues the American Jeremiad, a cultural tradition that goes well beyond merely critiquing the limitations of the existing social and political order; it also provides exhortation, admonishment, revelation, and enlightenment. By celebrating gospel music, Bell uses an African-American cultural tradition as a means of providing hope and encouragement to Americans confronting the enduring problem of racism.

I discuss and reflect on this text in four ways. First, I offer a brief description of Critical Race Theory, outline its principal themes and issues and examine its critical reception by scholars. Second, I discuss *Gospel Choirs* and examine Bell's conception of religion. Third, I illustrate the manner in which Bell's book is an instance of the literary and cultural tradition called the

American Jeremiad. Finally, I offer a few concluding remarks on Bell and his work.

Critical Race Theory is alternately referred to, by critics and practitioners alike, as a critique, a literature, a field of study, a discipline, a leftist movement, or some or all of these among minority legal scholars at such prestigious law schools as Harvard. Patricia Williams, a law professor at Columbia University Law School and a practitioner of Critical Race Theory, describes it as a "more-or-less annual conference."

> It is by no means a "black" movement, even if you think "race" excludes those who call themselves "white." Informal and interdisciplinary, there is more diversity and disagreement at its meetings than at most academic gatherings, and if there is any ideological coherence to the group, it is a decidedly – indeed insistently – intergrationist bent. Those who attend the conferences are black, white, Latino, Asian and South Asian, Native American, gay, straight, libertarian, Marxist, gentile, Jewish, Buddhist, feminist, Hindu, Muslim, Republican, pleasant, uncooperative and agnostic.[3]

Jeffrey Rosen, writing for *The New Republic*, sees something more spurious and insidious about Critical Race Theory and its practitioners. With its emphasis on the deconstruction of traditional legal practice and discourse, Critical Race Theory represents "a stark challenge to the liberal ideal of the rule of law." Rosen considers the now infamous O. J. Simpson case a disturbing example of the detrimental impact of Critical Race Theory and makes a provocative argument that the courtroom strategy of Johnnie Cochran, Simpson's defense attorney, was an instance of "applied critical race theory."[4]

Yet it seems both critics and practitioners agree that Critical Race Theory is an intellectual strategy designed to bring about legal, social, and political reform, especially in regard to racial justice and equality. Dissatisfied with the efforts, and many would argue the failure, of the civil rights movement to achieve equality and justice through litigation, Critical Race Theorists turn their attention to a more systematic critique of the law and legal institutions. Three features distinguish Critical Race Theory as an intellectual strategy.

First, Critical Race Theory aims its critique at traditional legal discourse, especially discussions about the nature, study, and practice of the law. Critical Race Theorists charge that traditional legal discourse is profoundly shaped and dominated by the racialized assumptions, concepts, principles, procedures, and cultural boundaries of Anglo-Americans. In contrast to a literary view of culture, critic R.W.B. Lewis once suggested, as an unfolding dialogue containing a number of voices and a debate over the ideas that preoccupy it, Critical Race Theorist would argue that American legal discourse is a monologue, a one-sided conversation that has taken place among a small group of Anglo-Americans to the exclusion of women, African Americans, and other people of color. To paraphrase the work of Lani Guinier, Critical Race Theorists challenge "the tyranny of the majority" over our understanding of the law.[5]

Second, Critical Race Theory is distinguished by an interdisciplinary methodology that employs new categories and concepts in the analysis of the law. Drawing on postmodern scholarship in philosophy, literary criticism, and the social sciences, practitioners of Critical Race Theory identify and deconstruct the assumptions, values, and beliefs veiled by the terms and categories used to define and frame the law, terms such as "neutrality," "objectivity," and "universality." The courts and law schools, they add, institutionalize this view of the law, reinscribing and reinforcing the very cultural assumptions that prevent a multiperspective view of the law.

To address this problem, Critical Race Theorists introduce a new set of categories into the discussion of how lawyers analyze, practice, and teach the law. These categories make visible and represent a range of issues, concerns, and experiences that have been present since the creation of American law and legal institutions yet rendered silent by the traditional practice and teaching of the law. Race, gender, class, and sexual orientation, among others, give voice to the silences in traditional legal discourse and correct the blindness of the law. Using race as a category of analysis, for example, allows theorists to demonstrate the extent to which racism is more than a set of isolated incidents; rather, it is endemic to American society (culture) and present in its institutions. Regarding racism, Charles Lawrence, a law professor at Georgetown University and a proponent of Critical Race Theory, writes:

> Racism in America is much more complex than either the conscious conspiracy of a power elite or the simple delusion of a few ignorant bigots. It is a part of our common historical experience and, therefore, a part of our culture. It arises from the assumptions we have learned to make about the world, ourselves, and others as well as from the patterns of our fundamental social activities.[6]

If the law is a social construction, as many of the critical Race Theorists argue, the introduction of new categories, perspectives, social histories, and concepts into the discussion of the law enriches and enlarges our understanding of what equality, justice, and fairness mean to different Americans. The law, Critical Race Theorists insist, should reflect that diversity of society.

Third, Critical Race Theory attempts to undermine the dominant narratives of traditional legal discourse by means of legal storytelling. This entails not only a critical analysis of conventional legal narratives used in legal histories, case studies, and courtroom proceedings but also the adoption of a wide range of literary forms that compel lawyers, legal scholars, and law students to view legal issues from the perspective of African Americans, women, and people of color. Critical Race Theorist use allegories, fantasies, autobiographies, parables, social histories, personal anecdotes, and stories to represent the experiences and cultures of people who are invisible before the law. This experimentation with literary form is more than a mere aesthetic consideration, a dissatisfaction with the linear, monotone notes found in law school reviews. It is an attempt to privilege the voices and social histories of people left out of traditional legal narratives and to document their experiences under the law. It also reflects a pedagogical mission. By using alternate forms of narratives and counter storytelling, theorists hope to teach their readers that there are many different ways to see, convey, and understand "reality" and the law.

The popular and academic response to the writings of some of the leading proponents of the theory has been varied. The Manhattan Institute's *City Journal* and *The Wall Street Journal* dismiss the theory as a threat to the law and legal institutions, as another form of political correctness that creates a conceptual ghetto inhabited by leftists, black radicals, and nihilistic law professors. In "The Bloods and the Crits," Rosen indiscriminately clumps together a number of recently published books on the subject of race in America and considers them sufficient evidence of the pervasive and detrimental influence of Critical Race Theory. Citing works by A. Leon Higginbotham, Jr., Jeffrey Toobin, Johnnie Cochran, Christopher Darden, Richard Delgado, and others, Rosen is skeptical, at best, regarding the benefits of Critical Race Theory as an intellectual strategy and legal reform movement.

Randall Kennedy, an African-American professor at Harvard Law School and a former colleague of Bell's, offers what many scholars consider to be the most substantive and well-argued critique of Critical Race Theory. In a 1989 essay on "Racial Critiques of Legal Academia," Kennedy reviews the writings of Bell, Delgado, and Mari Matsuda and analyzes what he identifies as the twofold thesis of most contemporary "racial critiques" such as Critical Race Theory: the exclusion thesis, the claim that the intellectual work of minority scholars has been undervalued in legal academia, and the distinctiveness thesis, the claim that minority legal scholars bring a unique perspective which white or Anglo-American scholars are unable to provide. Kennedy believes Critical Race Theory challenges the legal profession's understanding of itself, yet he has serious doubts about both its claims and its coherence as an intellectual strategy.[7]

Regarding the exclusion thesis, Kennedy finds no substantial evidence that contemporary law schools have attempted systematically to exclude black lawyers and scholarship from traditional legal discourse or institutions. Kennedy attributes the small numbers of black legal scholars in law school and the limited audience for their work to the absence of a strong black intellectual tradition in the study of the law. Where Bell, Delgado, Matsuda, and others are inclined to see racism as the primary reason for the low enrollment of black law students, small percentages of minority law faculty, and negative responses to government policies designed to address racial inequality, Kennedy considers a plethora of circumstances, some of which have nothing directly to do with racism, to be more of a factor. Kennedy believes recent developments, in particular the kind of self-critical examination of the academic establishment brought on by critical legal studies and the study of race relations and the law, promise a more receptive audience for black scholars and scholarship in the future.

Kennedy also doubts the additional claim that African-American students, lawyers, and law professors possess some special racial knowledge that entitles them to a place in the academy or makes their status at law schools unique. "One's racial (gender, religious, regional) identity," he writes, "is no substitute for the disciplined study essential to achieving expertise."[8] Knowledge of a specific racial group's experience neither qualifies one to be nor is a prerequisite for being a good lawyer. Ultimately, Kennedy questions the fundamental belief of Critical Race Theorists that their scholarship offers a unique, substantive, and coherent contribution to discussions of the nature, practice, and reform of the law.

One can find numerous examples of both the exclusion and the distinctiveness theses in Bell's writings. Kennedy's essay discusses at length evidence of Bell's reliance on both claims. At the heart of Bell's "racial critique" Kennedy finds a tendency to fault the racial prejudice of white academics for the underachievement of black intellectuals and legal scholars. Yet Kennedy's entire analysis is predicated on classifying Bell's writings, and those of most Critical Race Theorists, as racial critique literature, which use the category of race to examine "the nature and consequences of racial conflict within legal academia."[9] In *Gospel Choirs,* Bell attempts a new and slightly different intellectual strategy.

In a 1998 interview, Bell announced that his most recent books, *Gospel Choirs* and *Afrolantica,* marked a new departure in his writing and from his primary focus on legal reform. "In each of the books I was aiming beyond the law, beyond law students, beyond lawyers." Bell confessed: "I wanted to reach lay people, but I certainly had the others in mind." This is especially true of *Gospel Choirs*. "I think in *Gospel*," Bell reflected, "I'm less concerned with reaching the professional, the academics in law, than I was in say, the first book [*And We Are Not Saved*]... I just think it's fruitless to try, through legal analysis, to win a case when so much is caught up in the social and political situation." *Gospel Choirs,* Bell added, addresses the "spiritual nature of life" and offers gospel music to committed activists as a "source of strength" and a means to develop a "faith in something beyond our present situation."[10]

These insights notwithstanding, readers are left wondering how a text proposing gospel music as a solution for legal, social, economic, and political issues can remedy the very problems that legal reform and civil rights legislation failed to solve? Kennedy proposes that the writings of Critical Race Theorists are best read as "provocative thought pieces" designed primarily to jar the courts, law schools, and lawyers from their ideological slumber. Yet how can what Bell calls the "restructuring of our spiritual selves" supply the resources and solutions necessary for combating the social ills – racism, sexism, classism, homophobia – that plague American society?[11] What are the nature and the purpose of the strategies proposed by Bell? How can religion, or more specifically spirituality, achieve the reform and changes that Bell seeks through his work? The answers to these and other questions can be found in a discussion of the book's topics, narrative style, and conception of religion.

Gospel Choirs addresses many of the controversial themes and issues identified with Critical Race Theory: institutionalized racism, white skin privilege, racial hostility, black stereotypes, affirmative action programs, the limited social and political impact of civil rights litigation, and the history of hostility to and violence against blacks in America. In addition to these themes Bell adds new topics, ones that have more to do with the moral, spiritual, and communal life of African Americans. He turns his racial critique on the black community and reveals a number of ways in which African Americans have faltered in their efforts toward freedom. He explores particular manifestations of sexism, homophobia, elitism, and exploitation in the black community and offers an unflinching critique of the various ways in which blacks deny to each other the very freedoms withheld (from them) by the larger society.

The book also marks Bell's continued experimentation with form. As in his previous books, *Gospel Choirs* is an extraordinary demonstration of skill, using a variety of literary forms to convey a complex message. Each of the fourteen chapters and the prologue that compose the book adopts a different approach to the range of issues that have come to characterize the work of Critical Race Theorists. Chapter one uses the fantasy of the space traders tale to reveal the patriotism that leads a group of African Americans, abducted by aliens, to return to their earthly home after being abandoned and sold by their Anglo-American compatriots. Chapter six, a fictional encounter between Bell and his lawyer, who is African American and a lesbian, reveals the deep-rooted homophobia of the black community and the obvious yet overlooked connections between civil rights and gay issues. Chapters ten and eleven discuss black sexism and gender equality by means of a candid conversation between two black men, Bell and a cab driver, and a fantasy about the powerful and liberating effect of a million black women spontaneously and collectively dancing a popular step called the Electric Slide. Chapter fourteen, presented in the form of a sermon delivered by Bell's best-known character, the African-American lawyer Geneva Crenshaw, recounts how gospel music, once maligned and banned from black churches, eventually surmounted the resistance of the black community and became a source of hope and strength in the midst of the frequent hostilities of American society.

In *Confronting Authority,* Bell related how readers and audiences ask him, on more than one occasion, whether there are any remedies or solutions to the continuing problem of race in America. *Gospel Choirs* is his answer, one that proposes using African-American religion to address the permanence of racism. The topics and genres of *Gospel Choirs* are profoundly shaped by Bell's use of religion as a strategy for pursuing racial justice and overcoming the inevitable obstacles that one encounters. It is here that we begin to see the role that gospel music plays in the book.

This is not the first time Bell has drawn on religious ideas. There has always been an otherworldly or spiritual dimension to his writing. Beginning with "The Civil Rights Chronicles," Bell has introduced characters, scenarios, and themes that suggest to his readers that Bell is concerned with more than meets the eye. Geneva Crenshaw, Bell's fictional alter ego, who mysteriously appears and disappears throughout his writing, belongs to a "celestial curia" who travel back and forth in time, judging the world's progress toward racial justice and providing insight on the consequences of racism to everyone from the framers of the Constitution to black churchgoers.[12] In addition to this, each of Bell's books alludes to the power of religious faith and the need to bring about a religious conversion of American attitudes regarding racism.

Yet Bell has little interest in denominational religious practices and, despite his occasional reference to the black church, he is not seeking to win converts to an established religious tradition such as Christianity. Religion is a stratagem designed to give a new perspective from which to understand the relations between race and the law in America. To understand this point better it might help to reflect for a moment on precisely how Bell uses religion.

The anthropologist Clifford Geertz describes religion as a cultural system that provides both a conceptual order to the world and a set of symbols to which people develop strong attachment. Religion, Geertz writes in his now classic definition,

> is a system of symbols which acts to establish powerful, pervasive, and long- lasting moods and motivations in people by formulating conceptions of a general order of existence and clothing those conceptions with such an aura of factuality that the moods and motivations seem uniquely realistic.[13]

Following Geertz's definition, Bell's critique of the law can be viewed as an analysis of the fundamental faith Americans place in the civil order and civic discourse. Bell aims his critique at the conceptual order implicit in traditional legal discourse and expressed by symbolic language such as rights, justice, equality, and fairness. This conceptual order and symbolic language constitutes a system of symbols that shape American attitudes toward society, politics, economics, the law, and even African Americans. American faith in the democratic system, in what Herbert Croly called "the promise of American life," is the focal issue of *Gospel Choirs*.[14] Bell suggests applying African-American gospel music as a means of both critiquing the manner in which Americans have failed to realize the promise of American life and illustrating how African Americans have remained committed to the struggle for freedom. One way to illustrate the manner in which Bell both criticizes and reaffirms the promise of American life is to view *Gospel Choirs* as a moment in the rhetorical tradition known as the American Jeremiad. As I suggested earlier, there is a strategy at work here that draws affirmation, critical insight, and strength from African-American religious traditions.

Sacvan Bercovitch, a literary scholar and historian at Harvard University, first proposed the thesis that jeremiads, or political sermons, have been used throughout American history as a way of creating and maintaining the myth of America.[15] The jeremiad, Bercovitch explains, draws its name and character from the seventh-sixth century B.C.E. Hebrew prophet Jeremiah, who denounced the Jewish people for their failure to remain faithful to the Mosaic covenant. Jeremiah prophesied that God would allow the invading Babylonians to destroy Jerusalem and punish Jews for their apostasy. Yet Jeremiah assured the Hebrew people that their repentance would be rewarded with a new covenant with God. Bercovitch offers John Winthrop's 1630 speech, "A Modell of Christian Charity," as the prototypical American Jeremiad that firmly established, in the mind of New Englanders at least, the cultural myth that America is a divinely chosen nation with a special mission and sacred history. Winthrop's now-classic oration not only established that the political order was founded on a divine covenant with God but also warned that there would be disastrous consequences for the community if it failed to remember and remain steadfast in its commitment, or promise, to God.

Although Bercovitch is by no means the first scholar, nor the last, to recognize the Jeremiah-like lamentations, warnings, and exhortations in the sermons of the New England preachers as jeremiads, his innovation lies in arguing that the jeremiad is a cultural form, a rhetorical style, that had been wielded by generations of Americans to achieve ideological consensus regarding their identity, mission, and history. The jeremiad is one instance of America's larger cultural discourse, in which the meaning of America and being American are defined. Bercovitch finds evidence of the jeremiad not only in sermons, but also in "doctrinal treatises, histories, poems, biographies, personal narratives," and novels drawn from different periods of American history.[16]

Historians Wilson Jeremiah Moses and David Howard-Pitney take the idea one step further, identifying a black or Afro-American jeremiad, a rhetoric that takes the form of "constant warnings issued by blacks to whites, concerning the judgment that was to come for the sin of slavery." Elaborating on the idea, Moses writes,

> Blacks ingeniously adapted their rhetoric to the jeremiad tradition, which was one of the dominant forms of cultural expression in revivalistic ante-bellum America. Their use of the jeremiad revealed a conception of themselves as a chosen people, but it also showed a clever ability to play on the belief that America as a whole was a chosen nation with a covenantal duty to deal justly with the blacks.[17]

Howard-Pitney finds evidence of this rhetorical tradition in the speeches of Frederick Douglass, Booker T. Washington, Ida B. Wells, W.E.B. Du Bois, Mary Mcleod Bethune, Martin Luther King, Jr., and Jesse Jackson.[18] King's 1963 "I Have a Dream" speech is a masterful demonstration of not only the powerful and long-lasting effects jeremiads can have on their audiences but also of how the flexibility of the form allows a speaker to say two things at once. Referring to the Constitution of the United States and the Declaration of Independence as "promissory notes," King's jeremiad unflinchingly points out the impoverished social, political, and economic conditions of African Americans and condemns America for failing to make good on its promise. Yet he also reaffirms his belief that the promise of American life can be fulfilled.

Three features of the American Jeremiad can be found in *Gospel Choirs* and qualify it as a work in that rhetorical tradition. American jeremiads emphasize promise, declension, and prophecy. Bell's jeremiad stems from a profound belief in what

Herbert Croly, the founding editor of the *New Republic*, called "the promise of American life." This unspoken belief is fundamental for understanding the outrage, anger, and harsh tone of Bell's critical work. This promise, expressed in documents such as the Declaration of Independence and the Constitution, not only offers "unalienable Rights" (life, liberty, and the pursuit of happiness) to all its citizens but also commits the government to the formation of "a more perfect union." It is a promise expressed in presidential speeches, ritualized by Fourth of July and Thanksgiving celebrations, and ensconced at the heart of America's civic culture. More important though, it is a theme found in Bell's jeremiad.

The title of Bell's first book, *And We Are Not Saved,* is not only a direct quotation from the writings of Jeremiah ("the harvest is past, the summer is ended, and we are not saved": Jeremiah 8:20) but also a statement of the realization that, despite all the achievements and successes of the civil rights movement and legislation, African Americans still do not fully enjoy the rights and privileges of being American citizens. The civil rights movement was an expression of the African-American belief in the promise of American life, "a spiritual manifestation of the continuing faith of a people who have never truly gained their rights in a nation committed by its basic law to the freedom of all."[19]

Gospel Choirs affirms Bell's faith in America's promise and ideals, emphasizing the necessity of remaining committed to ideals, whether or not those goals are ever achieved.

> I realize that the effort to give life to symbolic terms like equality and justice and freedom is not only difficult, which we expect, but may be a misdirection of our energies and hopes. None of them encompasses the essence of human need. Rather, they are terms we try to equate with a good life, one without fear, threat, or domination... *Our belief in our rights gives them life and thus keeps alive our humanity whether or not those rights ever materialize... Our goal is not the achievement of rights – which may or may not happen – but the committed struggle.*[20]

Bell's jeremiad is also a response to America's failure to realize its promise as a nation, to commit itself to the achievement of "life, liberty and the pursuit of happiness" for all its citizens. The limited success of civil rights legislation, continued racial conflicts and hostilities, and ineffectual attempts at racial reforms are but a few examples of America's inability to make the promise of freedom a reality. *Gospel Choirs* is Bell's nagging, insistent reminder that all Americans do not fully enjoy the rights and privileges of being citizens. In the prologue, Bell informs readers that his book is a "written warning" regarding the "ineradicableness of racism" and the worsening conditions of African Americans.

> My immediate challenge was to transform ... evidence of our increasingly dire plight into a written warning, one sufficiently clear to challenge us to action, but not so devastating as to encourage denial or suggest surrender. A warning that would serve to confirm what many of us know but are afraid to acknowledge, that the present suffering of so many could foretell the future fate of us all.[21]

Bell gives his readers some sense of the "future fate" that awaits all Americans in "Nigger Free," chapter eight of *Gospel Choirs*. He repeatedly uses the offensive phrase to drive home an awareness of historically documented riots against African Americans that began as early as the Philadelphia mob gatherings of 1834 and continued well into the twentieth century. Though some critics have taken Bell to task for drawing comparisons between racial violence meted out against African Americans in the past and the outrage of contemporary Anglo-Americans responding to government-sponsored legislation such as Affirmative Action, Bell's jeremiad insists that both the violence of the past and the rage of the present spring from the same seeds of discontent and America's failure to create a more perfect union.

Third, *Gospel Choirs* does offer the possibility of hope, which is contingent on the ability of Americans to remain committed to the struggle for racial justice and equality. Herein lies the significance of the subtitle of the book, "Psalms of Survival in an Alien Land Called Home." Each chapter of the book is a "psalm" or sacred hymn crafted to forewarn, fortify, exhort, admonish, discipline, instruct, and guide readers through their encounters with racism and other forms of discrimination. Each chapter offers a model of the attitudes and conduct that distinguish, in Bell's mind, a person committed to the reform of American society. In chapter twelve, "Equality's Child," Bell imagines equality as a young, precocious child come to life, who is jailed after attempting to make equality and justice realities rather than ideals. "True equality," Bell writes, highlighting the hypocrisy of Americans, "can never be realized in a nation whose people view wealth and status as goals more important than justice and equality, and where the laws are designed to protect vested wealth." Bell encourages his readers to draw strength from these stories and parables, while he reminds them that this hope must be tempered with the under-standing that "the road of disciples and prophets is always hard."[22]

With *Gospel Choirs,* Derrick Bell moves beyond what one critic characterizes as racial critique and emerges with a new intellectual strategy, one rooted in the rhetorical tradition of the American jeremiad. Bell's use of the jeremiad reveals his fundamental belief in the democratic system and the promise of American life. It also gives a new dimension to his work as a Critical Race Theorist. Recommending the adoption of gospel music as a strategy for reform is not so much a claim regarding the superiority of one tradition over another, one cultural group over another, as it is the recognition of what contemporary Americans can learn from gospel music, a cultural tradition that bears witness to the steadfast commitment of African Americans to the ideals of freedom and justice.

Bell accomplishes a number of things with this new intellectual strategy. First, he offers a means for addressing the despair that often results from confronting the enduring problem of racism. *Gospel Choirs* serves as a "spiritual guide" to the kind of issues, questions, and difficulties one must face in order to make the promises of democracy a reality. It also provides models of the conduct that distinguishes the committed individual. Second, Bell's use of gospel music, an African-American cultural tradition, challenges other Americans to view the struggle for freedom from another perspective. This is not only consistent with the goals of Critical Race Theory but it also provides an occasion for other Americans to learn more about history, traditions, and experiences of African Americans. It literally privileges the voices of African Americans over the more dominant voices of American cultural discourse. It is the voice missing from what R.W.B. Lewis referred to as the ongoing conversation of American culture.[23] It counters the assumptions, misconceptions, and stereotypes implicit in the American cultural discourse and offers another perspective from which to understand such fundamental American concepts as justice, liberty, and equality. Finally though, this new strategy, like other jeremiads throughout American history, is a prophetic call from African Americans that criticizes white Americans for their failure to realize the promise of democracy yet encourages them to continue the struggle. For Derrick Bell, it is a call to each American to "sing the songs of Zion," the songs of freedom, in a strange land.

Notes

1. Derrick Bell, *And We Are Not Saved: The Elusive Quest for Racial Justice* (New York, 1987); *Faces at the Bottom of the Well: The Permanence of Racism* (New York, 1992); *Confronting Authority: Reflections of an Ardent Protester* (Boston, 1994).
2. Bell, *The Gospel Choirs: Psalms of Survival in an Alien Land Called Home* (New York, 1996).
3. Patricia J. Williams, "De Jure, De Facto, De Media," *The Nation,* June 2, 1997, 10.
4. Jeffrey Rosen, "The Bloods and Crits," *New Republic,* Dec. 9, 1996, 27.
5. R.W.B. Lewis, *The American Adam: Innocence, Tragedy, and Tradition in the Nineteenth Century* (Chicago, 1955), 1. Lani Guinier, *The Tyranny of the Majority: Fundamental Fairness in Representative Democracy* (New York, 1994).
6. Charles Lawrence, "The Id, the Ego, and Equal Protection: Reckoning with Unconscious Racism," *Stanford Law Review,* 39 (1987), 311, 330; quoted in Bell, *And We Are Not Saved,* 4.
7. Randall Kennedy, "Racial Critiques of Legal Academia," *Harvard Law Review,* 102 (1989), 1745.
8. Ibid., 1777.
9. Ibid., 1748.
10. Bell, "The Booklist Interview," *Booklist,* Feb. 15, 1995, 952. Bell, *Afrolantica Legacies* (Chicago, 1998).

11. Bell, *Gospel Choirs,* 201.
12. Bell, "The Civil Rights Chronicles," foreword to *Harvard Law Review,* 99 (1985), 4- 83.
13. Clifford Geertz, *The Interpretation of Culture: Selected Essays* (New York, 1973), 90.
14. Herbert Croly, *The Promise of American Life* (Cambridge, Mass., 1975; orig. pub. 1914), 1.
15. Sacvan Bercovitch, *The American Jeremiad* (New York, 1978).
16. Ibid., xiv.
17. Wilson Jeremiah Moses, *Black Messiahs and Uncle Toms: Social and Literary Manipulations of a Religious Myth* (University Park, Pa., 1982), 30, 31.
18. David Howard-Pitney, *The Afro-American Jeremiad: Appeals for Justice in America* (Philadelphia, 1990).
19. Bell, *And We Are Not Saved,* xi.
20. Ibid., 186.
21. Ibid., 4.
22. Ibid., 183, 196.
23. Lewis, *American Adam,* 2.

8
Hollywood Courtroom Dramas: The Politics of Judicial Realism

Christophe Den Tandt

In the development of American film, courtroom dramas have not enjoyed the critical attention bestowed, for instance, on the western or the crime thriller. Surprisingly, courtroom films are seldom granted the status of a full-fledged genre, even though they display perfectly circumscribed formal features – an easily identifiable setting and a highly codified narrative program.[1] Admittedly, these films, in spite of their structural consistency, have not created a world of references on a par with the Wild West or the urban jungle: the judicial universe of Spencer Tracy and Stanley Kramer is apparently a less visible film landmark than the mythologized America of John Wayne, James Cagney, John Ford, and Howard Hawks.[2] Nevertheless, judicial movies have proved peculiarly resilient during the course of Hollywood history. Whereas the western succumbed to the ideological upheavals of the 1960s and 1970s, courtroom dramas are still a potent force in the 1990s: Oliver Stone's *JFK* (1991) and Jonathan Demme's *Philadelphia* (1993) have been critical and commercial successes; more recent releases by prominent directors – Steven Spielberg (*Amistad,* 1997) and Francis Ford Coppola (*The Rainmaker,*

1997) – perpetuate the courtroom formula and leave it virtually unchanged.

Philadelphia, JFK, and *Amistad* fit what I call the "classical" paradigm of Hollywood courtroom dramas; they rank among the numerous judicial movies that, since the genre appeared in the 1930s, have promoted a basically positive image of American justice and have described the legal process as a model of good politics. Other instances of such classical courtroom films discussed here are Fritz Lang's *Fury* (1936), Frank Capra's *Mr Smith Goes to Washington* (1939), George Cukor's *Adam's Rib* (1949), Edward Dmytryk's *The Caine Mutiny* (1954), Sidney Lumet's *Twelve Angry Men* (1957), Robert Mulligan's *To Kill a Mockingbird* (1962), Jonathan Kaplan's *The Accused* (1988), Constantin Costa Gavras's *The Music Box* (1988), Michael Apted's *Class Action* (1990), and Marc Rocco's *Murder in the First* (1995). Though I have so far implied that the Hollywood judicial tradition is fairly continuous and homogeneous, it makes sense to argue that classical courtroom films such as these no longer address judicial issues as they are framed today. In this light, *Amistad* and *The Rainmaker* may be giving a new lease of life to a genre whose idealism may now appear disingenuous. Present-day American culture, shaped as it is by the O. J. Simpson case, the scandals surrounding the Clinton presidency, and the backlash against affirmative action, seems to leave little room for narratives in which justice may actually be pursued in a court of law. In the last fifteen years, Hollywood has acknowledged this change of climate by developing a more cynical type of courtroom drama, which we might call "litigation movies." The new subgenre came to prominence in the late 1980s, when the television series "L. A. Law" was first broadcast. Litigation movies, whose bad-lawyer thematics reverse many premises of classical courtroom films, are not my main focus here. I have, however, occasionally referred to some of them – Alan J. Pakula's *Presumed Innocent* (1990), Barry Levinson's *Disclosure* (1995), Arne Glimcher's *Just Cause* (1995), Taylor Hackford's *Devil's Advocate* (1996) – in order to contrast them with their liberal counterparts.

In these pages, I approach courtroom dramas from two complementary angles. First, my argument addresses the political didacticism of the genre. Indeed, legal thrillers have secured their place in the Hollywood canon because of a convergence among the formal possibilities of sound film, the theatricality of actual courtroom proceedings, and the desire to create a mass-culture showcase that can display the core values of the American political system. In other words, I contend that courtroom films have served as the soap-box orator's corner of a film tradition predominantly devoted to entertainment. Mark Tushnet, in a reading of *Class Action,* argues that judicially oriented films have consistently revolved around "the opposition between law and justice," that is, around the familiar presupposition that existing judicial institutions must conflict with an idealistic concept of what is essentially just. In political terms, this means that courtroom films stage a contest between what Max Lerner calls "the principle of constitutional democracy ('republic')," which celebrates positive law, and the principle of "majority action and passion ('democracy')," which is anchored in utopian moral realism.[3] As they articulate this thematics of politics, law, and justice, classical courtroom dramas have generally acted as channels for liberal ideas, sometimes even for the articulation of a left-wing program.[4] Indeed, against the severe limits imposed by industry self-censorship, courtroom films have consistently advertised the belief that political action, usually of a gradualist kind, is both necessary and rewarded with success. Because so many courtroom films carry this explicit political didacticism, it is necessary to distinguish "classical" courtroom dramas – and also, for that purpose, "litigation" films – from a third type of judicial movie, which is entirely devoted to the construction of suspense – works like Billy Wilder's *Witness for the Prosecution* (1957), Clint Eastwood's *Midnight in the Garden of Good and Evil* (1997), and made-for-television judicial mysteries in the Matlock or Perry Mason vein.

My interest in court dramas is rooted also in a theoretical concern for the workings of realist genres in literature and other media. Judicial thrillers, I argue, cultivate the referential illusion typical of the realist aesthetic – a semiotic process they rewrite along legalistic lines. Beyond its overt political dimension, the central concern of the genre – its unifying thematics – consists, I believe, in staging the spectacle of a supposedly impregnable political rhetoric. This display of judicial strategies concerns the problematic of realism because it supposedly offers a privileged access to what is held as real and essential in a democratic polity – the vital core of its political life and of its moral values. In other words, the movies fulfill a realist agenda because they naturalize, that is, legitimate, by depicting as self-evident a model of how political issues may be framed in the actual political world. This logic of ideological naturalization may, of course, be regarded as manipulative. Yet I argue that, if we bracket off the epistemologically naive presuppositions of the films' realist aesthetic, it is possible to tease out of these canonical Hollywood texts a valid reflection on the possibilities for political debate within a postmodern mass medium.

As advocates of Hollywood liberalism, courtroom narratives stage a battle for the definition of the American consensus. The most typical ideological gesture enacted in judicial thrillers is the attempt to cloak a specific political agenda in the supposedly neutral and consensual garb of judicial pronouncements. In other words, the history of the genre may be narrated as the sequence of the political appropriations of a judicial vital center. It is in these terms, we may measure the relations of continuity and distance that link a 1930s film such as *Mr. Smith Goes to Washington* (1939) and a 1980s work like *The Accused* (1988): the former turns the United States Congress into a law-school arena whose control is handed over to James Stewart, acting as a quaint representative of nostalgic small-town values; in the latter, where Jodie Foster plays the defendant, the law is made to work to the benefit of rape victims, regardless of their social class or previous sexual history. In these examples, capturing the vital center means either extending the boundaries of mainstream political discourse or reappropriating the scene of political power for the sake of a supposedly disempowered tradition. These complementary impulses are illustrated in two judicial thrillers of the 1990s: in *Philadelphia,* the scene of justice is made to include a recognition of the rights of AIDS victims; *JFK*, released during George Bush's presidency, uses the rituals of justice to cast a nostalgic glance on the passing of the Kennedy political legacy. Logically, because the tug-of-war enacted in these works focuses on the definition of the consensus, the movies deal with judicial issues at the most general or abstract level: court dramas always implicitly address the core ideals of the republic, issues of constitutional or civil rights, such as the presumption of innocence in *Twelve Angry Men* or racial discrimination in *To Kill a Mockingbird*.

It is, however, simplistic to imply that the political history of classical courtroom films reads like the smooth unfolding of a liberal teleology. More accurately, we should view each film's appropriation of the judicial consensus as the outcome of strenuously fought-over compromises: politically relevant screenplays were submitted to the restraints of culturally derived prohibitions, pressures from sponsors, industry self-regulation, or nationwide political campaigns such as the post-WWII Red Scare.[5] *Fury,* one of the earliest instances of a courtroom drama, offers exemplary instances of this difficult process of political accommodation. The film deals with lynch mobs and thus anticipates subsequent works about discrimination, although race relations are alluded to only very indirectly in *Fury*. The lynching victim, played by Spencer Tracy, is a white man suspected of kidnaping, not the stereotypical black scapegoat. African-American characters, though obviously involved in the film's thematics, appear only in the margins of the narrative.[6]

Self-regulation was the actual censorship tool that made such a displacement of political issues mandatory. This set of movie-making dos and don'ts, nicknamed the "Hays Code" after the first commissioner of the Motion Picture Producers and Distributors of America (MPPDA), was instituted in 1930 to satisfy complaints against the presumed immorality of late-silent-era movies; in more direct terms, it constituted the industry's response to embarrassing sexual scandals.[7] Though drafted to address sexual morality, the Hays Code acted as an efficient political gag: its practical purpose was to ensure that American movie productions remain pure entertainment products destined to the broadest possible audience – the very opposite of politically divisive movies. This resulted in piecemeal negotiations about what could be shown on the screen. Even so, the American film audience knew that the movies operated under restrictions and were in some way coded or submitted to conspicuous strategies of containment (unconvincing victories for the established order, melodramatic happy endings, for instance). A comic instance of the double consciousness thus induced occurs in the beginning of *Fury,* where Spencer Tracy and his fiancée Sylvia Sidney are contemplating the purchase of twin beds. According to Hollywood self-regulation, double beds sent too sexually explicit a signal for a family audience. The same logic of political or moralistic substitution justified casting of Spencer Tracy as a lynch victim.

Besides self-regulation, the factors that most significantly shaped the history of courtroom dramas were the late 1940s Red Scare and the civil rights movement. Anticommunism in the industry effectively put an end to the tradition of social-problem films that had developed in the thirties: blacklisting policies ensured that the left-wing artists who had found some degree of creative freedom during the Roosevelt Administration were prevented from working.[8] In some cases, the conservative backlash took the form of explicit propaganda on the screen: Gordon Douglas's *I Was a Communist for the FBI* (1951), for instance, used for its topic the investigations surrounding the House Committee of Un-American Activities (HUAC) hearings, and the movie's promotional campaign was meant to showcase the industry's efforts in rooting out leftist influences.[9] The long-term impact of the Red Scare consisted, however, in a broader cultural realignment: film production was reoriented toward family entertainment – thus simultaneously fulfilling the wishes of self-regulation censors.

HUAC affected liberal courtroom dramas particularly insofar as it questioned the moral legitimacy of the genre. A few years before the most critically acclaimed courtroom films were released (*The Caine Mutiny, Twelve Angry Men, Judgment at Nuremberg*), the hearings provided traumatic evidence that American justice could work in ways directly opposed to what was shown on the screen. HUAC defendants fighting for their civil rights were forced to resort to litigation tactics (technicalities in the use of the Fifth Amendment, particularly) and nevertheless lost their cases.[10] In this context, Peter Biskind is right to emphasize how politically loaded the notion of consensus building was to politically explicit movies of the 1950s. Biskind interprets *Twelve Angry Men,* in which the Henry Fonda character single-handedly manages to turn around a jury's verdict, precisely as a narrative that fetishizes the unifying virtues of centrist liberalism.[11] Political unanimity was the more explicitly welcome here as it compensated for the political damage inflicted in the beginning of the decade.

The development of the civil rights movement in the mid-1950s, on the contrary, reestablished the foundations of politically didactic films. The *Brown* v. *Board of Education of Topeka* Supreme Court decision of 1954, which banned discrimination in schools, provided courtroom dramas with the paradigm that informs them to this day. This new political energy was not exclusively channeled through the courtroom genre; above all, it generated films that seriously lagged behind the actual political context of their release. Some of the main Sidney Poitier antidiscrimination dramas perpetuated a gradualist political idiom whose optimism had been discredited after such violent upheavals as the Watts riots of 1965. Yet, even in its watered-down Hollywood version, the civil rights movement offered a model of judicially based politics that could be translated to other issues such as feminism and gay rights. Characteristically, it is precisely against this civil rights model that contemporary litigation movies are defined. The latter films express misgivings about, for instance, the newly won prerogatives of women professionals (in *Disclosure* or *Presumed Innocent*), or about liberal opposition to the death penalty (*Just Cause*). As such, they perform a paradoxical ideological gesture, redolent of right-wing populism: they implicitly condemn Reagan-era yuppiedom and simultaneously manifest a backlash against policies such as affirmative action and gender rights. It is uncertain at this stage whether this dystopian view of American justice will be able to drive out the older civil rights courtroom formula.

From this historical background emerges the image of a genre seemingly conveying moral self-confidence but also chronically struggling to uphold its political legitimacy – thus, a genre whose rhetorical powers must constantly be reasserted. The narrative formula itself has proved remarkably stable over time, even though actual social issues changed: the courtroom scenes of *Philadelphia* resort to devices that can be traced right back to *Fury*. My object in the rest of this essay is to show that these rhetorical strategies, which form the foundation of the political negotiation enacted in the films, revolve around the issue of the referentiality of language – the relation of texts to reality. The basic antagonism that the films posit between positive law and absolute justice – between the customs of the country (racial discrimination in *To Kill A Mockingbird*) and liberal values (the humanitarian conscience of *Mockingbird*'s lawyer-protagonist) – points back to an underlying semiotic dilemma: the movies intimate paradoxically that the prescribed workings of language, of judicial discourse, particularly, cannot articulate the ideals of a more democratic justice. Thus, these texts require that the grammar of law should not only be staged, but also momentarily transgressed or expanded. In *Adam's Rib,* for instance, courtroom protocol is disturbed as female acrobats and wrestlers are called to testify as the defendant's character witnesses. The burlesque scene that ensues is only an exaggeration, not an inversion, of the classical formula. Only through such crises of discourse can law be amended; only thus can it be made to approximate new values that are presented, not only as more equitable, but also, in quasi-Platonic logic, as anchored in a deeper level of reality. At its most utopian, this process helps the participants in the judicial game to gain an unmediated access to the world and thereby to secure the foundations of their politicized selfhood.

On the face of it, the systematic questioning of language and referentiality that characterizes courtroom drama seems out of place in a supposedly realistic genre. Realism is reputed to be the discourse that fosters what Jean Ricardou calls "referential illusion" (*"l'illusion référentielle"*), the power to render a text's own codes invisible – the capacity to make viewers or readers believe that artistic language is indeed the world.[12] Yet, in an influential discussion of late-nineteenth-century American fiction, Amy Beth Kaplan demonstrates that realism is always implicitly concerned with the limits of its own powers of representation.[13] She shows that late-nineteenth-century urban novels acknowledge their incapacity to portray the totality of urban experience in realist terms; those texts therefore mark out a boundary between the social domain representable according to realist verisimilitude – typically, the middle-class round of life – and the fields that this literary aesthetic must leave uncharted – working-class life or psychological experiences beyond accepted standards of normality, for instance. Conversely, when urban novels need to make visible these marginal domains, they do so according to the norms of romance – the sentimental or the gothic. Similar shifts toward romance, I argue, occur in courtroom movies, where they are used paradoxically to signify the accession to a higher level of realist representation.

By these standards, courtroom dramas are realistic primarily because they candidly evaluate the boundaries of what we might call "admissible reality" – what must pass as real in a judicial context. An emotionally laden narrative moment of judicial thrillers is indeed the "rules of evidence" motif – the business by which attorneys, prosecutors, and judges determine which witnesses or documents will be retained as relevant material in the judicial debate. The main plot articulations of *Judgment at Nuremberg* occur when the defense attorney (Maximilian Schell) attempts to keep Nazi racial legislation cases out of consideration, and when the prosecutor (Richard Widmark) decides to show in court documentary footage of the death camps. Likewise, the plot of *Class Action* revolves to a large extent on the prosecuting attorney's efforts to have an automobile safety report accepted as evidence and then to retrieve the document after the defense team has mislaid it. A comic inversion of this motif appears in *Devil's Advocate,* where wealthy New York attorneys seem endowed with a quasi-satanic ability to handpick favorable jurors and to make evidence speak in counterintuitive, even supernatural, directions.

Admittedly, evidence sorting in court dramas differs from the boundary effect described by Kaplan in that, at least from the viewers' perspective, it does not oppose two epistemologically distinct realities: viewers are explicitly made aware that the evidence in dispute is real and compelling; they are left to puzzle how such elements could be worthless with regard to the law. Yet I would argue that it is precisely this counterintuitive negotiation of evidence that typifies judicial realism: the movies stage a paradoxical, even scandalous, bargaining in which representatives of the law are given the power to define what components will contribute to the judicially sanctioned definition of the real. Simultaneously, the films signal that they are always able, by means of film language, to produce entirely conclusive evidence indicating that social reality does not fit these narrow criteria. Thus, judicial realism mobilizes two opposite impulses: the power of law to decree that a socially constructed boundary is as binding as an epistemological one and the political necessity to challenge this definition of what is real or unreal.

As they stage counterintuitive bargainings over a supposedly "admissible" reality, courtroom dramas bring about the delegitimation of the language of the law and, broadly speaking, raise suspicions about the trustworthiness of formal language as such. When the idiom of law is used in equivocations about the limits of the real, it becomes suspect of being disingenuous, unfalsifiable, deprived of referential value: the presumably self-evident bond between word and thing is called into question. The moment in courtroom dramas that best brings forward the basic ineffectuality of language is the proverbially inconclusive battle of experts. Among innumerable examples, we could mention the automobile safety case of *Class Action,* where experts for the plaintiff and for the defense fight it out to determine whether a car model was a fire hazard. Here as in other films the fact that professional opinions are uttered in the arena of the courtroom and thus cut off from the nonjudicial world induces defamiliarization: substance is turned into hollow argument, without referential power. The conspiratorial thrust of *JFK* is based precisely on this dissolution of reality at the hands of judicial language. The film, with its dizzying montage, marshals such a considerable body of evidence that any sense of the reality of the murder is fragmented or displaced, leaving room for conspiratorial hypotheses. In this, Stone's apparently innovative montage, his handling of history, evidence, and speculation, mobilize the sense of epistemological unreality inherent in the courtroom genre.

If, as courtroom dramas suggest, the judicial protocols of admissible reality are not the impregnable foundation of political life but rather stand on the side of the unreal, we may well wonder what standards will be retained for the definition of a valid testimony. The films suggest that any verbal utterance or any well-structured semiotic behavior, when integrated within the admissible reality of the law, are of necessity open to reasonable doubt. As *Twelve Angry Men* reveals, the only authentic judicial acts that can be performed in such circumstances are gestures of demystification. The liberal juror (Henry Fonda) of Lumet's movie manages to discredit the prosecution's evidence in two ways: first, classically, by pointing out material impossibilities (a witness claims he has heard the victim's cries for help over the deafening noise of an elevated train); second, by internally deconstructing seemingly reliable testimonies that cannot be substantiated by means of material evidence. The two most compelling witnesses in the case, he implies, are guilty of what we might call an excessive desire for semiotization: their testimony is as neatly packaged as their personal appearance on the stand. The jury must therefore question the motives that led to such impeccably narrated tales. We learn that one witness is an old man who relishes any opportunity to capture the attention of an audience; the other is a young woman who hides the fact that she wears glasses, an element relevant to her reliability as an eyewitness. At bottom, we understand that these witnesses are defeated by the very talent that enables them to rise up to the judicial occasion: they structured their stories and their own appearances according to their perception of the semiotic formalism of the court. By trying to fit the admissible real, however, they forfeited their value as creditable voices in the case. *Twelve Angry Men* seems therefore to leave no room whatsoever for trustworthy witnesses or for deliberations of a nondeconstructive kind: it implicitly discredits the judicial process altogether, in apparent contradiction with the liberal respect for the rule of law.

Just when judicial demystification seems to paint itself into a corner, courtroom dramas stage the narrative reversal that decisively empowers their political agenda: Audiences accustomed to the genre look forward to surprise revelations – unexpected testimonies, typically – or to other manipulations of due process that reverse power relations in court. In *Fury,* for instance, the film changes course when Spencer Tracy, presumed to have died in a prison fire, shows up in court and submits as evidence newsreel footage incriminating the rioters who laid siege to the prison. As a rhetorical gesture, Tracy's surprise return is what we might call a referential crisis – an abrupt reshuffling of rules of referentiality through which the movie's ideology finds itself regrounded. I argue in more detail below that such a narrative *coup de théâtre* is meant, as *Fury* indicates, to promote film language itself as the proper handmaiden of liberal politics. In the development of the plot, this redistribution of ideological authority is framed as a transition from judicial lies to pure filmic truth. From our point-of-view, it rather constitutes the moment when a boundary between two discourses is crossed, an instant of abrupt transition that is used as rhetorical shock tactic; the epistemological bargaining of the law is spectacularly cast aside in favor of filmic procedures that are touted as the very idiom of referentiality. In what follows, I show that the referential idiom thus established mobilizes two main strategies of legitimation: on the one hand, it displays supposedly natural signs that contribute to unimpeachable testimonies. On the other hand, it engineers a moment of revelation that we might call a "referential epiphany" or referent expansion: it brings to view a world outside the "admissible" real, a field of experience incommensurably larger or more complex than the legal institution allows.

Philadelphia contains what is arguably the clearest instances of a referential crisis based on pseudo natural signs. The movie's protagonist is Andrew Beckett (Tom Hanks), an AIDS patient who sues his former employer, a law firm, for firing him illegally. Beckett claims that his partners, unwilling to keep an AIDS patient among the staff, set him up to commit a professional mistake. In court, a large segment of the judicial debate is devoted to the ability to identify AIDS symptoms. Beckett was indeed fired after one of the firm's attorneys spotted an AIDS lesion on his forehead – a sign whose medical significance the attorney had previously learned to recognize. For their defense strategy, the law partners contend that they were totally ignorant of Beckett's condition. Their claim is substantiated by his appearance; by the fact that, at the time of the trial, his face shows no lesion of the type his colleague identified – a welcome coincidence that the defense attorney (Mary Steenburgen) exploits by having Beckett look at his own face in a mirror. At that juncture, Beckett's attorney (Denzel Washington) precipitates the referential crisis by asking his client to bare his chest. In this moving moment, evocative of the biblical story of Doubting Thomas, we are shown a body covered with scars that loudly proclaim the presence of the disease; the symptoms, visible to all, seem to be its natural signs.

In appearance a simple and powerful melodramatic moment, the climax of *Philadelphia* is the more compelling as it astutely fudges its own mechanisms of reference. The rhetorical momentum of the scene relies not only on the display of natural signs but also, more surprisingly, on the partial recognition that such a miraculous form of referentiality is impossible. The issue with which *Philadelphia* wrestles may be clarified by noting that, according to Saussurean semiology, there is no such thing as a "natural" sign: extralinguistic objects never spontaneously refer to – never "mean" – other objects; the smoke of a fire or the physical symptoms of a disease do not semiotically designate, respectively, the fire itself or the corresponding disease, even though the elements involved seem yoked by necessary bonds. Tzvétan Todorov voices the Saussurean point-of-view when he argues that "it is a misconception to believe that smoke is the 'natural' sign of fire; it is its consequence or one of its parts."[14] Thus, in Todorov's logic, identifying Andrew Beckett's lesions as AIDS symptoms involves a mental operation of a metonymic or synecdochic type. Rather than the fulfilment of a natural process, this form of diagnosis marks the acknowledgment of a relation of contiguity or the perception of the link between a part and its totality.[15] Signification is in this logic always the outcome of a social contract: "Only a community of language users can bestow upon [smoke] the status of sign."[16] *Philadelphia* does pay lip service to this view: the law firm employee who denounced Andrew first had to learn to recognize AIDS symptoms. The perjury he commits in court consists therefore in concealing his previously learned semiotic competence, not in refusing to acknowledge what would, in an essentialist perspective, be a universally recognizable medical fact. Nevertheless, the movie's impact requires that this learning process, which implies that reference is necessarily mediated through language, be eventually denied: the disrobing of Beckett's body is presented as the revelation of nature itself. The sense of unmediated referentiality thus created is furthered by the fact that the film medium makes the scene visible through what Charles Sanders Peirce calls "icons" or "likenesses." The visual language of cinema is made up of iconic signs that "partak[e] in the characters of th[eir] object" and therefore command an almost unchallengeable referential illusion.[17] Thus, the iconic depiction of pseudo natural signs is, for the courtroom genre, the very manifestation of the real.

In its predilection for pseudo natural signs, the courtroom drama genre comes to grant a privileged status to what we might call "borderline" semiotic (or "parasemiotic") processes. Under these terms, I refer to signifying mechanisms where language seems to merge with nature at least in so far as its signs escape deliberate, rational control. In practice, this means that judicial films, as they undermine the claims of verbal language, simultaneously confer epistemological legitimacy to gestures, tics, and uncontrollable behavior presumably rooted in the characters' idiosyncrasies. In *Twelve Angry Men,* a compulsive gesture by the most damaging witness – the shortsighted young woman, abruptly interrupts the seemingly endless deconstruction of evidence. Indeed, her myopia and her correlative decision not to wear her glasses in court are revealed when a juror points out that she compulsively rubbed the bridge of her nose while she was on the stand. Her testimony is therefore utterly discredited by parasemiotic means. The most memorable use of parasemiotic gestures to precipitate a referential crisis appears in *The Caine Mutiny,* where Humphrey Bogart impersonates Captain Philip Francis Queeg. The captain is the paranoid and compulsive-obsessive chief officer of a WW II destroyer. He testifies against one of his shipmates, who is court-martialed for relieving Queeg of his command when the latter's behavior seemed to threaten the safety of the ship. In court, Queeg attempts to project an image of self-disciplined leadership. This effort is pathetically undercut by his compulsion to juggle steel marbles in his hands as soon as facts unfavorable to his character are brought to light.

Because parasemiotic behavior plays such a key role in the rhetoric of court dramas, the most inarticulate witnesses, or at least those who are on the brink of losing control, turn out to be the most valuable assets in the development of the plot. *Judgment at Nuremberg* makes masterful use of this convention. The referential climax of this story is particularly spectacular in that it involves a reversal of roles: it is the defense attorney, not a mere witness or a defendant, who ends up losing his semiotic composure. Since the film seeks to explore how conscientious German officials agreed to enforce Nazi legislation, there is no better evidence than to let the otherwise highly respectable attorney be carried away by his argument and revert to the totalitarian attitudes his clients displayed in the recent past. Accordingly, the judge gives the young lawyer free rein to badger witnesses, thus letting the attorney's attitude manifest parasemiotic evidence of the metamorphosis from judicial fairness to barbarian totalitarianism. In an efficient melodramatic gesture, it is the defendant (Gary Cooper) who demands that the fascistic questioning be interrupted. Other instances of this form of characterization include a supposedly feeble-minded character who was sterilized according to Nazi legislation. The man, played by Montgomery Clift, lacks linguistic and behavioral restraint, a defect that serves as natural sign of his past trauma. Similarly, in *Murder in the First,* a film that denounces the solitary confinement system, the most compelling witness turns out to be a semiliterate inmate (Kevin Bacon) who, brought to near-madness by long periods of solitude, came to murder another convict. The apelike demeanor of the defendant and his heavily accented, subgrammatical speech embody a form a language that resists demystifying scrutiny.

As efficient as it is, the language of pseudo natural signification deployed by courtroom dramas can, by definition, only work with the abrupt concision of pure fact or with the indirectness of connotation. Although courtroom films seek to use such signs as the very idiom of the nonjudicial real, they can only let the referent thus evoked express itself in garbled or undecipherable form – inarticulate speech, indices, symptoms. The films therefore need narrative tools that simulate unmediated reference in a fashion that lends itself to a more extended fictional development. This is the function of referential epiphanies. This term designates such familiar devices of courtroom dramas as last-minute testimonies, unexpected reversals of judicial process, the submission of forgotten or eccentric evidence, elements that spectacularly expand the field of reference thus far represented in the film. Like pseudo natural signification, referential epiphanies involve the ability to manipulate or simulate the boundary between language and the extralinguistic. In pseudo natural signification and parasemiotics this simulation is effected by juxtaposing two contrasted idioms – untrustworthy words and reliable symptoms. Referential epiphanies, by comparison, rather than juxtapose two codes, present a contrast between two worlds, two distinct areas of experience: these moments of revelation contrast the admissible real, which is already articulated in language, with the soon-to-be-acknowledged field of forgotten evidence – the new world of reference to which the film gives a semiotic shape.

Referential epiphanies, because they manipulate two planes of reality, are at bottom a device of romance.[18] They introduce a connotation of magic to the otherwise realistic courtroom genre by implying that a domain of reference hitherto unavailable to the language of law can be made entirely visible to the camera – images, words, sounds, and all. Unmediated reference appears therefore as a newly discovered territory that opens up to the judicial gaze and that at first retains an aura of mystery. Accordingly, in *Fury,* Spencer Tracy's unexpected reappearance after the prison fire carries the eerie impact of a return from the dead – a connotation reinforced by the parasemiotic element that Tracy still exhibits burn scars. The crowning touch of magic in a scene like this consists in the implication that the two realms it posits, though ostensibly separate, are eventually revealed to be the same: the evidence that Tracy brings with him – film footage – is as real as anything due process takes into account. In this, courtroom films make a utopian and paradoxical gamble about the flexibility of admissible reality: they imply that it is possible to retrieve evidence from beyond the perimeter charted by the law.

The romance logic of referential epiphanies is skillfully exploited in *The Music Box,* a film that deals with an investigation into WW II atrocities. The heroine is Ann Talbot, a Hungarian-American lawyer (Jessica Lange) in Chicago, who attempts to defend Michael Lazslo, her father (Armin Mueller-Stahl), against war crime charges leveled at the instigation of the Hungarian communist government. Eventually, the young lawyer realizes that her father was indeed the pro-Nazi torturer infamously known as Mishka. Because the plot focuses on Talbot's coming to terms with her family past, the film quickly establishes the father's guilt for the viewer's sake – a task conclusively performed by means of pseudo natural signification. We see early on that the male bonding rituals Lazslo indulges in with his grandson – push-up exercises – are modeled on torture techniques Mishka used during the war: a witness mimics in court how the fascist officer let his victims perform the same gestures until they impaled themselves on bayonets. For the participants in the court debates, however, the case stalls: it is impossible to rule out the suspicion that the witnesses may be acting under the influence of Hungarian officials eager to punish Lazslo for his anticommunist activities. Above all, documents – photographs, ID cards – may have been falsified according to procedures familiar to Eastern Bloc secret services.

When the court debates move from Chicago to Budapest to interrogate a bed-ridden witness, we realize that the truth will come out by means of a radical broadening of the film's scope. Though the Budapest witness is unreliable and the case seems to reach a dead end, Talbot feels the psychological pressure of the European city's settings. Fascinated by the Danube River, along whose banks the fascist killings were carried out, she decides to investigate a lead she had so far ignored – the suggestion that her father may have been blackmailed by Tibor Zoldan, one of Mishka's henchmen, who later emigrated to the United States, where he died in dubious circumstances. Talbot pays a visit to Zoldan's sister, who gives her a pawnshop receipt her brother sent her from Chicago. The pawned item turns out to be a quaint music box that, when set in motion, disgorges a series of photographs showing Mishka – the very face displayed on Lazslo's immigrant card – performing executions. In the logic of the story, these pictures are unquestioningly real, yet also objects of romance. Unlike the documents discussed in court, their authenticity is guaranteed because they issue from another side of the real: they have been hoarded for a long time in a slightly mysterious world, far beyond the boundary of court proceedings. Thus, the music box device reduplicates in a more pronounced allegorical mode the movement of expansion initiated by the change of locale: it brings into the story fragments of history itself, images of a referent endowed with an uncanny aura that signifies its immunity to the corruption of judicial arguments.

It would be misguided to detect a call for the dismantling of law in the conflict that *The Music Box* and other courtroom dramas stage between a perennially limited judicial formalism and the search for unmediated reference and moral truth. These aspirations would be impossibly radical for the self-censored Hollywood medium, and, more pointedly, they would go against the civil rights paradigm of social reform, which attributes to the courts a crucial role in social change. In a more balanced appraisal of the status of justice and language in courtroom films, we should rather assume that the dialectic of admissible reality and referential crises is not simply homologous to the opposition between conservatism and radicalism. It makes more sense to contend that the films' rhetorical strategies are meant to manage contradictions in the liberal agenda itself. Max Lerner comments that, in liberal discourse, the broader political conflict between "the republic" and Whitmanesque "democracy" reappears in the form of difficulties in reconciling "pragmatic thought" and "the optimism of the idealist thinkers."[19] For courtroom films, this implies that neither contrasted term can be dispensed with permanently: the films' perpetual redrawing of the boundary separating the language of law from unmediated truth implies that, once moral realism is asserted, it will need the positive institution of law to acquire a concrete social shape.

The strategy of ideological management that allows films to keep in dialectic tension law and reality, pragmatic politics and commitment manifests itself visibly in what narratologists would call the "actantial model" of the genre – its handling of a stereotyped cast of character functions. Tushnet remarks that characters' roles are starkly dichotomized in courtroom dramas: in his view, the films pit against each other representatives of "the Dominant" and of "the Other"; in my reading, these types qualify respectively as watchdogs of admissible reality and referential questers – figures who are granted the ability to transgress existing rules of judicial reference. Yet I think it important to underline that this rigid binarism obtains only at the level of the deep actantial structure. At the surface of the text, this opposition is watered down by a game of permutations among actantial roles. In particular, out of respect for the progressive potential of legislation, the movies cannot systematically frame this actantial conflict as a battle between the defense and the prosecution. Thus, the actantial profiles described above are attributed in turn to characters with opposite functions in the judicial apparatus. In *Twelve Angry Men,* the referential quester – Henry Fonda and the jurors he progressively wins over to his cause – speaks for the defense. In *The Accused,* this actant makes up a collective entity that includes the attorney for the prosecution (Kelly McGillis), the rape victim (Jodie Foster), and one male witness who chooses to testify against his friends and thus qualifies as the heroine's adjuvant. In *The Music Box,* the defense attorney evolves from a wily advocate of the admissible real to the dignity of referential heroine when she sheds her blind attachment to family values, which act as her opponent in this story. She is helped in this psychological itinerary by the prosecutor, the Hungarian witnesses, and the music box itself. A similar switch of allegiances is depicted in *Class Action,* where the defense attorney (Mary Elizabeth Mastrantonio) becomes a referential quester in mid-narrative when she chooses to side with the prosecution team. In *Judgment at Nuremberg,* the most conspicuous referential quester is the judge (Spencer Tracy), with defense attorney Maximilian Schell as his unwitting adjudant. Through these games of actantial permutations courtroom films manage to balance their simultaneous critique and celebration of the judicial system.[20]

Whatever characters are eventually vindicated by the plots, the most important ideological gesture performed in courtroom films is the empowerment of the cinematic medium itself. Cinema, in this light, appears politically priceless because it is the site at which the regeneration of law in its confrontation with reality can be made visible. Films deploy a plurality of codes of representation, including iconic expression, which is often mistaken for realism itself. As such, they have the specific ability to stage pseudo natural signification and referential epiphanies. *Fury* illustrates very explicitly – or, as Tom Conley suggests, with the shrillness of self-parody – what kind of ideologically charged variety of political realism can be constructed along these lines.[21] Not only do the newsreel scenes projected for the jurors' sakes irrevocably prove the defendants' guilt, but they have clearly been filmed from camera angles – expressionistic tilted low-angle shots, for instance – obviously inaccessible to the film crews on the site, as if the cinematic gaze were magically ubiquitous and irrefutable in its claim to referentiality.

It is legitimate to discard the final court scene of *Fury* as a self-serving gesture by which the film industry naturalizes its consensual representation of American institutions. In this light, Lang's film aligns itself with the conventions of a genre that relies on manipulative twists – a film corpus in which the rights of the disempowered can only be vindicated through narratives that construct a dichotomized, cathartic view of the judicial process and that mistakenly present film as ideologically neutral. Yet, in my concluding remarks, I should like to paint a more optimistic picture of the political potential of the courtroom genre. Both the historical and the semiotic components of the present discussion indicate that judicial films have consistently opened up a space of political negotiation in one of the most ideologically powerful sites of American culture. The stake of this negotiation has essentially been the right to equitable representation – the right to see politically sensitive issues discussed on the screen and, particularly, to see them framed in films that depict the boundaries of the political mainstream as amenable to democratic change. This widening of political space is the meaning of the dialectic staged by courtroom movies between what I have called referential crises and the judicial real.

In this light, we may conclude that the semiotic mechanisms mobilized by courtroom films are more complex than what their sometimes formulaic plots suggest. In particular, in the present postmodern reading perspective, I argue that the courtroom genre proves an apt political medium insofar as it shows how civic negotiations are handled in a society aware of the power effects of its own ideological idioms. This potential for semiotic clear-sightedness is best illustrated in the tendency of courtroom films to scrutinize the authority of referential discourse – that is, to question anybody's appeals to the authority of the real. In Bakhtinian terms, we might argue that judicial plots, in their reflections on referentiality, foster a dialogizing of evidence or a deontology of heteroglossia.[22] By these terms, I mean to describe the judicial practice in which hard facts – referential epiphanies – are invoked only to be exposed as semiotic constructs and where disputes about evidence always mobilize a plurality of discourses with competing semiotic and legal prerogatives. The basically self-sub-versive riot footage of *Fury* illustrates this point: in their gothic excess, these shots suggest that truly decisive revelations, because they come from outside the admissible real, cannot initially exist on the same plane – within the same codes – as already acknowledged data. Thus, *Fury,* like other courtroom films, indicates that the most compelling form of evidence is the one that obliges us to evaluate disputed boundaries between conflicting idioms.

The present corpus offers several impressive instances of dialogized evidence. In *Adam's Rib,* Katharine Hepburn's decision to make a plea for women's equality by summoning a procession of grotesque performers, thereby disrupting court rituals, is more than a comic gimmick. It implicitly acknowledges that an abstract notion such as gender equality cannot be produced in front of a tinsel-town court: in a Hollywood comedy, it can only be cloaked in the idiom of slapstick. *Judgment at Nuremberg* displays this deontology of evidence in a more pessimistic context. The pivotal scene, in which the prosecutor projects images of the Nazi death camps in the court, brings about an intrusion of documentary discourse in a fiction film. Thus, Stanley Kramer does not attempt to represent World War II atrocities by means of a homogeneous, normative, and therefore questionable realist idiom. Instead, *Judgment at Nuremberg* both confronts us with devastating historical evidence and leaves us the interpretive liberty to determine the judicial and referential value of this data with regard to Hollywood narrative conventions, which continue to inform the other scenes of the film. A viewer adhering to a realist/reflectionist aesthetic might interpret this strategy as a shift from fiction into the realm of absolute reference. In the present framework, it qualifies rather as the most legitimate discursive tactic to signify past horrors whose full reality cannot be made present in the language of law or in any other idiom that would stake a claim for an unquestionable extralinguistic grounding. In scenes such as this one, we realize that the courtroom genre, by virtue of its seemingly clichéd depiction of judicial litigation, is indeed ideally equipped to stage a deontological reflection on the limits of political representation.

Notes

1. The extensive section on genre in Pam Cooke, *The Cinema Book* (London, 1985), 65-112, takes into consideration such canonical Hollywood forms as the western, melodrama, the gangster/crime film, *film noir*, the horror film, and the musical and thus bypasses courtroom films altogether. Courtroom dramas are equally ignored by historians, who underline the impact on the Hollywood genre system of the appearance of sound film in the late 1920s. David A Cook, in his *History of Narrative Films* (New York, 1996), 274-80, lists among the new sound genres the musical, the animated feature, the urban gangster film, the historical biography, and the screwball comedy. In Kristin Thompson and David Bordwell, *Film History: An Introduction* (New York, 1994), 257, Fritz Lang's courtroom drama *Fury* is categorized as a "social problem film." More surprising, among the essays collected in John Denvir, *Legal Realism: Movies as Legal Texts* (Urbana and Chicago, 1996), 244-59, only Mark Tushnet, "Class Action: One View of Gender and Law in Popular Culture," is devoted to a courtroom drama; Tushnet does not discuss this movie from the point of view of genre criticism. One might argue that judicial business on the screen lacks the semantic critical mass required for a genre and that it constitutes only a motif – a clichéd sequence of actions that fits many different types of stories and occasionally stretches over a whole film. I believe, however, that the courtroom formula is too distinctive and too ubiquitous among Hollywood releases to be assigned such a second-rank status.
2. The privileged status of the western as a cultural form expressive of American history was asserted, for instance, by French critic André Bazin, who describes the western as "the American Film par excellence" in *What Is Cinema?* vol. 2., ed. and trans. Hugh Gray (Berkeley, 1971), 143. Classical westerns (of John Ford, particularly) also fared well at the hands of later critics – the *Cahiers du Cinéma* group, for instance – who adopted a subversion model of reading and who deconstructed politically conservative texts, often with the attempt to identify in them oppositional elements. Courtroom dramas, on the contrary, are less propitious objects for the subversion approach, because instead of developing oppositional subtexts, they openly discuss such liberal issues as civil or gender rights. The problems raised by radical readings in this context are illustrated in Tom Conley, "The Laws of the Game: Jean Renoir, *La*

règle du jeu," in Denvir, *Legal Reelism,* 95-116, where the author applies to cinema Michel Foucault's and Gilles Deleuze's theories of power. In this interpretation, the purpose of Jonathan Demme's *Philadelphia* is no longer to increase public awareness about AIDS – this is merely what Conley calls the "ideological pabulum" of the film – but to make "the heterosexual male spectator ... feel the excitement of gay sex" (ibid., 96) guiltily enjoyed by the film's protagonist in shady movie theaters. Such an approach is, I believe, awkwardly elitist in its implicit claim that the political statements articulated by Hollywood products can be routinely disregarded.

3. Tushnet, "Class Action," 245; Max Lerner, *America as a Civilization* (New York, 1957), 365.
4. I do not use the term liberalism in the specialized meaning of political science, which would imply that film makers align themselves with well-defined schools of American political thought. Here liberalism carries the connotation it enjoys in everyday political journalism, where it designates, roughly, the agenda of left-wing Democrats from Franklin D. Roosevelt to the Kennedy Administration. As such, liberalism refers to the set of ideas likely to be recognized as progressive by the audience of a mass medium from the 1930s to the present: the defense of individuals against institutions such as monopolistic wealth or authoritarian government and the desire to broaden the rights of disempowered groups. According to Stephen Kautz, *Liberalism and Community* (Ithaca, 1995), 5, 19, this understanding of the term is typical of left-wing liberal thinkers who favor the claims of "community" against "classical liberalism," which privileges "the liberal idea of the free individual."
5. Ruth Vasey, *The World According to Hollywood: 1918-1939* (Exeter, Eng., 1997), provides a detailed account of the political impact of industry censorship on Hollywood plots. The specific principles of the production code are discussed in Ruth A. Inglis, "Self-Regulation in Operation," in Tino Balio, ed., *The American Film Industry* (Madison, 1985), 377-400.
6. Vasey, *World According to Hollywood,* 139, shows that, by the standards of 1930s censorship, studios that released films "featuring a southern lynching" were treading on "dangerous ground."
7. The willingness to purge the movie industry from presumably immoral influences is the keynote of Martin Quigley, *Decency in Motion Pictures* (New York, 1937), who describes his own contribution to the elaboration of the Hays Code. The official, industry-approved history of the production code is in Raymond Moley, *The Hays Office* (New York, 1945). Robert Sklar, *Movie-Made America: A Cultural History of American Movies* (New York, 1975), 78, and Vasey, *World According to Hollywood,* 27, indicate that this system of industry censorship was set up as a response to the perceived licentiousness of some late-silent comedies of manners and to a sex scandal involving silent-era comedy star Roscoe ("Fatty") Arbuckle. The writings of Moley and of industry commissioner Will Hays indicate, however, that in the name of keeping Hollywood movies pure entertainment products censorship could be directed against political content.

8. For a discussion of the impact of blacklisting and HUAC on Hollywood film making see John Cogley, *Report on Blacklisting*, vol. 1: *Movies* (New York, 1956), and Larry Ceplair and Steven Englund, *The Inquisition in Hollywood: Politics of the Film Community, 1930-60* (New York, 1980).
9. See Quigley's sympathetic review of the film in "Warner's Anti-Red Film Timely and Hard-Hitting," *Motion Picture Herald*, Apr. 21, 1947, 13.
10. See Cogley, "The Mass Hearings," in Balio, ed., *American Film Industry*, 492-93.
11. Peter Biskind, *Seeing Is Believing: How Hollywood Taught us to Stop Worrying and Love the Fifties* (New York, 1983), 32-38.
12. Jean Ricardou, *Le nouveau roman* (Paris, 1978), 30.
13. Amy Beth Kaplan, *The Social Construction of American Realism* (Chicago, 1985), 47, 160.
14. Tzvétan Todorov, "Signe," in Oswald Ducrot and Todorov, eds., *Dictionnaire encyclopédique des sciences du langage* (Paris, 1972), 132; translation mine.
15. The issue of natural signification – of the relation of language to things – is, however, more problematic than Saussureans such as Todorov allow. American semiotician Charles Sanders Peirce defines indexical signs ("Indexes") in a way that seems to acknowledge the possibility of natural signification. To him, the "footprint that Robinson Crusoe found in the sand" stands "unequivocally" as an index of a human presence on the island; Pierce, quoted in James Hoopes, ed., *Peirce on Signs: Writings on Semiotic by Charles Sanders Peirce* (Chapel Hill, N. C., and London, 1991), 252. In this light, the Saussurean principle according to which signs are created by the conventional decision of a community of speakers appears as an axiomatic, unfalsifiable hypothesis.
16. Todorov, "Signs," 132.
17. Peirce, quoted in Hoopes, ed., *Pierce on Signs*, 30, 251.
18. Fredric Jameson, in "Magical Narratives: On the Dialectical Use of Genre Criticism," *The Political Unconscious* (Ithaca, 1981), 141, argues that romance is a genre characterized by "the coexistence or tension between several generic modes or strains" – by the conflict between discourses of realism and magic. In this context, he discusses Northrop Frye's concept of the "romance 'epiphany,'" which refers to the "revelation of presence" of a "providential vision" in a desacralized world; ibid., 135. The concept of referential epiphany I use in these pages is similar to the romance epiphany, with the important difference that the object of its revelation turns out to be a new segment of reality.
19. Lerner, *America as a Civilization*, 729, 730.
20. In *Sémantique structurale: recherche de méthode* (Paris, 1966), 175-86, Algirdas Julien Greimas defines the "actants" contained in each narrative as a set of six stereotypical roles whose origin lies in sentence syntax itself. The actants are, respectively, the Subject (hero), the Object, the Donor, the Receiver (destinataire), the Adjuvant, and the Opponent. In most cases, each actual "actor" (character) performs several actantial

roles in the course of a story. Greimas calls this phenomenon actantial "syncretism." Tushnet, *"Class Action,"* 247.
21. Conley, "Laws of the Game," 100.
22. Mikhail Bakhtin, *The Dialogic Imagination: Four Essays by M. M. Bakhtin,* ed. Michael Holquist, trans. Caryl Emerson and Holquist (Austin, 1981), 271, uses "heteroglossia" to describe his belief that any linguistic utterance is shaped by a dialogue among several voices – that the voice of others is always implicitly embedded in language. An aesthetic consequence of heteroglossia, which Bakhtin analyses mostly in the context of the novel, is that no text can be homogeneous in terms of genre: it always consists of a dialogue involving several socially connoted idioms. A deontology of heteroglossia would therefore be the principles that allow authors to manage this implicit dialogue in the most responsible and equitable ways.

Films

Accused, The. Dir. Jonathan Kaplan. With Jodie Foster and Kelly McGillis. Paramount, 1988.
Adam's Rib. Dir. George Cukor. With Spencer Tracy and Katharine Hepburn. MGM, 1949.
Amistad. Dir. Steven Spielberg. With Morgan Freeman, Anthony Hopkins, Djimon Hounsou, Matthew McConaughey, and Nigel Hawthorne. Dreamworks Pictures, 1997.
Caine Mutiny, The. Dir. Edward Dmytryk. With Humphrey Bogart. Columbia, 1954.
Class Action. Dir. Michael Apted. With Gene Hackman and Mary Elizabeth Mastrantonio. Twentieth Century Fox, 1990.
Devil's Advocate, The. Dir. Taylor Hackford. With Al Pacino, Keanu Reeves, and Charlize Theron. Warner Brothers, 1997.
Disclosure. Dir. Barry Levinson. With Michael Douglas and Demi Moore. Warner Brothers, 1994.
Fury. Dir. Fritz Lang. With Spencer Tracy and Sylvia Sidney. MGM, 1936.
I Was a Communist for the FBI. Dir. Gordon Douglas. With Frank Lovejoy and Dorothy Hart. Warner Brothers, 1951.
JFK. Dir. Oliver Stone. With Kevin Costner and Sissy Spacek. Camelot Productions/Warner Bros./New Regency Films/Canal Plus/Ixtlan, 1991.
Judgment at Nuremberg. Dir. Stanley Kramer. With Spencer Tracy, Burt Lancaster, Richard Widmark, Marlene Dietrich, Judy Garland and Maximilian Shell. Roxlom, 1961.
Just Cause. Dir. Arne Glimcher. With Sean Connery, Lawrence Fishbourne, Kate Capshaw, and Ruby Dee. Warner Brothers, 1995.
Midnight in the Garden of Good and Evil. Dir. Clint Eastwood. With Kevin Spacey, John Cusack, The Lady Chablis, and Alison Eastwood. Warner Brothers, 1997.

Murder in the First. Dir. Mark Rocco. With Christian Slater and Kevin Bacon. Twentieth- Century Fox, 1995.
Music Box. Dir. Constantin Costa-Gavras. With Jessica Lange and Armin Mueller-Stahl. Carolco, 1989.
Philadelphia. Dir. Jonathan Demme. With Tom Hanks and Denzel Washington. Tristar Pictures, 1993.
Presumed Innocent. Dir. Alan J. Pakula. With Harrison Ford, Bonnie Bedelia, Brian Dennehy, and Greta Scacchi. Warner Brothers, 1990.
Rainmaker, The. Dir. Francis Ford Coppola. With Matt Damon, Danny De Vito, Claire Danes, and Mary Kay Place. Mirage Productions/Paramount Pictures, 1997.
To Kill a Mockingbird. Dir. Robert Mulligan. Prod. Alan J. Pakula. With Gregory Peck and Mary Badham. Universal, 1962.
Twelve Angry Men. Dir. Sidney Lumet. With Henry Fonda. Orion/Nova, 1957.
Witness for the Prosecution. Dir. Billy Wilder. With Tyrone Power, Marlene Dietrich, and Charles Laughton. United Artists, 1957.

9
A Brief Cultural History of Corporate Legal Theory and Why American Studies Should Care About It

Eric Guthey

From various perspectives, the essays in this volume explore the notion that the interdiscipline of American studies would do well to recognize more fully the importance of the law, legal institutions, and legal cultures as fundamental components of American culture and cultures, in both the singular and the plural. To American studies scholars in thrall to the latest literary/theoretical fashions, this may seem at first like a downright stodgy premise. Those scholars will find ample ammunition for that charge in this essay, which will discuss what no doubt will sound to many like the most boring and potentially hegemonic aspect of legal thought – corporate legal theory. Most contemporary American and cultural studies scholarship treats the corporation from afar as a "power bloc" – a threatening, monolithic institution whose stranglehold on American society should be resented, resisted, but not accorded the same amount of attention as other, supposedly more authentic, forms of culture. I argue, however, that the study of corporations, corporate cultures, and corporate legal theory ought to be included at the center of an American studies agenda informed by the theoretical concerns of cultural materialism, for the corporation represents a site where cultural and symbolic discourses meld together with material structures – with capital itself – to the point where the two become indistinguishable.

In a provocative book on the history of broadcast regulation in the United States, sociologist Thomas Streeter makes a strong case for the notion that the law represents just such a dynamic site for the practice of cultural materialism. From the outset, Streeter contests the view that the law is an arcane and rigid structure far removed from the realities of everyday cultural life. "Law … even if arcane, is hardly mechanical," Streeter states. "Law is fluid both in meaning and in boundaries: its interpretation shifts dramatically from context to context, and its relevance flows in unexpected ways into areas normally thought of as remote from law." With a nod to the exceedingly text-based nature of much contemporary cultural criticism, he adds that, although law is a highly symbolic activity that foregrounds the ritual interpretation of texts, it also controls individual and social behavior and the distribution of resources, so that it is inherently political. "Law thus forces us to look simultaneously at the textual quality of power and the powerful quality of texts." Because, as Streeter states, "law is a lived set of social relations," it lends itself to scholarly analysis predicated on the exploration of social context – the very kind of analysis that characterizes the field of American studies.[1]

I discuss the extent to which contemporary American studies scholarship appears unwilling or unable to consider the lived sets of social relations that constitute corporations and business cultures in the United States as appropriate objects of extended critical analysis. I conjecture about the possible reasons for this lack and propose that the problem may stem from a sense on the part of American studies scholars that it is their responsibility to champion a grass-roots ideal of cultural agency in the face of the perceived encroachment of an array of powerful determining structures, including business and corporate structures. Then I canvass the history of corporate legal theory to suggest that these sentiments are, ironically, misplaced. For the last thirty years, the most neoconservative theorists in corporate law have themselves eschewed any definition of the corporation predicated on structure, instead embracing their own extremely atomizing and individualistic emphasis on pure agency as the fundamental building block of corporate activity. By tacitly lumping all corporate activity together as structural and therefore hegemonic, American studies scholars have allowed this important shift in the legal and ideological legitimization of corporate license to pass largely unnoticed. Through a description of how my research on celebrity media owner Ted Turner addresses this shift, I will demonstrate how the critical concerns central to the field of American studies – including concerns with gender, shifting cultural context, symbolic imagery, and popular cultural forms – can inform and enhance our understanding of corporate law as a dynamic discourse that creates and sustains the most powerful institutions on the American landscape, and that deserves more serious critical scrutiny by interdisciplinary scholars of American culture.

In February 1997, the *Wall Street Journal* reported that the volume of corporate mergers that had occurred in the previous year added up to $1 trillion worldwide, with $650 billion of this activity taking place in the United States – a figure nearly double the volume of similar deals that marked the infamous 1980s. "It is a merger boom the likes of which the business world hasn't seen since the buyout-crazy mid-1980s or since the go-go 1960s," the paper observed. "If anything, [it] is more reminiscent of a wave of combinations in the late 19th century that created the nation's first corporate behemoths and helped reinforce a climate of popular mistrust of concentrated industrial power."[2] But the current merger mania seems to have inspired no comparable wave of antitrust fervor, with the result that the megadeals continue at a fever pitch without significant opposition, even though studies show that roughly 80 percent of all corporate mergers fail. In June 1998, the *New York Times* reported that the value of mergers and acquisitions in the United States during the first half of the year had already topped $910 billion, up 153 percent from the same period in 1997. The companies involved run the gamut of industries Americans work for and do business with every day. Office Depot and Viking Office Products; Chrysler Motors and Daimler-Benz; AT&T and Telecommunications Inc.; Coopers and Lybrand and Price-Waterhouse; Travelers Group and

Salomon Brothers; Citicorp and Travelers Group; Nations Bank and Bank-America; British Petroleum and Amoco; Worldcom and MCI Communications; Mrs. Fields Cookies and the Great American Cookie Company; and so on and so on and so on.

In spring 1998, I encouraged the undergraduates in my American Business History class at the University of Michigan Business School to debate the social ramifications of such large-scale corporate mergers. The debate was rather one-sided; the most vocal students felt that if a private company wanted to get bigger, that was its right as a private entity. They were much more incensed, in fact, about a seventy-six-year-old Florida woman, Ina Brown, who had the gall to pursue a class action lawsuit against the American Family Publishers company for the thoroughly misleading language in its sweepstakes mailings. If she was "stupid" enough to believe what she read in her junk mail, the students insisted, that was her problem. In their opinion, the sweepstakes company was simply exercising its right to try to turn a profit, and the court should throw out her case as frivolous and unwarranted. I worked with the class (to varying degrees of success) to examine the underlying assumptions that would lead them to defend the rights of powerful, multi-billion-dollar commercial giants while heaping scorn on the attempt of a single elderly woman to curb one such company's excesses. Such assumptions are difficult to get at, because they stem from complex historical and social constructions of corporate rights and privileges, the paradoxical status of vast, collective corporate ventures as natural persons before the law, and the manner in which legal doctrine, popular culture, and corporate public relations alike have draped such large capitalist collectives with American individualist and free market ideals. The students' venom toward Ina Brown bears witness to considerable confusion about the terms "public" and "private" and about what corporations actually are and how they rose to such prominence that these intersecting factors have created.[3]

Perhaps it is too much to expect to sort out such issues in a business school (although American business school faculty and students are not as monochromatically procorporation as one might think). It would be nice to think that my home field of American studies could provide the diverse interdisciplinary intellectual environment where faculty and students could explore the roots and ramifications of the wholesale incorporation of American society. After all, as sociologist William Roy points out, "Few features of contemporary American society are more far-reaching or awesome than its large industrial corporations, the largest of which command more resources than the majority of nations in the world, employ more people than live in many cities, and shape our daily life more thoroughly than previously dominant institutions such as religion."[4] While very few people in American studies would dispute this claim, even fewer of them appear interested in taking the time to investigate this major feature of the American landscape very closely. The pedagogical and intellectual mission of American studies – the interdisciplinary investigation of the institutions and cultures of the United States – does not include at present a serious examination of the institution of the corporation or of American business cultures from the inside out. One would never imagine from scanning the programs of any of the recent major conferences in American studies, for example, that we are living through a period of unprecedented corporate conglomeration and market ascendancy. The 1998 meeting of the American Studies Association, convened around the theme "American Studies and the Question of Empire," devotes just one session to examining American cultures in the corporate empire (only three papers out of several hundred appear to focus on the corporation, and none of the presenters of these papers list an institutional affiliation with American studies).[5] Likewise, the workshops at the 1998 conference of the European Association of American Studies addressed a range of vital issues – gender, race, ethnicity, regionalism, landscape, literature, poetry, otherness, critical theory, semiotics, identity, the family, sexuality, morality, and marginalized language groups. Yet of more than 225 papers presented, only one (this one) claimed as its topic the centrality of the corporation and business activity in American cultural life.

This gaping hole in American studies scholarship is bound to affect students. A graduating senior from Michigan's Program in American Cultures, where I have been a faculty associate, came to me at the end of her last semester to ask for some advice. She had thoroughly enjoyed her degree and her concentration in ethnic studies and planned to pursue graduate work in American studies as soon as possible. Because she needed money, however, she had taken a job as a buyer with Abercrombie and Fitch's corporate headquarters in Ohio, which actively reaches out to graduating seniors – and not just business majors – for management positions ("You're fun, outgoing and have great personal style," the company's web site tells prospective applicants. "You live the Abercrombie lifestyle, and you believe work and play can go together."[6]) Not only did this woman say that she had encountered nothing in her American studies degree that would have directly prepared her to understand and negotiate the corporate world she was about to enter, but she actually felt that, according to what she had learned, her decision to work in the corporate sector was somehow wrong. She is probably not the only American studies graduate to absorb such a guilt complex. The Crossroads American Studies web site contains more than fifty very useful syllabuses representing a broad spectrum of what faculty in the field are teaching. The majority of these syllabuses claim that they will cover "major themes, issues, and institutions in American culture." But only three of those courses even mention business or corporate culture, and none of them presents students with any extended studies of how corporations have evolved, how corporations differ, or how so many people regularly negotiate their role as corporate citizens simultaneously with their roles as American citizens, as members of ethnic majorities or minorities, and as men and women with different class and professional affiliations.[7]

Where is our collective sense of proportion? Isn't this a bit like oceanographers refusing to acknowledge the existence of water? Imagine the historian who stumbles across the Crossroads web site or an ASA conference program while surfing the web in the year 3000, when there may be no more United States or other nation states, but only global corporations. This historian will probably work – without tenure – as a content provider for the Microsoft University of the Internet. Won't she look back in wonder at how so many highly trained, intelligent, and critical cultural scholars could have chosen to overlook so completely the burgeoning incorporation of American culture that will have shaped her very existence? How can American studies as a discipline afford largely to ignore the most powerful institutions on the American landscape?

Granted, some fine investigations of business and corporate life have come out of American studies – work by David Noble, David Nye, Susan Porter Benson, Alan Trachtenberg, and the late Roland Marchand spring immediately to mind.[8] And there is a small coterie of emerging scholars who are trying to apply the latest in critical cultural theories to the study of corporate and business cultures.[9] But the field as a whole is not following their lead, certainly not at the moment. It is easy to find scholars of American culture, especially those who consider themselves to be doing cultural studies, who are very concerned about "corporate hegemony" in a vaguely oppositional sense. And many in American studies, as well as in the humanities at large, are downright angry or scared – with good reason – about the encroachment of the corporation and bottom-line calculations into the sacred halls of academia itself. But these concerns have not inspired many American studies scholars to examine the corporation from the inside out. They have produced the opposite effect – an almost defiant focus on those aspects of American culture at the farthest remove from the corporate boardroom, or even the corporate cubicle.

Part of this selective focus no doubt stems from what Elaine Tyler May calls the "radical roots of American Studies" and from the emergence of the field as an offshoot of American literary studies.[10] But I would like to suggest another potential reason for this gulf. American studies scholars have been very concerned to distance themselves from a crude model of determinism, exemplified in many people's minds by the Frankfurt School, whereby material base governs cultural superstructure. In defiance of this model, these same scholars proclaim the power of the superstructure to fight back against the base. Culture is important, we argue. On this basis, American studies has taken up the project of restoring a sense of agency to marginalized cultural groups. We insist that power and agency reside in places most do not expect to find it – in texts and interpretive practices, in material artifacts, in forms of artistic expression, in the coping strategies of ethnic and racial minorities, in everyday life. In aggregate the discipline of

American studies is now pretty much all about the championing of cultural agency.

This is an extremely valuable body of work. But, viewed as a whole, as the comprehensive and interdisciplinary study of American culture, our field remains incomplete, and one might even say evasive. In large part this is because we have come to define the corporation and business tacitly as, *not* agency, but as structure. And because we proceed on the premise that structure is bad and agency is good, we avoid any sustained study of corporate cultures as American cultures. This head-over-heels romance with cultural agency ends up replicating the very crude determinism it seeks to counteract and renders American studies incapable of criticizing corporate and business structures themselves in any meaningful way. Not only have we adjusted our collective disciplinary lens in such a way that we cannot focus clearly or for sustained periods of time on corporate structures, but also the structures themselves have moved during the last thirty years to redefine themselves as somehow *not* structure, but pure agency. Management literature and discourse, for example, is now full of diatribes against the evils of bureaucracies and celebrations of culture, diversity, individual empowerment, and the flattening of hierarchies. Since the 1970s, corporate legal theory has largely abandoned a structuralist definition of the corporation as an autonomous managerial hierarchy in favor of a view of the business firm as nothing more than a cluster of proliferating market activities, as a site of pure agency.

"One of the essential and central notions which give our industrial feudalism logical symmetry is the personification of great industrial enterprise," observed legendary antitrust attorney and Yale Law School professor Thurman Arnold. "The ideal that a great corporation is endowed with the rights and prerogatives of a free individual is as essential to the acceptance of corporate rule in temporal affairs as was the ideal of the divine right of kings / in an earlier day." Arnold devoted a whole chapter of his book to lampooning the notion, already hardened into legal orthodoxy, that the corporation is a person before the law. "The arguments often appeared nonsensical," he complained, "but it should be remembered that for the purpose of binding organizations together nothing makes as much sense as nonsense, and hence nonsense always wins."[11] Contemporary law professor Morton J. Horwitz explores the roots of corporate personhood less sarcastically in a 1985 law review article "Santa Clara Revisited." According to Horwitz, nineteenth-century concession theories, which held that corporations exist only as artificial creations of state charters, provided too strong a basis for state regulatory intervention to suit the interests of capital. Another nineteenth-century alternative, the aggregate theory of the firm as a collection of individual stockholders, threatened to make those individuals personally liable for the corporation's actions, above and beyond the dollar amount of their initial investment. Both approaches thus provided the basis for severe restrictions on corporate activity and investment. The "real entity" theory of the corporation maintained that the firm was a natural "person" before the law, neither created by state fiat nor reducible to the sum of its stockholders. "The main effect of the natural entity theory of the business corporation was to legitimate large scale enterprise and to destroy any special basis for state regulation of the corporation that derived from its creation by the state," says Horwitz.[12] Not surprisingly, then, the real entity theory of the firm gained prominence during the same period that bore witness to the rise of the mammoth managerial corporation itself.

The corporation did not become such a giant dominating the American landscape without considerable struggle and dissent. In the words of Allen Kaufman and Lawrence Zacharias, "the preeminent institution of the modern marketplace, the managerial corporation, has regularly incited debates over its benefits for democratic practices, the market, and liberty itself," because "modern corporate society [threatens] to reduce the individual, America's basic element of constitutional logic, to apparent sociological irrelevance."[13] This "corporation problem" was the very reason for the progressive antitrust movement of which Arnold became such an important figurehead. In essence, the problem is that such un precedented levels of market concentration and privilege challenged an American liberal imagination predicated on the Jeffersonian ideal of a democracy of small propertyholders. "It needs no sleep, takes no vacations," one commentator has written of this strange creature called the corporation. "If you prick it, it does not bleed; if you tickle it, it does not laugh. It can scream, however, if taxed or otherwise annoyed." Streeter describes the burgeoning threat this strange creature poses to the liberal ideal this way: "If the legitimacy of a market society rests on its control by individuals, how can one justify a capitalism dominated by the giant impersonal collectivities we call corporations?" Streeter and several other scholars have highlighted how *corporate* liberalism developed as a set of interrelated strategies for resolving this quandary by reconciling traditional liberal ideals with corporate capitalist imperatives. In this context, the real entity theory of the firm appears as a central tool in the corporate liberal arsenal because it justifies powerful capitalist collectivities in vividly individualist terms.[14]

The legal device by means of which real entity theorists achieved this feat was the separation of ownership from control. Managers would serve as neutral trustees situated halfway between shareholders and society at large, responsible for weighing the interests of both but invested with an authority of their own. Management expertise would ensure that shareholders received an optimal return on their investment, while managers' autonomy and social responsibility would guarantee that the staggering levels of economic power inherent in the corporate form would not threaten the rights of individual citizens. "Indeed, it seems almost essential if the corporate system is to survive," stated Adolf A. Berle and Gardiner C. Means in 1932, "that the 'control' of the great corporations should develop into a purely neutral technocracy, balancing a variety of claims by various groups in the community and assigning to each a portion of the income stream on the basis of public policy rather than private cupidity."[15] Berle and Means's work has come to serve as the *locus classicus* of the corporate legal doctrine known as "managerialism."

As Streeter argues in *Selling the Air,* the central ideals of corporate liberal managerialism undergirded more than forty years of federal regulation of the radio and television industries. Although legal doctrine long had held that the airwaves belonged to the citizens of the United States, the Radio Act of 1927 and the Communications Act of 1934 charged the Federal Communications Commission (FCC) to dole out access to the electromagnetic spectrum to private corporations. Even though managed by private companies, commercial broadcasting would remain a truly democratic system, so the argument went, because individual licensees would serve their communities as public trustees, provide programs of local interest and concern, and facilitate a broad range of local expression over the airwaves. This rationale did pave the way for a limited amount of positive state control over corporate broadcasting – at least compared to what came after. It also legitimized such a wide range of managerial discretion that it ended up promoting and protecting a virtual oligopoly of three all-powerful national networks through the 1970s.

That managerialism buttressed massive corporate hierarchies even as it paid lip service to individual rights should not be too surprising, given that it was so stridently paternalistic. The separation of ownership from control and the corporate liberal emphasis on technocratic expertise were predicated on the belief that sturdy, autonomous management hierarchies, like fathers, know best. The real entity theory contributed to this paternalistic mode of legitimizing corporate power, as Mark McGurl observes, because insisting on the tangible reality and sturdiness of its existence "was a way for the corporation to lay visible claim to a privileged, indeed dominating, place on the landscape of American market culture." McGurl provides a vivid description of the masculine presumptions behind this effort in a discussion of what he calls "those fantastic, phallomaniacal monuments to corporate identity, the skyscrapers." He cites a 1930s architectural critic who celebrated skyscrapers as "a natural growth, and a symbol of the American spirit ... ruthless, tireless, assured energism, delightedly proclaiming, 'What a great boy am I!'"[16]

That observation could just as easily apply to Ted Turner, the subject of my current research. But Turner would direct his own phallomaniacal energies *against* the towers of paternalist managerialism. Seeking to hurdle broadcasting's formidable regulatory barriers to entry throughout the 1970s, Turner charged that the networks had not lived up to their responsibilities as public trustees. He went on to attack the foundational managerialist principle of neutral trusteeship itself in the name of technological abundance and open competition.

Cable and satellite technology had solved the problem of spectrum scarcity, Turner argued, and he should suffer no federally imposed compunction to serve as a trustee of the public good. Instead, Congress should abolish restrictions to entry in the television industry based on that principle and let the market hold sway. "We should be thankful that the marketplace is allowing more competition and diversification," Turner said, holding up his "superstation" as an example of the benefits of deregulation during Senate hearings in 1979. "Television is becoming a consumer product. That's the big difference between what the future holds and what the networks want to keep giving us."[17]

These arguments did not spring fully grown from Ted Turner's head. They floated thick in the air he had been breathing long before he bought into the broadcasting industry in 1968, and they combined elements from many sources, including the movement for corporate responsibility, the work of consumer advocates such as Ralph Nader, the broadcast reform movement, and the deregulatory struggles of Turner's own primary distributor, the cable industry. Rage against the managerial establishment had become a hot cultural commodity during the 1960s, and not exclusively among hippie dropouts. In the *Conquest of Cool,* Thomas Frank makes clear that even members of the corporate establishment began to adopt rebellious postures during this period. "Capitalism was entering the space age in the sixties, and Organization Man was a drag not only as a parent, but as an executive," Frank argues. "The values of caution, deference, and hierarchy drowned creativity and denied flexibility; they enervated not only the human spirit but the consuming spirit and the entrepreneurial spirit as well."[18]

A large part of Ted Turner's veneer comes from the fact that he did not just mouth these arguments, he *embodied* them – his personal success story, his status as a sailing hero, his southern bravura, his cleft chin, his Rhett Butler mustache, even his fabled womanizing and the parable of his Oedipal struggles with his own overbearing father all combined to make him a natural leader in the assault on paternalist managerialism. Turner is such a creature of the market, in fact, that his personal biography is also the biography of the new ways corporate capital has come to represent and legitimate itself over the last thirty years. More than anything he actually said during the 1980s, his image as a figure of raw male energy and entrepreneurial aggression carried its own rhetorical force. "What makes me root for Turner is not his self-proclaimed virtue but his wild vitality, his unruliness," enthused one commentator in the *New York Times* during Turner's 1985 bid for CBS. "No force short of Turner could shock [CBS] out of its tedious complacency."[19]

The shift in the rhetorical construction of corporate management for which Ted Turner has served as the premier poster boy occurred simultaneously with a transformation in the legal construction of the American corporation. Starting in the 1970s, economists and legal scholars developed a new theory of the corporation that sought to wield the raw energies of the market, to erode the foundations of federal regulation, and to topple complacent managerial hierarchies. In the year that Ted Turner's company launched the nation's first cable superstation and rose to national notoriety as the scourge of the broadcasting establishment, economists Michael Jensen and William Meckling called for a new economic theory of the firm.[20] In stark contrast to the real entity theory, their theory insisted that the corporation was a nexus of contracts, a bundle of intersecting market transactions that defies embodiment or, conveniently, regulatory containment. The new theory professes to be egalitarian, because these supposed contracts are drawn up among a variety of rationally self-interested actors – managers, shareholders, employees, customers, and suppliers, who all seek to reduce their literal or figurative transaction costs in order to maximize outcomes. Thus contract theory does not even acknowledge the existence of a power imbalance that threatens individual liberties and that necessitates the corrective separation of ownership and control. The very concepts of "ownership" and "control" lose their meaning, as does the point of insisting that corporations exist as separate, natural entities with legal standing. The contractarian picture of the firm performed the magic trick of dissolving managerial hierarchies altogether – at least in theory.[21] The corporation is reconceived as simply a site of bustling activity, a figure of pure agency.

At first blush, the definition of "agency" employed by Jensen and other agency theorists appears strange to cultural theorists who use the same term in the humanities. Agency theorists are economists, so they presume that all human actions are motivated by rational self-interest and utility maximizing, or what we call "greed." "We define an agency relationship as a contract under which one or more persons (the principal(s)) engage another person (the agent) to perform some service on their behalf which involves delegating some decision making authority to the agent." In plain language, people with money, "principals," engage other people, called "agents," to manage their money for them. But because everyone is presumably greedy, the principals cannot be sure that the agents will watch over their money carefully enough or that the agents will not try to skim some money off the top for themselves. The value of whatever agents do manage to take for themselves, together with the costs incurred by the principal to monitor all of this skimming, are called "agency costs." As Doug Henwood points out, we might just as well call these "perks" and the costs of controlling them, but Jensen and other agency theorists plot all of this "perk grabbing" with complicated vectors to lend their theory "the prestige of mathematics for those easily seduced by subscripts."[22] The point of all of this talk of agency costs is to contrast a picture of the corporation predicated on structure, the managerialist picture, with a new definition of the corporation as an intense concentration of self-determining individual activity, or agency as we usually speak of it in the humanities.

The real world "agents" of this understanding of the firm turned out to be the corporate takeover artists of the 1980s. To the delight of agency theorists, corporate takeovers and leveraged buyouts toppled managerial hierarchies, broke them up into their aggregate parts, and sold them off in chains of transactions that rendered the boundaries between individual firms and the market itself increasingly fluid. The takeover era also transformed the gendered image of American business leadership – patriarchal, austere managerialists were violently overthrown by hyperaggressive, even sexually predatory, raiders and pirates. During the 1980s, takeover events were often framed as "rapes," with target companies cast as "sleeping beauties" or "brides" dragged to the altar.[23] "When Ted Turner came a-courtin' to CBS a few years back, this most proud and disdainful of maidens turned him a cold shoulder," declared the *New*

York Times commentary on Ted Turner's hostile bid for CBS in 1983. "Now he's threatening to carry the network off kicking and screaming, and I for one hope he gets away with it." The cartoon that ran with the piece celebrated Turner's latest business adventure with equally macho imagery. Turner appeared as a robust sailor with a ring in his ear, ready to harpoon a monstrous white whale with the CBS logo for an eye.[24]

Despite this oppositional posture toward managerial hierarchies, corporate takeovers and the new economic theory of the firm that legitimized them ended up promoting even greater levels of economic concentration and managerial discretion. Law professor William Bratton explains this by noting that "treating hierarchy as if it does not exist offers wonderful support to those at the top of the hierarchy." He concludes that the picture of the firm as contract is "merely the latest in a long series of attempts to describe and justify the phenomenon of collective production in individualist terms." It would be a mistake, however, to conclude that contract theory is therefore liberal. Modeling all corporate activity on predatory market transactions rather than on familial relationships, it shares none of the paternalistic characteristics of corporate liberalism. Moreover, contract theory refuses to acknowledge the existence of the central problem – the collective corporate threat to the unfettered agency of the liberal individual – that gave rise to corporate liberal ideology in the first place. "Since no cognizable corporate collectivity appears amidst the nexus of contracts," says Bratton, "no tension arises between collective and individual interests."[25]

During the 1970s and early 1980s, Ted Turner functioned as a transitional figure between paternalist managerialism and the real entity theory of the firm, on the one hand, and predatory market adventurism and the new economic theories of the firm on the other. Turner acknowledged the corporate threat to liberal individualism but fundamentally altered the corporate liberal solution to the problem. His symbolic effect has been to supplant the bureaucratic rationality of corporate liberalism with market efficiencies, its technological expertise with an "aw-shucks" enthusiasm for satellite gadgetry, and its paternalistic trusteeship with the vicarious virtues of youthful and regenerative entrepreneurship. This is why he has never legitimized corporate media management in the top-down, paternalistic mode of a Thomas Edison, a David Sarnoff, or a William Paley. No matter how gray-haired Turner gets, he maintains a youthful, rebellious, seductive, and boyish aura of naiveté and acquisitiveness. But as the merger of his company with the massive media conglomerate Time Warner demonstrates, Turner does not dissolve the real entity of the corporation completely. Rather than separate ownership from control or do away with both, Turner combines ownership and control back together again in his own person, presenting himself as a new, tangible, antibureaucratic, and competitive-masculine embodiment of corporate activity and managerial trusteeship. "A lot of people expected Mr. Turner would ride off into the sunset after he sold his Turner Broadcasting System Inc. to Time Warner," stated an article in the *Wall Street Journal* in March 1997. "Instead, he is off on a wild ride through the world's biggest media empire, crashing into top executives' personal fiefdoms, abruptly canceling deals, asking impertinent questions about lavish expenses, and generally giving Time Warner a one-man dose of culture shock."[26]

"Institutions are fundamentally historical," insists William Roy in his recent book. "They do not just exist, but are constantly being created, reproduced, and transformed." Roy provides a much-needed corrective to prevailing technoeconomic and functionalist historical accounts of the rise of the large corporation, epitomized in his view by the work of Alfred Chandler. Such accounts adhere to an ahistorical efficiency theory, he argues, that views the economies of scale made possible by the large, multidivisional corporation run by salaried managers as the logical and natural result of a set of technological and economic needs and developments. By contrast, Roy insists that "the rise of the corporation was neither inevitable nor natural." Instead, he argues, "it was the work of specific individuals and groups acting within the context of constraints and facilitators, setting goals, mobilizing resources, and influencing others to act in concert, shape meanings, and mobilize resources." Roy demonstrates forcefully that the rise of the large corporation was a thoroughly socialized and politicized phenomenon – hence the title of his book. He concludes, "Power relationships that create new structures become embedded within social institutions that take on a life of their own, a process set within history, so that to understand the reasons why a system like corporate capitalism arose requires that we understand its roots as well as its immediate precipitants."[27]

Roy's exciting work should be taken as a challenge to scholars in American studies who share his interests in lived social relations, in the dynamics of power, and in the historical contingency of supposedly "natural" institutions to take a closer look at the corporation through the lens of interdisciplinary cultural history and criticism. They would be surprised at what they will find. Progressive, anticorporate American studies scholars who take up the project of championing cultural agency, for example, will be disturbed to discover that some of the most conservative advocates of corporate legal theory also have seized upon and elevated a notion of agency as a moral imperative and transcendent value. I do not mean to imply that the emphasis on agency in new economic theories of the corporation calls into question the legitimacy of the way American studies scholars use the term. But American studies scholars should recognize that even a realm as apparently monolithic and arcane as corporate legal theory has a dynamic history and the outcome of that history matters for the balance of power relations in American society.

A more thorough investigation of corporate legal theory from an American studies perspective needs to include many important developments that I have left out here for the sake of brevity. Many progressive legal scholars have taken up the project of combating the agency theorists, refusing to allow legal theory to serve merely as the servant of corporate power.[28] Looked at historically, corporate legal theory turns out to be a complex debate about agency versus structure, individuality versus collectivity, private versus public, and democratic representation versus concentrated economic power. To put all of this in the currently fashionable American Studies terminology, corporate legal theory is all about boundaries and borderlands. The fixing of the corporate border enfranchises some and disenfranchises others. It inscribes the individual in relation to the collective and negotiates the ever-shifting divide between public and private spheres. The place to find this debate is in the law journals. They contain a vibrant, exciting, and sophisticated literature on the nature of the corporation, a literature full of fierce struggles and piercing insights about American culture. American studies has many things to contribute to this discussion. Interdisciplinary perspectives on race, class, gender, culture, power, and history can bring corporate legal theory alive and make its relevance clear to students of American culture. Given that the struggles over diversity, difference, representation, and justice so central to American studies are likely to take place hidden from public view, in larger and larger commercial institutions, the investigation of corporate structures and business cultures ought to be included at the center of the interdisciplinary study of American cultures.

Notes

1. Thomas Streeter, *Selling the Air: A Critique of the Policy of Commercial Broadcasting in the United States* (Chicago, 1996), 8, 15.
2. Steven Lipin, "Amalgamated America – Concentration: Corporations' Dreams Converge in One Idea: It's Time to Do a Deal," *Wall Street Journal*, Feb. 26, 1997, A1.
3. "Sweepstakes 'winners' seek victory in lawsuits; Companies sued over 'aggressive, deceptive' language in letters," *Baltimore Sun*, Mar. 8, 1998, 4A.
4. William Roy, *Socializing Capital: The Rise of the Large Industrial Corporation in America* (Princeton, N. J., 1997), xiii.
5. American Studies Association Web Pages, <http://www.press.jhu.edu/associations/asa/program98/asa_1998.html>
6. Abercrombie and Fitch Web Pages, <http://www.abercrombie.com>
7. American Studies Electronic Crossroads Web Pages, <http://www.georgetown.edu/crossroads/as_syllabi.html>
8. David Noble, *America By Design: Science, Technology, and the Rise of Corporate Capitalism* (New York, 1977); David E. Nye, *Image Worlds: Corporate Identities at General Electric, 1890-1930* (Cambridge, Mass., 1985); Susan Porter Benson, *Counter Cultures: Saleswomen, Managers, and Customers in American Department Stores, 1890-1940* (Urbana, Ill., 1986); Alan Trachtenberg, *The Incorporation of America: Culture and Society in the Gilded Age* (New York, 1982); Roland Marchand, *Creating the Corporate Soul: The Rise of Public Relations and Corporate Imagery in American Big Business* (Berkeley, 1998).
9. See, for example, Christopher Newfield, "Corporate Culture Wars" and the other essays in *Corporate Futures: The Diffusion of the Culturally Sensitive Corporate Form* (Chicago, 1998); Angel Kwolek-Folland, *Engendering Business: Men and Women in the Corporate Office, 1870-1930*

(Baltimore, 1998), and *Incorporating Women: A History of Women and Business in the United States* (forthcoming); Thomas Frank, *The Conquest of Cool: Business Culture, Counterculture, and Hip Consumerism* (Chicago, 1997), as well as Frank's and other essays in the independent magazine, *The Baffler*. For a scathing left critique of corporate finance from the inside out, see Doug Henwood, *Wall Street: How it Works and for Whom* (London, 1998).

10. Elaine Tyler May, "The Radical Roots of American Studies: Presidential Address to the American Studies Association, November 9, 1995," *American Quarterly,* 48 (1996), 179-200.
11. Thurman Arnold, *The Folklore of Capitalism* (New Haven, 1937), 185.
12. Morton J. Horwitz, "Santa Clara Revisited: The Development of Corporate Theory," *West Virginia Law Review,* 88 (1985), 173-224.
13. Allen Kaufman and Lawrence Zacharias, "From Trust to Contract: The Legal Language of Managerial Ideology, 1920-1980," *Business History Review,* 66:3 (1992), 16.
14. Martin Mayer, *Wall Street: Men and Money* (New York, 1955), 33, quoted in R. Jeffrey Lustig, *Corporate Liberalism: The Origins of Modern American Political Theory, 1890-1920* (Berkeley, 1982), 10; Streeter, *Selling the Air: A Critique of the Idea of Commercial Broadcasting in the United States* (Chicago, 1996), 51.
15. Adolf A. Berle and Gardiner C. Means, *The Modern Corporation and Private Property,* rev. ed. (New York, 1967; orig. pub. 1932), 312.
16. Mark McGurl, "Making It Big: Picturing the Radio Age in King Kong," *Critical Inquiry,* 22:4 (1996), 17.
17. United States Senate, 96th Congress, 1st Session, Committee on Commerce, Science, and Transportation, Subcommittee on Communications, Hearings on Amendments to the Communications Act of 1934, May 10- June 7, 1979 (Washington, D. C., 1979), 2145.
18. Frank, *The Conquest of Cool: Business Culture, Counterculture, and Hip Consumerism*, 28.
19. James Traub "Turner Might Save CBS From Itself," *New York Times,* May 1, 1985, A 27.
20. Michael Jensen and William Meckling "Theory of the Firm: Managerial Behavior, Agency Costs, and Ownership Structure," *Journal of Financial Economics,* 3 (1976), 305-60. Jensen and Meckling traced the roots of their theory to two other articles, Armen A. Alchian and Harold Demsetz, "Production, Information Costs, and Economic Organization," *American Economic Review,* 62 (1972), 777-95, and Ronald H. Coase, "The Nature of the Firm," *Economica,* 4 (1937), 390-94.
21. William W. Bratton, Jr., "The New Economic Theory of the Firm: Critical Perspectives from History," *Stanford Law Review,* 41 (1989), 1499.
22. Henwood, *Wall Street,* 267.
23. Paul M. Hirsch, "From Ambushes to Golden Parachutes: Corporate Takeovers as an Instance of Cultural Framing and Institutional Integration," *American Journal of Sociology,* 91 (1986), 800-37.
24. Traub "Turner Might Save CBS From Itself," A 27.

25. Bratton, "New Economic Theory of the Firm," 1499.
26. Eben Shapiro, "Ted's Way: Brash as Ever, Turner Is Giving Time Warner Dose of Culture Shock," *Wall Street Journal,* Mar. 24, 1997, A1.
27. Roy, *Socializing Capital,* 259. See Alfred Chandler, *The Visible Hand: The Managerial Revolution in American Business* (Cambridge, Mass., 1977).
28. See, for example, the essays in Lawrence E. Mitchell, *Progressive Corporate Law* (Boulder, Colo., 1995).

10

American Links to Legal Reform in Ireland, 1937-1997: A Study in the International Impact of American Constitutional Law

Michael Böss

In a recent biography of Mary Robinson (née Bourke), *Irish Times* journalist Lorna Siggins describes how, in 1967, the young law graduate left Trinity College, Dublin, to discover the meaning of "direct action" at Harvard Law School. Mary Bourke went to the United States in 1966 at the urging of Harvard's Arthur van Mehren, whom she met at a session of the Hague Conference on Private International Law the year before. There she had functioned as an official note taker and *secrétaire rédactrice*. At Harvard she obtained the master of laws degree (LL.M), in addition to her master's degree in law from Trinity College, her barrister-at-law degree from King's Inns, Dublin, and her experience as auditor of the TCD Law Society and editor of the student law review, *Justice*.[1] She had taken six subjects at Harvard: conflict of laws, the prediction and prevention of harmful conduct, an introduction to urban legal studies, international transactions and relations, legal aspects of the European Common Market, and the civil law system. This choice reflected her growing interest in international law and the social problems of modern urban societies.

In hindsight it seems to have been less the academic challenge at Harvard than the contemporary intellectual and political climate in the United States (and at Harvard) that were to mean most for her later career as a lawyer and a member of the upper house of the Irish parliament, the Seanad. Later in life, she would cite her time in Cambridge, Massachusetts, as one of the most influential experiences of her life, particularly for what it taught her about the relation between law and society. In a 1980 interview in the *Sunday Independent,* she recalled how social issues were suddenly articulated in the debate among American law student, and how she personally was affected by the new interest in matters of personal conscience:

> The Vietnam War forced a lot of young people to re-think. There was a great deal of discussion on socialism, on equality, civil rights, and poverty. Many of the very bright students were turning down large law firm salaries, [sic] to get involved in projects and counsel for legal education, which was a totally transformed approach. When I came home, I related all this to Ireland and have continued to do so.[2]

What Mary Bourke Robinson brought home with her from Harvard, then, was greater awareness of law as one of the structural dimensions of culture; law as the "hidden infrastructure which conditions our society and pervades almost every aspect of our lives," as she put it much later.[3] To this should be added a growing perception of the need for Irish judges to play an active role in policy making. The model was the United States Supreme Court under Chief Justice Earl Warren.

Seen in a wide perspective, "the education of Mary Robinson" reflects the way in which American constitutional law influenced a new generation of European lawyers after the Second World War. In a particular, Irish, perspective, it is a good example of the way in which calls for social and legal reform in Ireland often respond to events and developments in the United States. In this essay, I argue that American law played an implicit role in the drafting of the Constitution of Ireland in 1936-1937, most significantly in the creation of a Supreme Court with the power of judicial review. I demonstrate how this "American" institution produced unforeseen results in the 1960s, when Irish Supreme Court judges Cearbhall O Dalaigh and Brian Walsh changed the face of Irish law under direct inspiration from the United States Supreme Court. I also wish to show how constitutional politics in the United States, in the wake of *Roe* v. *Wade* and the rise of the New Right put a brake on liberal legal reforms in Ireland in the 1980s. Finally, I argue that in her career as a lawyer and senator, Robinson epitomized the impact of American legal culture on Ireland in the 1970s and 1980s. Finally, I conclude that Robinson's appointment to the post of United Nations High Commissioner for Human Rights in 1997, with the strong support of the United States, represents the latest chapter in a story of how American law has interacted with European law on issues that are of vital importance in any modern, liberal democracy: how to balance the rights of the individual with the "common good," that is, with the interests of the community as a whole, and how to adhere to universal principles of justice while respecting the values and norms of the local and national community. Thus this essay aims to be both a contribution to the study of the international scope of American law and a study of the general social, cultural, and political aspects of constitutional law.

The Constitution of Ireland is sometimes called "De Valera's Constitution."[4] No wonder! In the 1930s Eamon de Valera, the embodiment of Irish republican nationalism and four times prime minister between 1932 and 1958, personally campaigned for a replacement of the Irish Free State Constitution of 1922. During 1935-1937 he played an active role in supervising the drafting of a new constitution by a small group of civil servants led by John Hearne, who at that time was legal adviser in the Department of External Affairs and had international legal experience from his attendance at sessions in the League of Nations.

Even from its narrow passage by popular referendum in July 1937 (685,105 votes to 526,945), the Constitution of Ireland was an advanced piece of constitutional law for a political system built on the principle of responsible democracy.[5] The Constitution created a bicameral parliament (Oireachtas) with a lower house (Dáil) and an upper house (Seanad), the office of a popularly elected president as head of state, and an independent judiciary. The Bunreacht nah Éireann – its official title in Irish – can reasonably well be decribed as a written version of the (unwritten) British constitutional tradition, if it were not for three features, two of which give it an "American" character: the referendum, the establishment of a Supreme Court with special functions, and the integration of a Bill of Rights. All three provisions came to play an important role for the introduction of legal reform in Ireland from the 1960s on, although when the Draft Constitution was debated in Parliament in 1937, they were hardly mentioned. At that time, both de Valera and the opposition parties did not regard them as central to the constitutional project.

The Constitution explicitly protects the basic political and civil rights of citizens. This gives it the appearance of a moderately liberal document, given the conservative and authoritarian social values that characterized Irish society and most members of the nationalist movement in the 1930s. Eamon de Valera had taken great pains to emphasize that from then on "the people [would be] the masters" and "above the lawyers and above Government and all others."[6] His republican ideal is also stated in the Preamble: "We, the people of Éire ... do hereby adopt, enact, and give to ourselves this Constitution," it says, with an echo from the American Constitution, which had inspired Irish republican nationalists since the end of the eighteenth century.

Nevertheless, the Draft Constitution did give rise to accusations of discrimination against the rights of individuals. The criticism was based on the status in society it was alleged to give women, especially in its articles on the "fundamental rights" of the family. The way in which de Valera dealt with this issue is a key to understanding how he generally balanced individual against communal rights, that is, the interests of individual citizens against the interests of the "common good" of the Irish state.

During the debate in the Dáil on May 11, 1937, two deputies claimed that the Constitution, if passed, would reduce the rights and opportunities of women. In doing this, they voiced inside the Dáil the extraparliamentary criticism raised by a number of Irish women's groups, who feared that "the proposed constitution [left] the door open for reactionary legislation against women in every department" and that the proposed constitution would deny women the "equal rights and equal opportunities [that] Irishmen and Irishwomen" had been guaranteed in 1916, in connection with the first proclamation of an Irish republic.[7] The argument that had been raised during the debate did not concern women's political rights but the delimitation of their social and economic rights by Articles 40.1, 41.2, and 45.[8] Article 40.1 read (and still reads):

> All citizens shall, as human persons, be held equal before the law. This shall not be held to mean that the State shall not in its enactments have due regard to differences of capacity, physical and moral, and of social function.

The "moral" and "social function" of women was further stated in Article 41.2:

> 1. In particular the State recognises that by her life within the home, woman gives to the State a support within the home without which the common good cannot be achieved.
> 2. The State shall, therefore, endeavour to ensure that mothers shall not be obliged by economic necessity to engage in labour to the neglect of their duties in the home.

De Valera clearly did not understand how the wording of Article 41.2 discriminated against women. On the contrary, he was convinced that the article gave protection to women (including widows, unmarried mothers, mothers married to neglectful or disabled husbands, and mothers with handicapped children) in that it prevented them from being forced by economic necessity to work outside the home. He spent much of his speaking time defending his own reasons for including the article. His defense was obviously motivated by the unease he felt about the social consequences of the international market economy that Ireland was becoming part of.[9]

De Valera's concern with the potential social effects of Ireland's economic modernization had further led him to include an article (Article 45) that states a number of Directive Principles of Social Policy intended for "the general guidance of the Oireachtas." In general, the directives can be said to have laid the moral basis, in principle, for the creation of an Irish welfare state. Thus it is the obligation of the State, for instance, "to promote the welfare of the whole people by securing and protecting as effectively as it may a social order in which justice and charity shall inform all the institutions of the national life." Further, the State is obliged to secure that "men and women equally [will have] an adequate means of livelihood" and to regulate the economy in such a way as to serve "the common good" and "the welfare of the people as a whole."

It is important to underline that the Constitution expressly guarantees the rights of religious minorities. Still, in practice de Valera tended toward a majoritarian conception of democracy. He found that if 99 percent of all Irish women shared his views – and in all likelihood they did at the time – he was justified in disregarding the interests of the 1 percent who did not.[10] This had implications for the largest religious minority of the State, Irish Protestants, with whom the preceding government had clashed in 1923. Also in that case the contested issue had been divorce.

The 1937 Constitution integrated the existing statute law against divorce under the rights of the family (Article 41.3). The new constitutional ban originated in the social teaching of the Catholic church and deprived the Protestant minority of a right that did not conflict with the doctrines of their own church. De Valera admitted that the ban reflected the ethos of the religious majority of the state. But his defense was based on a secular argument, namely, the interest of the common good: "This is not *merely* a question of religious teaching ... even from the purely social side, apart from all that, I would propose here that we would not sanction divorce [emphasis added]."[11]

De Valera's argument was based on his notion of Ireland as a national family ideally kept together in a tight social order by popular common will. In his ideas of a national democracy, one may find elements of Rousseau (*volonté générale*), Herder (*Volk*), and "romantic" social philosophy, whether rooted in the teaching of the Catholic church or in communitarian ideals of a Tönnies extraction (*Gemeinschaft*). This is why a reading of the social directives may make the Irish Constitution look less like a legal document than a social manifest; a program about how to save society from breaking apart as a community under the strains of modernity: the laws of the free market, commercialization, secularization, mass popular culture, and individualism. De Valera feared that the values and norms of traditional Irish culture – and, with this, the sense of living in a community based on a common ethos – would come under threat if individual interests and rights superceded communal rights and interests. The "interests of the community as a whole" must therefore delimit and qualify the rights of individuals. There was no such thing as an absolute individual right, he stressed.[12]

The political implication of this mode of thinking is that minorities and individuals must be expected to make sacrifices and to be loyal to the Irish nation. They must resign themselves to the will of the majority, for if they chose not to, then the glue that holds society together may dissolve, and the social body will fall apart.[13] Hence, de Valera did not regard questions of personal and private morality as issues pertaining exclusively to individual citizens. They were concerns of the whole state.

De Valera was convinced that the State could not exert its authority without the assistance of other institutions, especially the church and the schools, if the "body of tradition" were not to be torn apart.[14] Addressing the annual congress of primary school teachers assembled at Killarney in 1940 – and with a clear but unstated reference to the United States – he reminded his audience that the twentieth century had already seen many examples of societies that had suffered under the impact of modernity. The implicit argument was that they had been based on an individualist ideology and not on national cooperation and Christian principles.[15]

During the debates over the Draft Constitution in 1937, most of the critical voices were more concerned with the role of the president than with the issue of individual rights. Suspicious of de Valera's democratic disposition, members of the opposition feared that, given the president's election by direct vote of the people (Article 12.2.1) and the possibility of conferring additional powers and functions on him (Article 13.10), de Valera would be able to turn Ireland into a personal dictatorship.[16] To prevent any such future situation, parliament amended Articles 13.9 and 13.10 and inserted a new Article 13.11. These articles make clear that "the powers and functions conferred on the President by this Constitution shall be exercisable and performable by him only on the advice of the Government" and that "no power or function conferred on the President by law shall be exercisable or performable by him save only on the advice of the Government." On his own part, de Valera claimed that he merely saw the president's role as a guardian of the Constitution and of the peoples' rights against government or parliament.[17] Despite the presidency's potential for wielding considerable political power, the Irish system of government as the presidency evolved in the following years did not develop into the type of "semi-presidential" system that is known in countries such as Finland, France, and Portugal.[18]

One of the six discretionary powers of the president that de Valera had found it necessary to defend is in Article 26, which gives the president the privilege to refer any bill passed or deemed to have been passed by both houses of the Oireachtas other than a money bill to the Supreme Court "for a decision on the question as to whether such Bill or any specified provision or provisions of such Bill is or are repugnant to this Constitution or to any provision thereof." As the debate and closer scrutiny showed, this provision, in effect, rather than giving greater power to the presidency, invests it in the Supreme Court.

On the model of the system in force before and after the Irish Free State Constitution of 1922 (which was based on the Anglo-Irish Treaty of 1921), the 1937 Constitution sets up a hierarchy of Courts of First Instance, including a High Court invested with full original jurisdiction in both civil and criminal law, and a Court of Final Appeal, the Supreme Court. The Supreme Court is given appellate jurisdiction from all decisions of the High Court (Article 34.4.3).[19]

In addition to being the highest court of appeal, the Supreme Court determines constitutional construction. This judicial review provision is foreign to the British Constitution and also to the Constitution of 1922. In 1937, it did have some European precedents in the form of constitutional courts, but it is the United States Supreme Court that it most immediately copied. There are certain differences betweeen the American and the Irish supreme courts. In contrast to the U. S. court, no *stare decisis* principle applies in the Irish court . In Ireland, judicial review is deliberately mentioned in the Constitution, whereas in the United States it is implied by the Constitution's provisions.

It is evident from the debates in the Dáil that de Valera himself did not intend the courts to play the governmental role that the judiciary has come to do in the United States. This is also reflected in the text of the Constitution. The power of judicial review in Ireland is clearly not an absolute power. It may, for instance (under Article 28, in cases of national emergency), be superseded by resolutions of the Oireachtas. De Valera saw the Dáil as the center of the political power in the State. It was there that the Irish people could claim its sovereign authority.[20]

Many of de Valera's statements show that he regarded the Constitution as a finished product. In a public address on the eve of polling day, July 1, 1937, he said that he saw it as "a renewed declaration of national independence." Its enactment would "mark the attainment of one definite objective in the national struggle." Although he left the Constitution open for future amendments through popular referendum, he obviously did not envisage a process of a constitutional development in which judicial review ended up affecting not only statute law but also, indirectly, the Constitution itself.[21]

Given the judges' unfamiliarity with judicial review, there was indeed great hesitancy throughout the first twenty-five years about putting it to any practical use.[22] Normally Irish judges would interpret the constitutional rights of the citizens conservatively. Even in the mid-1950s, they refrained from adopting the "policy-oriented" approach that characterized the American Supreme Court under Chief Justice Warren[23] Irish Supreme Court justices instead followed the principle held by de Valera that the courts had not been given the authority to control the parliament or to cause social change. In 1940, they declared that the duty of determining the extent to which the rights of any particular citizen, or class of citizen, can properly be harmonized with the rights of the citizens as a whole seems to us to be a matter which is peculiarly within the province of the Oireachtas, and any attempt by this Court to control the Oireachtas in the exercise of this function would, in our opinion, be a usurpation of its authority.[24]

A few judges, in particular Mr. Justice Gavan Duffy, a convinced republican and strong supporter of de Valera, took a more activist view. Duffy saw in the new Constitution an opportunity to catholicize Irish law by introducing natural law principles, as understood by the Catholic church, into the judgments of the courts. Together with a few others who thought along the same lines, Duffy felt that the Constitution offered an opening for a legal system that was particularly fitted to Irish cultural tradition and that was at variance with the inherited, but more or less foreign, common law tradition of the United Kingdom.[25]

Not until well into the sixties did the Irish Supreme Court begin to play a new "American" role as policy maker rather than as mere intrepeter of the law. It started when two judges, Chief Justice Cearbhall O Dalaigh and Mr. Justice Brian Walsh, sought to exploit the new opportunities in cases of a constitutional nature under inspiration from the legal culture of the United States. In his analysis of the effects of what he calls the "revolution in the interpretation of the Irish legal system," journalist and writer Colm Tóibín concludes that the new development was motivated by two wishes: first, a wish to "nationalize" – or "de-Anglicize" – the Irish legal system by making the court system less formal and more humane and, second, a wish to realize de Valera's original ambition of giving sovereign authority to the people.[26] But although O Dalaigh and Walsh were both supporters of Fianna Fáil (de Valera's party), the implementation of these wishes had implications that de Valera would probably not have consented to, because it would mean that the interests and rights of the individual would be given greater weight than those of the state and the community. In practice, this was exactly what happened. From now on, the Supreme Court would rule against the government in cases in which individual rights had been violated. In doing so, the court turned itself into an independent branch of government and became a kind of third house of legislation.

Among Irish legal scholars, the decision of the U. S. Supreme Court in *Brown v. Board of Education of Topeka* (1954) had already created considerable attention. In 1957, Chief Justice Warren was awarded an honorary degree from the National University of Ireland.[27] Later on, in the early 1960s, both O Dalaigh and Walsh used the United States Supreme Court as a model for the Irish court. For a number of years, Walsh had been an avid student of the judgments of the U. S. court. He was personally acquainted with a number of its members, including Associate Justice William Brennan. In court, both he and O Dalaigh developed the practice of regularly asking counsel if they were able to cite American precedents in their argument. At the time, access to American court decisions had been made easier because an Irish-American organization had donated a large number of American law books to the Bar Library.[28]

The most significant Irish Supreme Court judgments made under American inspiration can be divided into three categories: first, the curbing of the arbitrary powers that the government, individual ministers, and other bodies had formerly tended to give themselves; second, the attempt to define the individual's rights in the area of criminal law and to protect the rights of citizens; and third, the attempt to expand the rights of the individual on the basis of the Constitution.[29]

The accumulated effects of judicial review and constitutional construction as influenced by American jurisprudence and legal culture since the 1960s have been so dramatic that it no longer makes any real sense to characterize the present Constitution of Ireland as the personal heritage of Eamon de Valera. Professor James Casey emphasizes, however, that the main significance of judicial review in Ireland cannot be assessed only by a head count of statutes invalidated. Rather, it lies in the effect that it had, in the 1960s and 1970s, on the Irish public in creating "a heightened awareness of citizens' rights and of the Constitution's role in diffusing and restricting power." Casey explains the increased invocation of the Constitution by several interdependent cultural, social, and political factors:

It took place during a period in which Ireland gave up its protectionist policies, both economically and culturally, and opened up towards the outside world, not least to American culture and social values.

There was the stimulus of economic development; the opening to the outside world caused by that and by the advent of television. There was plainly also a heightened awareness of, and concern for, rights, stimulated perhaps by the civil rights campaigns in the United States and in Northern Ireland. And as well as this, legal practioners, and a new generation of judges, had become more conscious of the Constitution's potential for safeguarding – and indeed extending – existing rights.[30]

The adjustment to a new social climate attuned to modern notions of individual freedom and personal rights implied a loosening from the moorings of tradition. In the courts this meant a weakening of (Anglo-Irish) common law tradition in favor of more abstract principles. Also, it meant more innovative – at times even creative – approaches to constitutional interpretation. The established historical approach to constitutional construction was largely supplanted by a judicially activist approach inspired by the human rights legal philosophy of the secular natural law tradition. This happened in continental Europe as well in the postwar period.[31] The Americanization of Irish legal practice, therefore, should be seen as part of a general process of Americanization of European law after the war.[32]

It was in the course of this process that the notion of unenumerated rights turned up in Irish courts in 1965. Not incidentally, it happened in the same year that the notion was first introduced in the United States Supreme Court in connection with *Griswold* v. *Connecticut*.[33] In *Griswold*, it will be remembered, the plaintiff had held that an anticontraception law enacted in 1879 infringed on the right of a married couple to marital privacy. The majority of the justices had argued that specific guarantees in the Bill of Rights had "penumbras" that gave them life and substance. Among these was a right of privacy. Associate Justice William O. Douglas had even hinted at the existence of "a right of privacy older than the Bill of Rights," that is, a natural right. Associate Justice Arthur Goldberg, in his concurring opinion, argued that the concept of liberty mentioned in the Fourteenth Amendment "protects those personal rights which are fundamental and is not confined in specific terms to the Bill of Rights."[34]

The same line of argument occurs in a landmark judgment by Mr. Justice Kenny in a case brought before the High Court in 1965, *Ryan* v. *Attorney General*. The American Supreme Court had earlier made significant decisions in very minor cases and had not waited for the perfect case to come along. The Irish Supreme Court was to follow the same policy. *Ryan* is not about contraception but about a plaintiff who was opposed to a new practice of flouridating water supplies. In his judgment, Mr. Justice Kenny referred to the existence of "personal rights" that are "not confined to those specified in Article 40 but include all those rights which result from the Christian and democratic nature of the state."[35] This judgment allowed for the creation of several other rights not stated in but implied by the Constitution.

The personal rights recognized thus far by the Irish courts, apart from the right to privacy, are the right to strike, the right to earn one's living, the right to communicate, the right to legal protection on criminal charges, the right to protection of one's health, the right to travel in the state, the right to travel abroad, the right to marry and found a family, the right to fair procedures in decision making, the right of association, and the right of access to the courts.[36] The gradual recognition of unenumerated rights has also run parallel to a similar development in American constitutional jurisprudence on issues such as contraception, homosexuality, and abortion.

An example of how rulings in the United States Supreme Court directly affected constitutional interpretation in Ireland is another Irish watershed judgment – especially for the relationship between state and church – *McGee* v. *Attorney General* (1974). In this case, two of the judges based their argument for a right of privacy squarely on the interpretation of the United States Constitution in *Griswold* v. *Connecticut,* while citing *Poe* v. *Ullmann* in support. In *McGee,* the majority of the Supreme Court held Section 17 of the Criminal Law (Amendment) Act of 1935, prohibiting the importation of contraceptives, to be unconstitutional, arguing that it impugned the right of marital privacy as protected by Articles 40 and 41. In his attack on Section 17, Mr. Justice Henchy ended his opinion by quoting from the judgments of Associate Justices John Marshall Harlan and Goldberg on the right to privacy.[37]

Concurring with this opinion, Chief Justice Walsh invoked natural law principles of justice, not in order to specify the rights of married parents, but to support his view that the family had unenumerated rights over which the State could not have any control. Walsh argued that Articles 41, 42, and 43 "emphatically reject the theory that there are no rights without laws, no rights contrary to the law and no rights anterior to the law." Justice was placed "above the [positive] law." This meant that the "individual has natural and human rights over which the State has no authority." Walsh admitted, however, that the specific content of natural law was far from clear.[38]

What was clear was that the way the chief justice interpreted the Constitution did not accord with the way the hierarchy of the Catholic church read it. Church hierarchy was strongly opposed to a liberalization of the existing law, which banned the importation and sale of means of contraception. The bishops found that "the increased availability of contraceptives" would have a negative effect on "the quality of life in the Republic of Ireland."[39] The Chief Justice rejected the view that, in a pluralist society, the Catholic church could possess any privileged authority to interpret the Irish Constitution or to determine the scope of personal rights. It is the exclusive privilege of the judges, he argued, to determine which rights are to be considered prior to positive law and which should be considered inviolable and uninfrangible. The judges should do this exclusively on the basis of the fundamental principles and values of the Constitution, their professional education and experience, and in accordance with the predominant ethos of their own age.[40]

McGee v. *Attorney General* may be characterized as the *Brown* v. *Board of Education of Topeka* of Irish legal and political history in that, by sanctioning a future change in the law, the Irish Supreme Court from that day made social change possible in areas where legislators had long hesitated to act. Irish governments went on hesitating on this point for another six years – although with less complacency – until finally, in 1979, Section 17 was abandoned and the sale of contraceptives for "family planning or adequate medical reasons" was legalized.[41] *Mc Gee* may also be said to be a key indicator of the degree to which American jurisprudence in the period from the mid-1960s through the 1970s "took root" in Ireland, as Professor Gerard Hogan puts it.[42]

This and earlier judgments in defense of specified and unspecified constitutional rights of the individual citizen were instrumental in gradually turning Ireland into the liberal, pluralist democracy it is today. Fifty years from now, this process of social change through legal reform may be seen as having been swift and dramatic. To the liberal participant of the day, however, it often appears as a slow and unpredictable course of development with moments of frustrating and serious setbacks. For one thing, at that time the legal profession itself was far from agreed on the extent to which the law should be used at all as a political instrument. As we saw earlier, the notion of the Supreme Court as an independent branch of government was foreign to the intentions of the "founding father" of the Constitution. Because judges in Ireland are appointed, not elected, it would have meant the creation of a body capable of bypassing the people's representatives in parliament and thus outside the democratic control of the people to whom de Valera meant to give sovereign power. A second delaying factor was the rise of divisions in the major political parties between "modernizers" and "traditionalists." Finally, and of greatest importance perhaps, was popular resistance to legal reform in areas of morality. For the fact is that in the Irish political system – with the great powers conferred on the institution of the referendum – it is indeed the voters who are masters.

This was reaffirmed in the early 1980s when Irish society was once again affected by events in the United States. This time it was the ruling of the Supreme Court in *Roe* v. *Wade* (1973) that gave occasion to a new round of constitutional politics. It began when lay Catholics of a neotraditionalist persuasion were encouraged by the rise of the New Right in the United States to launch a counteroffensive against the "liberal values" perceived to be spreading throughout Irish society. *McGee* caused considerable concern in many Catholic lay organizations about the ultimate effects of the court's ruling:

would the next step of the Irish courts be to overturn the 1861 statute banning abortion in the case of a future plaintiff claiming abortion to be a constitutional right protected by Article 40.3? This concern led to the forming, in 1981, of the Pro-Life Amendment Campaign (PLAC), an umbrella group of fourteen organizations. In 1982-1983 PLAC campaigned successfully for a constitutional ban against abortion. The amendment was carried by 67 percent of the votes in a referendum held in September 1983. Now inserted in the Constitution as Article 40.3, it obliges the state to acknowledge "the right to life of the unborn and, with due regard to the equal right to life of the mother ... in its laws to respect, and, as far as practicable, by its laws to defend and vindicate that right."[43]

Debating at Second Stage the Eighth Amendment of the Constitution Bill (the abortion amendment), the minister for justice recognized the impact that the United States Supreme Court had hitherto had on constitutional development in Ireland:

> It has become apparent that judicial decisions can alter fundamentally what had been accepted to be the law even to the extent of introducing what is virtually a system of abortion on demand... . Our constitutional law is in a continuous state of development. In this context, it is only necessary to think of the U.S. Supreme Court decisions on marital privacy.[44]

In the Senate, the independent senator, Mary Robinson, spoke out strongly against passage of such an amendment, asking the assembled members: "Do we want a Roman Catholic confessional State or a pluralist society in the Republican tradition of Tone and Davis? We can't have it both ways."[45]

Mary Robinson is, next to Garret FitzGerald, the person who more than any other public figure in this period was identified with liberal reforms.[46] Her senatorial record from the 1970s and 1980s reveals a persistent defender of individual rights and freedoms in many different areas. It is evident that her career as a political activist in matters of legal and social reform was given a significant impetus after the year she spent in the United States.

As initially described, Robinson's experiences at Harvard Law School had convinced her that the judicial system might have a reforming function in the government of Ireland: "I saw Ireland quite different – how we needed change, law reform and that even our parliamentary structures needed opening up," she told a journalist from the *Irish Times* in 1978.[47] Twenty-three years later, she confirmed that her sharpened awareness of the relation between law reform and politics is one of the fruits of her American experience. She had initially been "very interested in the importance of the [American] Constitution and the federal Supreme Court." She pointed out that the parallels between the constitutions of Ireland and the United States had caused her to see

> The potential for issues to be raised and indeed social change to come about as a result of court decisions. I saw, as did others, the potential in an Irish context, where it was hard to get a parliamentary majority for change on issues of law and morality. It was difficult for politicians to take stands partly because of our electoral system. The multiseat constituency means that nobody is sure of his or her seat, and so you do not have very courageous stands being taken. The other way of getting change, then, [is] to bring up a constitutional case and hopefully have a court decision that could open up the situation.[48]

As a lawyer, Robinson would, mostly successfully, take on cases of alleged violation of the rights of individual citizens.[49] Many of these involved women: the de Burca-Anderson case (1976), challenging the existing jury system (which banned women from sitting in juries); the Murphy case (1982), changing the taxation of married couples, and the Hyland case (1988), ensuring equality of social welfare benefits for married couples. Her other cases were concerned with the protection of civil rights and liberties, as, for instance, the Norris case (1984) against part of the 1861 Offences Against the Person Act (which outlawed homosexual practices between adults), and *Dublin Well Woman Centre v. Ireland* (1988), on the right to inform the public about abortion. A convinced human rights lawyer and judicial activist since her student days at Harvard, Robinson went to international courts in cases where her clients were defeated in Irish courts.[50]

As a senator, Robinson initiated and supported legislation on, among other concerns, adoption, marital breakdown, equal pay, free legal aid, and other issues relating to equality. She thought that many of the existing laws of the Irish State, including the Constitution, reflected a society of the past and not the complex identity and modern values of contemporary Irish citizens. She frequently accused Irish politicians of shirking their responsibility as legislators. They failed to "take a lead" in adjusting legislation to present social conditions, she would say. This had resulted in a kind of democratic deficit. She found that the administration of the Irish state was too centralized. In many areas, it was "outside the control of the democratic process." As a result, many young people were getting "disillusioned" and felt it "increasingly difficult to play an active part in the country."[51]

Robinson found particularly fault with the narrowly confessional values of the Constitution, as for instance expressed in Articles 41 and 42. The State should not "enshrine a particular denominational viewpoint, even a majority one, in its Constitution to the outlawing of all others." This was "an infringement on human liberty," because it meant that Ireland had taken on itself to legislate on issues of private morality. Whether in matters of family planning, censorship, illegitimacy, or adoption, she saw it as the task of the legislator to protect basic human rights as guaranteed under the Constitution. Insofar as she found that the Constitution did not live up to international conventions, she would argue that Ireland's status as a co-signer of such conventions required the government to amend its laws accordingly. Early in her career, she saw the future legal implications of Ireland's membership in the European Economic Community (EEC). In 1971, she predicted that it would have significant cultural implications and would mean "a fundamental constitutional change." But she was also greatly concerned about the "lack of democracy" in the existing structures of the EEC.[52]

Broad constitutional reform in the republic, she hoped, would help create a more stable relationship between the two states on the island of Ireland. For better North-South relations to be achieved, it was also necessary to revise Articles 2 and 3 (on the territorial claim of the Constitution). Instead of expressing the desire for a political takeover of Northern Ireland, revised articles should express an "aspiration for coexistence" in "viable [political] units which offer the basic protections of peace and security, of respect for the dignity of human persons and of absence of discrimination and terrorism." Realizing that this was likely to be a long-term goal, fundamental human rights should not be sacrificed in the meantime, however. In the 1970s, she set herself off from other liberals, such as Labour's Conor Cruise O'Brien, by criticizing emergency measures that limited the rights of free speech and the standard requirements of due process in the fight against political terrorism.[53]

In such cases Robinson often drew on her knowledge of American legal precedents. In criticizing the Offences against the State Bill in 1972, for example, she found that many sections of the bill reflected "a conflict between the protection of the individual and the interests of maintaining law and order." She undergirded her criticism with a reference to American Justice Felix Frankfurter, who, in 1943, said that "the history of liberty [had] largely been the history of procedural safeguards." She went on to cite a couple of American constitutional cases. These references provoked one of her opponents, Senator Tomas Maoláin, to respond: "It's a pity that Senator Robinson in her lauding of the various obscure things that they have in America is so selective and that she does not tell us all of what happens over there."[54]

As president of Ireland from 1990 to 1997, Robinson often returned by invitation to the United States. In 1995, five years after her election, she gave an address at Stanford University on "Constitutional Shifts in Europe and the United States."[55] The speech reflects her growing recognition, enhanced by her new role as president, that the law protects both individuals and communities. In the speech, she acknowledges that laws protecting individual rights, although crucial for the health of society, should not conflict with basic community values.[56] She reflects on the fundamental issues of democracy: how political power should best be exercised in a balancing the interests of the individual and the interests of the community. Ideally, this is done by combining universal principles of justice with the general ethos of the community, reconciling codified law (a Bill of Rights) and common law. She reminds her audience that this is the way it is done in both the United States and in Ireland and that this feature has made the Irish judicial system unique in Europe. The combination – and tension – of common law and constitutionalism, she argues, may leave necessary room for the protection of community values without violating the rights of the individual citizen. She sees a tendency toward a similar beneficial tension between common and codified law in Europe today, describing the way in which decisions made in the European Court of Justice are now in the forefront of every nation's legal system.

She also recognizes the significance of the recent "new shift away from the centre" and the "alternative drive to the new Europe," in which there will be room for "more localised decision making" and for the protection of national values. But she emphasizes that "localism, or subsidiarity, or special treatment or however it is described, has its limits. Local autonomy can never be allowed to become a shelter in which the abuse of our human rights is permitted out of too deferential a reverence for a national authority."[57]

Robinson goes on to say that she considers the creation of the right balance between localism and universal human rights one of the greatest challenges for Europe today. This challenge is mirrored in the historical evolution of American federalism. It is therefore useful for present-day Europeans to reflect on the coming into existence of a United States of America, for the courts have played a key role in transforming the United States into a modern democracy. Without the "vital role" of the courts, the American Constitution would have become a dead letter and the democratic base of the union would have been weakened through less participation and less accountability.

The courts ought to play a similar role for a developing Europe, she thinks, calling for an express Bill of Rights for the Euopean Union taking its example from the United States. As for judicial interpretation, Robinson emphasizes the vital importance that the courts give effect to what is "explicitly expressed" in the Constitution and also to what is implied, the unenumerated rights of the citizen. This activist approach, she reminds her audience, was something Irish judges had learned from the American Supreme Court when they started the process of turning the Constitution of Ireland into "a modern rights-based document." This has been part of an ongoing process of Europe and the United States "learning from each other":

> It was to the pioneering creativity of the Warren Court of the late 1950s and early 1960s that our own Supreme Court in Dublin looked when it began in the mid 1960s to fashion our 1937 Constitution into the modern rights-based document it is today. The Irish judges learned from their American contemporaries, just as earlier generations of American colonists had learned about the control of power from such continental scholars as Montesquieu and Rousseau; and just as both you Americans and we Irish had learned about representative government from the British when our respective founders were planning our States. This process of learning from each other is at least as old as our nations, and its role in our development as nations has been incalculably beneficial.[58]

The symbolic conclusion to the story of how American legal culture and jurisprudence have influenced constitutional development and led to legal reform in Ireland in this century was written two years after Mary Robinson gave this speech. In 1997, she was appointed United Nations High Commissioner for Human Rights with the discreet but strong backing of the United States. The support for her candidacy came, it must be remembered, from an American president who appreciated and deliberately sought to revive the historical links between Ireland and the United States, not least through his active and successful involvement in the peace process in Northern Ireland.[59] The president, furthermore, sympathized with Robinson's visions and hopes for a "New Ireland" and for international order in which community values would be respected but would no longer be allowed to conflict with universal principles of justice. As of the moment of writing, however, the results of Robinson's attempt as high commissioner to balance two such potentially opposing demands, for example in her dealings with China, have been met with some scepticism by human rights activists, not least in the United States. The interaction between American and European legal traditions goes on.

Notes

1. Lorna Siggins, *Mary Robinson: The Woman Who Took Power in the Park* (Edinburgh, 1997), 46-49.
2. Jacqui Dunne, *Sunday Independent,* June 15,1980, quoted ibid., 51.
3. "Women and the Law in Ireland," in Ailbhe Smyth, ed., *Irish Women's Studies Reader* (Dublin, 1993), 100.
4. Ronan Fanning, "Mr de Valera Drafts a Constitution," in Brian Farrell, ed., *De Valera's Constitution and Ours* (Dublin, 1988), 36.
5. Responsible democracy is defined as a political system in which the government can be held accountable for its actions and the basic rights of the citizens are protected. See Alan J. Ward, *The Irish Constitutional Tradition: Responsible Government and Modern Ireland, 1782-1992* (Blackrock, 1994), 1-11.
6. Parliamentary Debates, Dáil, vol. 67 (1937), cols. 40, 74.
7. Quoted in Rosemary Cullen Owens, *Smashing Times: A History of the Irish Women's Suffrage Movement, 1889-1922* (Dublin, 1984), 132.
8. Yvonne Scannell, "The Constitution and the Role of Women," in Farrell, ed., *De Valera's Constitution and Ours,* 124-27.
9. See Parliamentary Debates, Dail, vol. 67, col. 70.
10. Ibid., col. 66.
11. Ibid., col. 63.
12. de Valera, debating the Constitution of Ireland in Dáil Éireann, May 11, 1937, quoted in Maurice Moynihan, ed., *Speeches and Statements by Eamon de Valera, 1917-73* (Dublin, 1980), 320.
13. At times, especially when he wanted to make the point that Ireland ideally was a cultural, social, national, and geographical unity, de Valera had recourse to organicist metaphors. Ireland, he would say, is a "combination of chemical elements," a "living body" inspired by a national "soul." See ibid., 525, and Tim Pat Coogan, *Eamon de Valera: Long Fellow, Long Shadow* (London, 1995), 324.
14. Moynihan, ed., *Speeches and Statements by Eamon de Valera,* 423.
15. Ibid., 430-32.
16. Parliamentary Debates, Dail, vol. 67 (1937), cols. 229, 303, 1007-09. See also Michael Gallagher, "The President, the People and the Constitution," in Farrell, ed., *De Valera's Constitution and Ours,* 78.
17. Parliamentary Debates, Dail, vol. 67 (1937), cols. 40, 51.
18. For a discussion of "semi-presidential systems" see Maurice Duverger, "A New Political System Model: Semi-presidential Government," *European Journal of Political Research,* 8 (1980), 165-87.

19. Although the system of courts was authorized in 1937, it was not established until the Courts (Establishment and Constitution) Act 1961.
20. See Moynihan, ed., *Speeches and Statements by Eamon de Valera,* 306.
21. De Valera, quoted in earl of Longford and Thomas P. O'Neill, *Eamon de Valera* (London, 1970), 300; James Casey, "Changing the Constitution: Amendment and Judicial Review," in Farrell, ed., *De Valera's Constitution and Ours,* 157.
22. There are some important examples of its use in this period, such as *National Union of Railwaymen* v. *Sullivan* (1947), IR 77; *Buckley* v. *Attorney General* (1950), Irish Reports (IR)67; and *In re Irish Employers' Mutual Insurance Association Ltd.* (1955), IR 176.
23. See Kenneth Holland, "Judicial Activism in the United States," in Holland, ed., *Judicial Activism in Comparative Perspective* (London, 1991), 18.
24. *In re Article 26 of the Constitution and the Offences against the State (Amendment) Bill, 1940* (1940), IR 470, 481.
25. Gerard Hogan, "Law and Religion: Church-State Relations in Ireland from Independence to the Present Day," *American Journal of Comparative Law,* 35 (1987),47-96, quotation on 56; Basil Chubb, *Politics of the Irish Constitution,* 42-44.
26. Colm Tóibín, "Inside the Supreme Court," *Magill* (Feb. 1985), 8-35.
27. Jack Harrison Pollack, *Earl Warren: The Judge Who Changed America* (Englewood Cliffs, N. J., 1979), 193.
28. The tendency, since 1959, to cite American precedent may be exemplified by *O'Byrne* v. *Minister for Finance* (1959) IR 1; *Quinn's Supermarket Ltd.* v. *Attorney General* (1972) IR 1; *McGee* v. *Attorney General* (1974) IR 284; *The State (Healy)* v. *Donoghue* (1976) IR 325; *The State (M.)* v. *Attorney General* (1979) IR 73; *King* v. *Attorney General* (1981) IR 233; *Murphy* v. *Attorney General* (1982) IR 241; *O'Brien* v. *Sullivan* (1984) IR 316; and *Clancy* v. *Ireland* (1988) IR 326. The practice of using American precedents has become an established feature of Irish legal culture. Today important decisions in American courts are cited and referred in a regular column in the *Irish Law Times*. This is an addition to the earlier tradition of citing and referring cases from the House of Lords and the lower courts of the United Kingdom. American court decisions, along with decisions from the European Court of Human Rights and the European Court of Justice, are an important part of the context in which law is practised in Ireland. See Hogan and Gerry Whyte, eds., *J. M. Kelly: The Irish Constitution,* 3d ed. (Dublin, 1994), 451, and Patrick McEntee, interview with Gerard Hogan and Justice Barrington, "The Constitution, Law and Ideology," *The Crane Bag,* 9: 1 (1985), 104-09.
29. Tóibín, "Inside the Supreme Court," 12.
30. James Casey, *Constitutional Law in Ireland* (London, 1987), 29, 156.
31. For a discussion of constitutional interpretation and its development in Ireland see Hogan and Whyte, eds., *J. M. Kelly,* xcviii-cxviii, and Casey, *Constitutional Law in Ireland,* 297-305. For the reference to the rebirth of natural law thinking see Roger Cotterell, *The Politics of Jurispru-*

dence: A Critical Introduction to Legal Philosophy (London, 1989), 127-32.
32. See, e. g., Casey, "The Devlopment of Constitutional Law under Chief Justice O'Higgins," *Irish Jurist,* 21 (1986), 22-23; Francis X. Beytagh, "Equality under the Irish and American Constitutions," ibid., 18 (1983), 252-53; and L. Henkin and A. J. Rosenthal, eds., *Constitutionalism and Rights: The Influence of the United States Constitution Abroad* (New York, 1990).
33. 381 U.S. 479 (1964).
34. Kermit L. Hall et al., eds., *American Legal History: Cases and Materials* (New York, 1991), 520; 381 U.S. 479 (1964), p. 486 (Justice Goldberg, concurring).
35. *Ryan v. Attorney General* (1965) IR 294, p. 312.
36. Casey, *Constitutional Law in Ireland,* 306; Hogan and Whyte, eds., *J. M. Kelly,* 755-89.
37. Hogan, "Law and Religion," 69; *McGee v. Attorney General* (1974) IR, 326-28 (Justice Henchy) IR, 335-36 (Justice Griffin); *Griswold v. Connecticut,* 367 U.S. 497 (1961); *McGee v. Attorney General* (1974), IR, 326.
38. *McGee v. Attorney General* (1974) IR, 310.
39. *Irish Independent,* Nov. 26, 1973.
40. *McGee v. Attorney General* (1974), IR 284, 318.
41. Section 3 of the Health (Family Planning) Act (1979). Further liberalization was made in 1985 and 1992.
42. Hogan, "Legal Aspects of Church/State Relations in Ireland," *Saint Louis University Public Law Review,* 7 (1988), 281. From the late 1970s, the impact of European constitutional law has arguably been greater than that of American law in Ireland. See, e.g., Síofra O'Leary, "The Reciprocal Relationship between Irish Constitutional Law and the Law of the European Communities," in Tim Murphy and Patrick Twomey, eds., *Ireland's Evolving Constitution, 1937-1997* (Oxford, 1998).
43. For an analysis of the historical origins of the amendment initiative see Tom Hesketh, *The Second Partitioning of Ireland: The Abortion Referendum of 1983* (Dublin, 1990).
44. Parliamentary Debates, Dail, Feb. 9, 1983, vol. 99, cols. 1354-56.
45. Parliamentary Debates, Seanad, May 4, 1983, vol. 100, cols. 549-53.
46. Although FitzGerald in many ways personified modern Irish liberalism with his pluralist attitude and call for constitutional reform, he never succeeded in implementing his reform ideas. On the contrary, he lost credibility in the eyes of many liberals in 1982-1983 after his clumsy handling of the abortion amendment initiative.
47. Robinson, quoted in *Irish Times,* Feb. 26, 1977, and in Siggins, *Mary Robinson,* 52.
48. Michael Böss, interview with Robinson, June 1995.
49. For a select, alphabetically arranged index of reported cases in which Robinson appears, see Michael O'Sullivan, *Mary Robinson: The Life and Times of an Irish Liberal* (Dublin, 1993), 217-19.
50. Mostly successfully, except in one case, in Application No. 15404/89.

51. See, e.g., Marital Breakdown Problems: Motion, Parliamentary Debates: Senate, June 15, 1983, vol. 101, cols. 102-03; see also ibid., col. 100; ibid., Mar. 20, 1974, vol. 74, col. 441; Fourth Amendment to the Constitution Bill, 1972, ibid., Senate, July 15, vol. 95, col. 413.
52. Parliamentary Debates, Senate, May 4, 1983, vol. 100, col. 551; Family Planning Bill, 1973, Parliamentary Debates: Senate, Feb. 20, 1974, vol. 77, col. 212. See also her contributions to debates on illegitimacy, ibid., vol. 79, 1974, col. 55, and Illegitimacy Status: Motion, ibid., May 16, 1984, vol. 103, col. 1368. See, e.g., Joint Committee on Women's Rights: Motion, ibid., July 6, 1983, vol. 101, col. 813; ibid., Mar. 11, 1971, vol. 69, col. 1291; and ibid., Nov. 22, 1972, vol. 73, col. 859.
53. Parliamentary Debates, Senate, July 3, 1974, col. 786; Offences Against the State Bill, 1972, ibid., Dec. 2, 1972, vol. 85, cols. 1145ff; Emergency Powers Bill, ibid., Sept. 14, 1976, vol. 85, col. 279.
54. Offences Against the State Bill, ibid., cols. 1184, 1186, 1236-37.
55. Robinson, "Constitutional Shifts in Europe and the United States: Learning from Each Other," speech given at Stanford University, Oct. 18, 1995, 1.
56. Robinson has always declared herself against free access to abortion in Ireland.
57. Robinson, "Constitutional Shifts in Europe and the United States," 4-6.
58. Ibid, 2.
59. On securing the support of President Bill Clinton see John Horgan, *Mary Robinson: An Independent Voice* (Dublin, 1997), 195-96, and Siggins, *Mary Robinson,* 228. For analyses of the relationship between the United States under President Clinton and Ireland, see Conor O'Cleary, *The Greening of the White House* (Dublin, 1996), and Andrew J. Wilson, *Irish America and the Ulster Conflict, 1968-1995* (Belfast, 1995), chap. 10.

The Authors

Niels Bjerre-Poulsen is Associate Professor of American politics and society at the Copenhagen Business School. He holds an M.A. in History from the University of Copenhagen and a Ph.D. in American History from the University of California, Santa Barbara. He has written extensively on American politics, especially on the American right. He is the author of *Right Face: Organizing the American Conservative Movement 1945-65* (Copenhagen: Museum Tusculanum Press, 2001), *USA: Historie og identitet* (USA: History and Identity) (Copenhagen: Gads Forlag, 2000) and the co-author with Peter Kurrild-Klitgaard of *American Isolationism: From Old to New* (Uppsala: The Swedish Institute for North American Studies, 1997).

Marcus C. Bruce is Associate Professor of Religion at Bates College, Maine. He received his Master of Divinity from the Yale Divinity School and his Ph.D. in American Studies from the Yale Graduate School. While at Bates College, he has been teaching courses in Religion, American Cultural Studies, and African-American Cultural Studies. He has co-authored with Barbara Ballard, *Debating the Negro Problem: Booker T. Washington, W.E.B. Du Bois, and the Twentieth Century* (forthcoming with Rowman and Littlefield Press, 2001), and is currently working on African-Americans in Paris. He is on the Board of Trustees for The Maine Humanities Council and The Carnegie Council on Ethics and International Affairs.

Michael Böss is Associate Professor at the Department of English, Århus University, where he teaches history and Irish studies. In 1987, he published *Den irske verden: Historie, kultur og identitet i det moderne samfund* (The Irish World: History, Culture and Identity in a Modern Society) and in 1998 he co-edited *Ireland – Towards New Identities?*

Saul Cornell is Associate Professor of History at The Ohio State University. He is a graduate of Amherst College and the University of Pennsylvania. His main research interest is early American history and culture, and he is the author of *The Other Founders: Anti-Federalism and the Dissenting Tradition in America, 1788-1828* (Institute of Early American History and Culture, University of North Carolina Press, 1999) and the editor of *Whose Right to bear Arms Did the Second Amendment Protect?* (Bedforrd/St. Martins, 2000)

Bo G. Ekelund is Lecturer at Stockholm University. He is currently involved in a research project at Uppsala University, "Literary Generations and Social Authority: A Study of American Prose-Fiction Debut Writers, 1940-2000." He has published an extensive study of the U.S. novelist John Gardner, *In the Pathless Forest: John Gardner's Literary Project*, as well as articles on Gardner, Pierre Bourdieu and Julian Barnes. At present he is finishing a book entitled *Studies in an Undead Culture: Social Forms of Fictional Recognition, 1980-2000*.

Mark P. Gibney is Belk Distinguished Professor of International Ethics at the University of North Carolina-Asheville. He received his J.D. at the Villanova University School of Law and his Ph.D. in Political Science at the University of Michigan. His main research interest is American politics and human rights, and he has published widely in law reviews and political science journals. He has edited a number of volumes, most recently *Judicial Protection of Human Rights: Myth or Reality?* (Praeger Publ., 1999).

Eric R. Guthey is Associate Professor of American studies at the Copenhagen Business School. He holds an M.A. in Biblical Literature and Religion from Columbia University and a Ph.D. in American Studies from Emory University. He is the author of *Ted Turner, Media Legend/Market Reality* (University of California Press, forthcoming) and has taught and published on American mass media, popular culture, and corporate culture.

Helle Porsdam is Associate Professor at the Center for American Studies, University of Southern Denmark, Odense University, where she teaches American history and culture. Her main research interest is the centrality of law in American culture and society. She is the author of *Legally Speaking: Contemporary American Culture and the Law* (Amherst, MA: University of Massachusetts Press, 1999) and is currently working on a project on Danish legalization as a form of Americanization. She spent the fall of 2000 as a Liberal Arts Fellow at the Harvard Law School.

Ernst Peter Schneck is Assistant Professor in the Department of American Literature at the Amerika-Institut, Ludwig-Maximilians-Universität in Munich, Germany. After studying American Studies and Media Studies at the John F. Kennedy-Institut, Berlin and Yale University, he received a Ph.D. from the Free University, Berlin. He has published on 19th Century American literature and painting, on word and image studies, cultural studies, and electronic media and is currently working on rhetoric and evidence and the representation of the judicial process in American literature and culture. He is also the co-editor of 'PhiN. Philologie im Netz' (http://www.phin.de).

Christophe Den Tandt is a graduate of the Universite Libre de Bruxelles and of Yale University. He teaches English and American literature as well as literary theory at the University of Brussels. He has published an essay on American literary naturalism entitled *The Urban Sublime in Literary Naturalism* (University of Illinois Press, 1998), as well as articles on postmodern science fiction and the contemporary detective novel. His current research interest is the status of realism within postmodern culture.

Irmina Wawrzyczek is Professor of History at the Maria Curie-Sklodowska University in Lublin, Poland. She has specialized in the Anglo-American history of the early modern period, and has published books and articles on the cultural history of early colonial America. She is the author of *Unfree Labour in Early Modern English Culture* (1990) and *Planting and Loving: Popular Sexual Mores in Seventeenth-Century Virginia* (1998). Her major editorial work consists of two volumes in the five-volume *Historia Stanow Zjednoczonych* (Warsaw, 1995). She has served as secretary of the Polish Association for American Studies and is currently on the editorial board of *American Studies* (University of Warsaw).